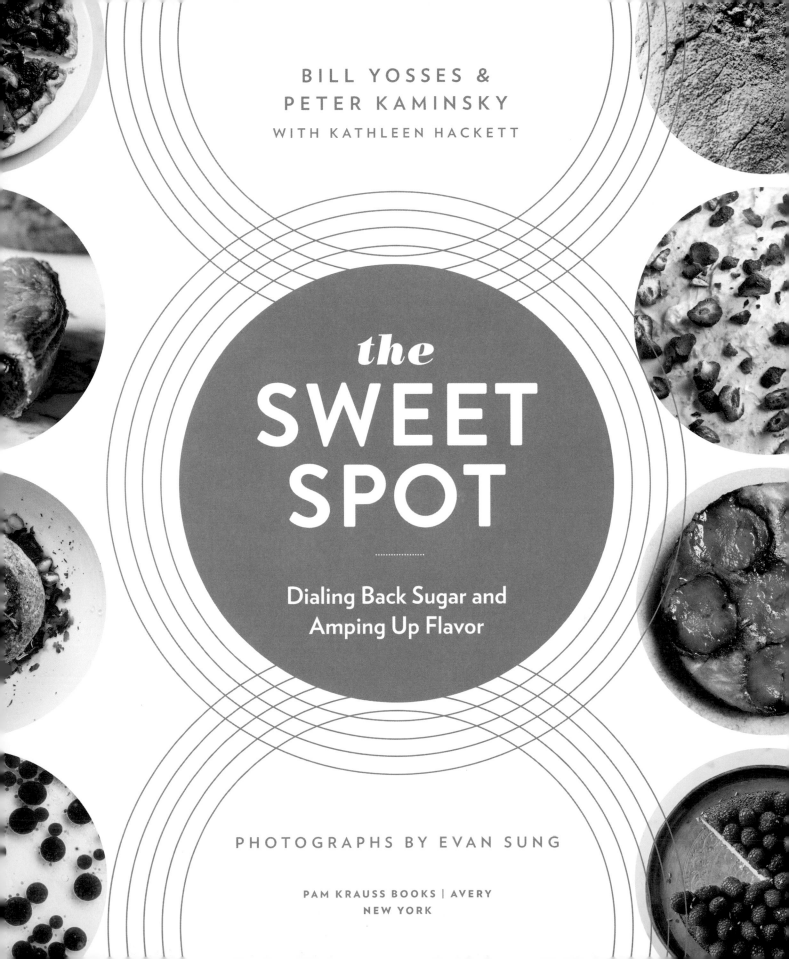

BILL YOSSES &
PETER KAMINSKY

WITH KATHLEEN HACKETT

the SWEET SPOT

Dialing Back Sugar and
Amping Up Flavor

PHOTOGRAPHS BY EVAN SUNG

PAM KRAUSS BOOKS | AVERY
NEW YORK

Pam Krauss Books / Avery
an imprint of Penguin Random House LLC
375 Hudson Street, New York, New York 10014

Most Avery books are available at special quantity discounts for bulk purchase for sales promotions, premiums, fund-raising, and educational needs. Special books or book excerpts also can be created to fit specific needs. For details, write SpecialMarkets@penguinrandomhouse.com.

ISBN 9780804189019

Printed in Germany

10 9 8 7 6 5 4 3 2 1

Book design by Ashley Tucker

For Michel Richard,
The Magician

contents

THINKING OUTSIDE THE *sugar* BOWL

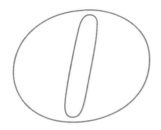ne universal fact is true of all desserts: Nobody *needs* them but everybody *wants* some. Whether the dessert in question is a molecular cuisine pomegranate gel for a state dinner at the White House or a school-night special as simple as my mother's coconut cake, a bite of something sweet is the finishing touch that puts a bow on a good meal.

Like music, or dance, or a well-played game of dominoes, the purpose of dessert is to delight and even amuse. It is all too easy, however, to "over-delight" ourselves with desserts that deliver unhealthy and unnecessary amounts of fats, calories, and, most especially, sugar. In considering how to create desserts that are no less seductive yet healthier, I've taken a hard look at such things as portion size and quality and quantity of ingredients, all of which come into play when rethinking the sweet final act of a satisfying meal. Throughout this process, discovering the point at which each recipe can be made with just enough sugar to leave dessert lovers fed and happy—the sweet spot, if you will—has been my Holy Grail.

The inspiration for a number of the recipes in this book can be traced to my work under two administrations in the White House, where I baked for the Bushes and the Obamas, who dubbed me Crustmaster-in-Chief. A turning point for me occurred about two weeks after President Obama was inaugurated (I had already spent two years as dessert chef under Bush 43). Mrs. Obama called a meeting of the cooking staff. The same thought went through everybody's mind: *Who's getting fired?* Happily that wasn't the purpose of the meeting. She started talking about their kids and told us that, during the campaign, eating schedules and family dinners went to shreds. The children's pediatrician advised her to be more careful about what the kids were eating. "If that's happening to me," she said, "I'm sure it's happening to mothers everywhere."

Healthier eating became our prime directive for mealtime at the White House. More vegetables, smaller portions, more fruits, less sugar. Through much delicious trial and error, I have continued in that direction to come up with the healthier desserts you'll encounter in these pages.

It all starts from four simple words that should be the dessert chef's mantra: *Treat sugar like salt.* In other words, rather than starting to create a recipe with sweetness in mind and then adding ingredients and creating texture, I look to ingredients first (more fruits and herbs and more well-executed fun-to-eat textures) and only then do I add just enough sweetener to make something that is recognizably a dessert rather than a savory course.

I fervently believe that, with the exception of such no-no's as trans fats and many industrial additives, foods cannot be definitively labeled healthy or unhealthy and that too much energy is wasted parsing these categories. In terms of health, it makes much more sense to focus on the *quality* of the ingredients, *how* they are prepared, and the *size of portions.*

But while I don't believe that sugar is inherently terrible, in the confusing and constantly changing world of nutritional advice there is rare unanimity among food scientists that the *amount* of refined sugar in our diet is a leading cause of obesity and a grim list of life-threatening ailments. *Overdoing* sugar is the real issue.

One of the reasons that desserts have become so laden with sugar is that sweeteners are often a quick, easy way to compensate for inferior—usually inexpensive—ingredients. And while it's true that when you drown out the lack of flavor with more and more sugar, your desserts will be eaten, even enjoyed, these are just cheap thrills. Better ingredients combined with good technique always yield more sensual satisfaction.

These recipes are equally the result of my time in the White House kitchen and the half-dozen years before that working as a fine-dining pastry chef, when I became increasingly attracted by what the winemaker calls "terroir"—the magical combination of soil, pedigree, and climate that makes an apple from Oregon different than one from upstate New York, or gives chocolate from Trinidad a cherry flavor and makes cacao beans from Ghana taste mild and smooth. In the course of my march toward healthier food, a fundamental truth revealed itself, one that is obvious once you hear it: If you make desserts with the most flavorful ingredients, you will be no less happy with less on your plate. In other words, desserts may not be a health food, strictly speaking, but they are a pleasure that can be made healthier.

One of the ways to increase flavor while cutting back on sugar is by unlocking the sorcerer's cabinet of herbs and spices that have long been the exclusive province of the savory chef. Herbs, spices, even vinegars and essential oils in desserts are like grace notes on a beautiful musical passage. I have found, time and again, that these add-ons can work luscious magic: sharpening, intensifying, layering flavor.

Likewise, the flowers of herbs usually carry the same flavor elements as the more commonly used leaves, but they bring the added benefit of color and beauty. Desserts want to be pretty. This doesn't mean ornate. It just means pleasing to the eye. You need a bit of that to rekindle your interest at the end of a long and substantial meal.

Refined white flour (all-purpose or pastry) is versatile and creates wonderful texture, but nutritionally it is a lightweight. Still, because of the structure that it uniquely adds to baked goods, it has an important place in the pastry kitchen. Whole grain flours—which contain all the nutrients and fiber of ripe grain—can be used to great effect in crusts, cakes, and cookies as a healthy and more fully flavored supplement to white flour.

Working with NASA scientist Steve Howell, I have gone around the country, even teaching an annual course on the physics of food at Harvard (so I guess you could say my desserts *are* rocket science . . . in a way). I have incorporated some of what I have learned in the lab to expand your repertoire of desserts to include treats that please the eye, extend flavor, enhance the textural experience, and, in so doing, bring diners to their bliss point more quickly, with smaller portions and less sweetener.

This new approach rests on what I call the Seven Pillars of Healthier Desserts. (Thank you, T. E. Lawrence!)

THE SEVEN PILLARS *of healthier desserts*

○ LESS SUGAR: **Cut back on the sugar calories—especially refined sugar. Let the full flavor of prime ingredients shine through.**

○ MORE WHOLE GRAINS: **Although I am not a Puritan about using white flour, I now include more nutritionally beneficial whole grains wherever possible.**

○ BETTER, FULLER-FLAVORED INGREDIENTS: **Fruits picked at their peak, cacao raised for its flavor profile, more use of nuts, more honey and agave nectar.**

○ NO FAKE FOODS: **No Cool Whip, Splenda, fake maple syrup (that has no maple), or processed "food substances" straight from the test tube.**

○ REDUCED FAT: **Although fat, in the right proportion, is necessary for good health and good flavor, reducing it means fewer calories. No trans fat!**

○ HERBS, SPICES, ESSENTIAL OILS: **They add elegance, nuance, and complexity so you can cut down on sugar and fat but keep the pleasure.**

○ SUBSTITUTE: **By adding a fruit compote or puree to a dessert you also add levels of flavor and contrast without resorting to extra butter, or cream. Also, working with generally accessible ingredients and techniques from modern food science, I'll show how to enhance texture and mouthfeel with less fat.**

My true north is always to delight, and anything that adds fun, interest, and flavor to a dessert while subtracting calories is a win. The interesting and exciting new recipes in this book come out of my efforts to reach that goal.

In order to enjoy pleasure-giving desserts that finish off a great meal, just use the best ingredients with the best, often simplest techniques, and, critically, serve smaller portions. It turns out, you can have your cake and eat it, too.

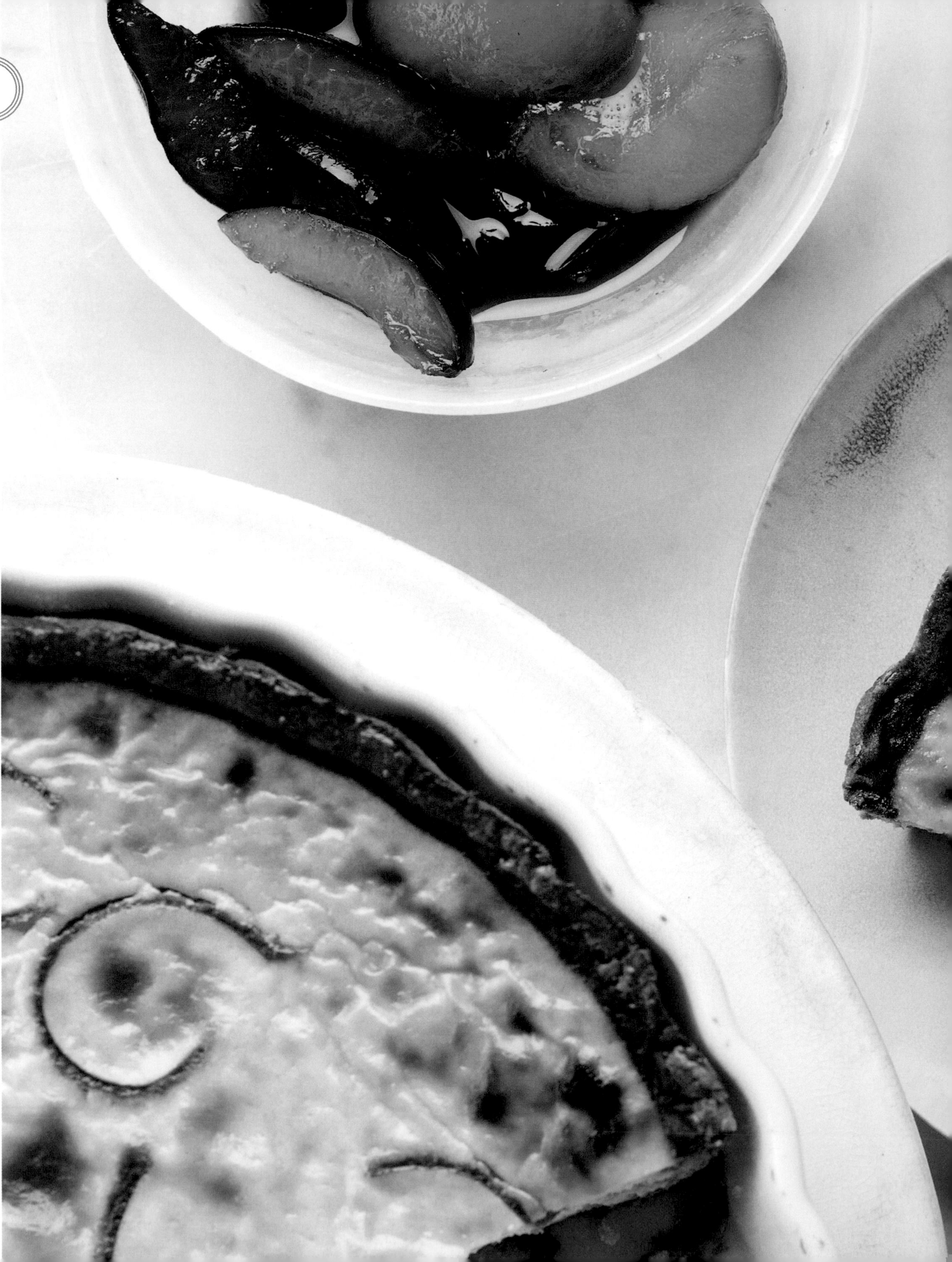

MY PANTRY

In developing the recipes for this book I asked myself three questions:

○ *Could this dessert be equally satisfying—or even more so—with less sweetener?*

○ *Can I reduce the total amount of calories from sweetener, fat, and eggs?*

○ *What would make each bite more interesting and flavorful?*

To answer these questions I had to rethink old assumptions, test (and retest) new ideas, and importantly, restock my pantry with much more than a canister of sugar and flour, some eggs, and some salt.

Let me start out by explaining how I use, and don't use, sugar, butter, and white flour. While it is a fact that many cookies, cakes, pies, and puddings would be impossible without them, it is also true that their overuse has earned the disapproval that many nutritionists—mistakenly—apply to all desserts. The architects, philosophers, dramatists, and poets of ancient Greece had a motto: "Nothing in excess and everything in proportion." That same principle has animated me to reexamine my craft as I created new desserts. I incorporate sugar, butter, and white flour only where necessary and compensate for using less by introducing other flavor components that excite the palate. Then I apply this yardstick: Does the result please me and, perhaps more importantly, will kids eat it?

Sugar

The main source of sweetness in desserts is sugar—glucose, sucrose, fructose, and, to a lesser degree, lactose. Desserts could no more do without sugar than a Mozart violin concerto could be performed without a violin. But as I indicated earlier, the solution to the sweetness puzzle is, first and foremost, use less. By testing, cutting back, and retesting multiple times, I found the point for each recipe at which it is still sweet enough to be a dessert but not so much so that it crowds out other flavors. The surprise was how far you can go in reducing sugar.

You'll encounter a number of alternative sweeteners in this book, but refined white sugar—a product obtained from sugarcane—uniquely adds to structure in doughs, batters, meringues, and puddings. I use it when I have to, and in those cases my preference is for organic cane sugar. As far as taste goes, white sugar is just sweet, with no other distinguishing characteristics. Demerara, muscovado, turbinado, and brown sugar—also made from sugarcane—are less refined than white sugar. Although they have the same effect on structure, their taste is brawnier with hints of molasses, which is desirable when you want a more robust flavor.

Unlike refined white sugar, honey, agave nectar, and maple syrup add flavor in addition to sweetness. Maple syrup adds a buttery, nutty accent. Agave carries a faint hint of tequila. Honey can be as varied in its floral and fruity undertones as the hundreds of species of flowers that bees gather to create this concentrated nutrient. Whenever possible, use a local honey, one produced near where you live. By eating local honey you ingest tiny amounts of pollen from your region, which many scientists say allows your body to develop resistance to those hay fever–causing irritants. All of these sweeteners are less processed than cane sugar, and some studies suggest they have a slightly lower glycemic index (so are absorbed less rapidly by your liver). They also contribute to flavor, and flavor is what is needed in a dessert if you are cutting down on the overall amount of sugar. As most nutritionists will tell you, "Sugar is sugar no matter if you get it from cane sugar, honey, or any other natural product," so even though my desserts call for other sweeteners in addition to the stuff in your sugar bowl, I also use these more "virtuous" sweeteners judiciously as well.

"But wait," you say, "aren't fruits loaded with sugar?" Yes, indeed, but the sugar in fresh fruits comes with fiber, which slows down its absorption into the bloodstream. This is why I always recommend using fruit in season; it is inherently sweet, and recipes require much less additional sweetener.

Butter

There's no getting around the fact that butter has taken a bum rap in recent decades as fats have been demonized in general and butter in particular. Yet, as fat-phobia took over our diets in the last fifty years, a majority of Americans have become overweight. Clearly fat alone is not at the heart of our obesity epidemic. We need fat. Without it, humans would never have evolved the big brains that put high-energy demands on our food. Fat delivers more concentrated energy than protein or carbohydrates. Yes, butter contains saturated fats. Equally true, butter is essential to many desserts. It is an article of faith among old-school chefs that almost any deficiency in a recipe can be solved by adding more butter. Like many common beliefs, there is an element of truth to this. Butter tastes great. It has gorgeous texture. It can help make baked goods lighter, airier, and crisper. In almost every recipe in this book, I have cut back the amount of butter that a more traditional dessert chef would call for, using just what is necessary for taste and texture. But not all butters

Millet Grains
and Flour

Amaranth Grains
and Flour

are equal. Unsalted butter made from the milk of grass-fed cows is the only kind I use. While high in fat, it is also high in healthful omega-3.

Flours

The vast majority of baked desserts rely on flour for their body and structure. Without flour, a pie is just a puddle of fruits; a cake is all filling and frosting. Most flours are made from pulverized grains, nuts, or seeds and they all contribute protein and carbohydrates to a recipe. Depending on how refined or processed they are, they can also contribute vitamins, minerals, and healthier unsaturated fats. Adding other flours (detailed below) in addition to—or sometimes instead of—traditional white flour can up the nutritional value of desserts while broadening the range of flavors and texture of baked goods. Nationwide, the best brand of high-quality white flour is King Arthur, however I've noticed recently that local growers and millers have been turning out superb flours with more flavorful strains of wheat. If you have such farmers and millers in your area, seek them out.

ALL-PURPOSE: This is the white flour—made from wheat—that most home bakers use for everything. On the plus side it contains protein. On the other side of the ledger it has a high amount of simple carbohydrates that your body rapidly turns into sugar. Because it has gluten (for most of us this protein is a good thing), it is uniquely able to create an airy structure or crumb that is essential for many cakes, pies, and pastries.

WHOLE WHEAT: Too long relegated to the stodgy-sounding "health food" category, whole wheat flour produced by modern milling methods carries the full flavor of wheat without the off-putting texture of mulch. Because it includes every part of the grain it is rich in vitamins, minerals, and antioxidants and, most importantly, it contains fiber, which helps slow down the absorption of sugar. Rustic desserts such as pies and crisps that incorporate whole wheat in the dough have more forceful overall flavor and texture.

CORN FLOUR (FINELY GROUND CORNMEAL): Adds sweetness, fiber, and a pleasantly sandy—but not gritty—texture. It is rich in minerals such as selenium, which promotes utilization of vitamins C and E. It is also a good source of B vitamins. It comes in various degrees of grinding, which allows you to vary the texture of the finished recipe. Many varieties of corn are naturally sweet; by using them I found I could reduce white sugar.

CHICKPEA FLOUR: High in protein and gluten-free, chickpeas (also known as the ubiquitous garbanzo in Spanish cooking) have a pleasantly strong nutlike flavor that goes well with the bold effect of spices.

QUINOA FLOUR: A relative of beets and spinach, quinoa isn't a true grain, but it is very much like a grain in its nutritional properties. In addition to having vitamins, minerals, and fiber, it is the only grainlike food that has complete protein with all nine amino acids. Gluten-phobes take heart: There is none here.

AMARANTH: Not to be outdone by the Incas, who are often associated with quinoa, the Aztecs loved their amaranth. It has more protein than wheat and is a source of iron, potassium, and magnesium. When used with wheat it helps maintain moistness in the crumb. NASA has recommended it as a part of the diet on space missions.

MILLET: Millet is nearly as high in protein as wheat and, importantly, high in fiber, which slows down the uptake of sugar. It is rich in minerals and B vitamins and often contains heart-healthy Omega-3s that help lower bad cholesterol.

FLAXSEED FLOUR (FLAX MEAL): It's very nutty, high in Omega-3, protein, B vitamins, and many minerals. Make sure to get milder-tasting golden flaxseeds or flour.

BUCKWHEAT: A relative of sorrel and rhubarb—but without their strong tartness—buckwheat has an earthy flavor that evokes cold winter mornings and a crackling fireplace. What pioneer chronicle would be complete without a scene of a farmhouse breakfast with a stack of buckwheat pancakes? Buckwheat is rich in fiber and complex carbohydrates, so it slows down sugar absorption.

Nuts

People have been eating nuts for as long as there have been people. All nuts are rich in protein, vitamins, and minerals and contain no gluten. They are also high in heart-healthy fats. Roasting brings out that special toasted quality that we think of when we describe an ingredient as nutty—which, when used to describe other foods, is meant as a high form of compliment.

WHOLE OR CHOPPED NUTS: When eaten whole or lightly chopped they are the very essence of crunchiness, which is the first quality that your palate searches out before deciding how something tastes. In this book you'll find recipes with almonds, walnuts, pecans, cashews, pine nuts, pistachios, and hazelnuts. They are forceful and delicious players in any filling or topping.

NUT MILKS: Soaked, steeped, and blended with water, nut milks are popular with people who are lactose intolerant or avoid animal products, and anyone looking for new and satisfying flavors. They have much of the nutritional value of whole nuts in

note

You can find some of the less traditional flours used in this book under the Bob's Red Mill brand at supermarkets, natural food stores, and online. You can also mill your own flours and meals easily at home; with one of the machines on page 26.

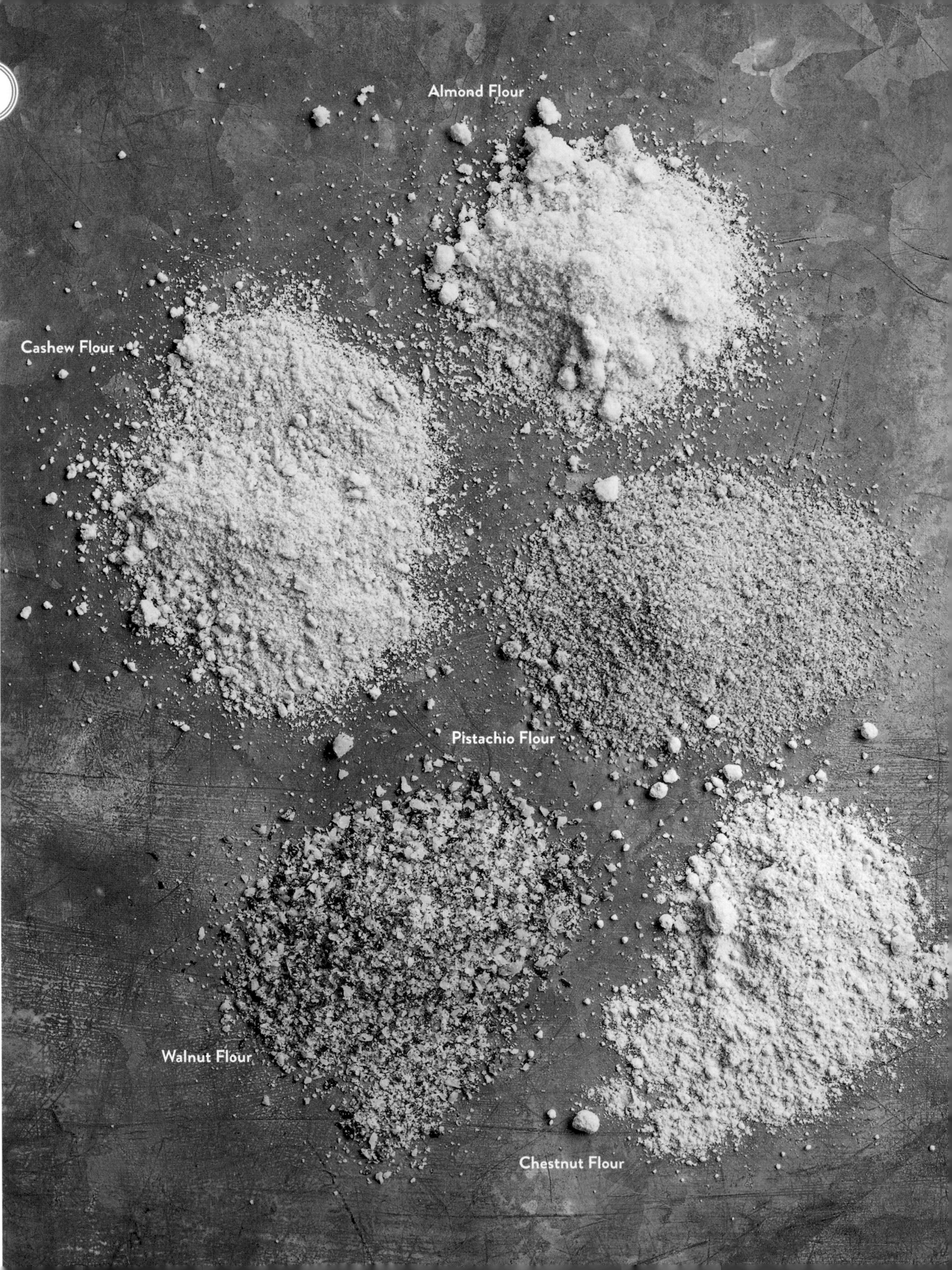

Almond Flour

Cashew Flour

Pistachio Flour

Walnut Flour

Chestnut Flour

a less concentrated form (because they are blended with and diluted with water). Importantly, in recipes that seek to increase depth of flavor while holding back on sweetener, they contribute complex flavors not found in dairy products. I recommend making your own fresh almond milk (page 244) when possible.

NUT OILS: Many of the desserts in this book take advantage of the full and round mouthfeel that fat lends to a recipe. Nut oils are invaluable as a textural and tenderizing agent. Apart from the fact that they are very low in saturated fat, their deep flavors suffuse the crust and crumb in every recipe where I call for them, sometimes instead of butter, sometimes along with it. With the exception of a few high-quality brands, noted in the recipes, I avoid extract, which is usually synthetic . . . and tastes like it!

Nut Flours

Nut-based baked goods are popular with people who seek to avoid gluten. The rest of us like nut-flour desserts because they are delicious, nuanced, and highly nutritious. Since they are relatively high in fat (the good kind), nut flours preserve moistness in the crumb of baked desserts. Although you can buy many nut flours, you might find that you don't use some of them often enough to keep them fresh or justify the expense. Dedicated DIY home chefs can grind their own beautifully fresh nut flours using one of the mills recommended on page 26.

ALMOND FLOUR: The most-used nut flour in Europe. No doubt the popularity of almonds stems in part from the fact that Arab and Turkish pastry chefs relied on them heavily and it is through them that we have inherited many of our dessert traditions. Of course that begs the question: "Why were the caliph's bakers so in love with almonds?" The answer would be: "Because they taste great." Packed with nutrients, no nut delivers more nutrition than almonds, a feature that I regard as "free gift with purchase." As a dessert maker, I value them first for their deliciousness.

CHESTNUT FLOUR: Before wheat and other cultivated grains made their way into Western Europe, ancient peoples ate a lot of chestnuts and acorns. They fed the acorns to their pigs (where they help produce the world's most coveted hams), but saved the chestnuts for their own consumption. To this day, they have maintained a place in the European diet. They are particularly high in vitamin C and B vitamins and lower in fat than many nuts. Anyone who has ever gotten a whiff of chestnuts roasting on an open fire knows their lush sweet aroma.

PISTACHIO FLOUR: As Kermit once lamented, "It's not easy being green," but this is especially so for many so-called pistachio cakes, cookies, and pastries. That's because there is very little real pistachio in them. In all probability what you have been eating is pistachio paste, which is loaded with sugary ground almonds and food coloring. I don't know why anyone would want to mask the flavor of pistachio. It is so elegant. Thankfully, you can buy 100 percent pistachio flour or make your own quite easily.

WALNUT FLOUR: Of all the nuts, I find these most evoke the sense of a forest. This is not to say that they taste like lumber or leaves. Instead, they have a hint of the heady aroma of freshly felled timber and are brimming with heart-healthy monounsaturated fats. Walnut flour delivers a powerful taste note that suffuses and supports the more delicate tones in a recipe.

HAZELNUT FLOUR: European bakers have long prized and used hazelnuts, but Americans are just catching on. They have the most monounsaturated (heart-healthy) fat of commonly eaten nuts (pecans are a close second). Along with almonds, they are the most chocolate-friendly of the nuts used in baking and desserts.

Chocolate

Its scientific name, *Theobroma cacao*, means "food of the gods," and if I were a deity, I would certainly prefer it to ambrosia, the beverage of choice on Mount Olympus. I was pleased to read a few years ago that chocolate has the same health-boosting ingredient as red wine, resveratrol. It's loaded with antioxidants, and its fat, though saturated, is largely converted into monounsaturated fat during digestion. It is also high in substances known as flavonoids that are very heart protective. So I'm good with chocolate . . . *but only high-quality chocolate with a relatively low percentage of sugar.* In its original state in the jungles of Brazil, cacao nibs (the part of the plant made into chocolate) are very tannic, i.e., astringent and bitter, but over the years the Aztecs and the Mayans bred their cacao for less tannins so that high-quality chocolate made from these cultivated forms of cacao require much less sugar in order to be palatable. The Harvard T.H. Chan of School Public Health recommends that if you eat desserts, the healthiest ones will contain fruit, nuts, or chocolate (or all three). In these recipes I recommend chocolate that is 70% cacao (which means it is made with less sugar).

Vanilla Beans and Paste

Vanilla beans—which contribute attractive aroma—are actually the fermented dried seeds of the vanilla orchid. They add depth of flavor and roundness on the palate.

Vanilla paste is pulverized seeds and I use them for convenience. I avoid commercial extract because of its synthetic flavor.

Herbs

We all know that leafy green herbs can wake up sauces, marinades, roasts, and everything you grill. When added at the last minute—while a dish is still warm—their oils disperse into the air, carrying their own tantalizing scents as well as aromas they pick up from that grilled ribeye. In baking—or in any cooking involved with desserts—they play the same role that cooked herbs do in a soup or stew, adding depth and complexity, producing fuller flavor. Remember when you cut down on sweetener you have to compensate with something else, because only fuller flavor will satisfy you, especially if you strive for the reduced portions that I recommend. You are always looking for a knockout punch of flavor. Mint has long been included in the dessert canon. Basil brings the fragrant freshness of cool spring air to the palate as well as a hint of licorice (which always seeks out sweetness and showcases it). Lemon verbena contributes all the citrusy/floral notes of lemon without adding more tartness. Rosemary and caramelized stone fruits pair well (careful, though, because rosemary tends to hog the palate). Even parsley can work in a dessert, exhibit A being the parsley-flavored Very Fresh Green Cake (page 130) I created just to prove to myself that it could be done. I plan to serve it every St. Patrick's Day from now until I am pushing daisies . . . or shamrocks.

Spices

I have to wonder who started the rumor that spices gained popularity in European cuisine because they masked the taste of rotten meat, fish, and poultry. Talk about lipstick on a pig! Once a thing has gone rotten there's no disguising it. I believe that spices were prized because they accent certain flavors, because they contribute their own taste, and because they help to focus and sharpen diffuse flavors. Almost all spices contain volatile oils—aromatic compounds that dissipate rapidly and infuse every mouthful of cake, pie, cookie, or pudding. They also bring antifungal and antibacterial properties as a side benefit, which is why just about every spice plays a role in folk medicine. As a chef, however, what interests me most is how they coax out other flavors and add their own powerful notes to a dessert. Like herbs, spices accentuate complexity and play on sweetness, which allows us to use less sweetener.

Chances are when you use spices in your desserts, cinnamon is your default; from bear claws to Danish pastries, it is the one spice you can be sure to find in any bake shop or any dessert cookbook. I like cinnamon, especially the way it helps marry the flavors of butter and baked flour, but for the adventurous dessert chef, there is much more to the spice world. Nutmeg and mace, which are made from different parts of the same plant, are standbys in holiday recipes. They are both pungent and complement sweetness. Cloves are potent; there is no mistaking or hiding their flavor, which is why I use them in desserts with other strong flavors. Star anise, fennel seed, and licorice root all tend to highlight sweetness, so when I cut back on sugar, I find that these spices underscore what remains and convince the palate that it's getting more sweetener than is actually there. Cardamom works similarly but with its own signature taste rather than the licorice notes of anise and fennel. Ginger has fruity overtones and peppery heat. Although I'm not a fan of the chipotle-and-chocolate trend—a combo that can pummel and thereby deaden the palate—the right amount of spicy heat can kick-start the tasting experience. Thai chiles do the same and add vegetal flavor. White and black pepper contribute mild heat and subtle floral accents. Black pepper with peaches and sea salt with watermelon are two combinations that I never could have imagined in childhood, but now that I have survived my extended adolescence, I adore these pairings.

Bottom line: Spice-driven cuisine is fascinating and I have just scratched the surface in this book. I encourage you to devise your own combinations. I think you will be surprised to find how extensively the dessert chef can draw from his or her spice rack. No, let me restate that. Forget the spice rack! You probably have spices in there that have been hanging around longer than your oldest pair of shoes. They have likely lost most of their flavor. Buy your spices fresh; roast and grind them just before using. No need to buy a special spice grinder for this purpose; a clean coffee grinder works beautifully.

Specialty Ingredients

Every time I go shopping in a foreign country or walk into an ethnic market here at home, I'm always on the lookout for new ingredients to liven up my next dessert. One of my goals in this book is to encourage readers to seek out new ingredients from around the world to include in their desserts. Here are a few of the more unfamiliar ones that we use in this book.

NOTE: ABOUT SOURCES: When I first started writing cookbooks, I would have to include page after page of specialty markets, mail-order houses in hard-to-spell countries, and cranky farmers, but every unusual ingredient or tool in this book is now available online. When appropriate I have noted sources for especially unusual ingredients throughout.

Drinking Vinegars (Shrubs)

One of the chance discoveries of this book came about when I visited the Brooklyn outpost of Pok Pok, Andy Ricker's celebrated Thai restaurant in Portland, Oregon. It was a sultry day, the kind when even the leaves seem to wilt and forget that throwing cooling shade is part of their job description. At the front of the restaurant I was surprised to see a list of shrubs, beverages made by combining drinking vinegars with seltzer. Other than superexpensive twenty-year-old balsamic vinegar, I had never thought of vinegars as a sweetener (although there is no better way of bringing out the full summer flavor of strawberries even in February). After one sip of the sweet/tart, refreshing drink, I was sold, and realized this intensely flavored ingredient, perfectly balanced between sweet and sour, would provide fireworks of flavor in a reduced-sugar recipe.

I've since learned that drinking vinegars have been prized since biblical times and that they were widely used as a vitamin C supplement in the colonial era. In our own era they have become the darlings of hipster mixologists. From panna cotta to tea cakes to macerated fruit, anything that wants a splash of syrup is livened up with these vinegars. Tamarind is my favorite flavor (maybe because it has hints of caramelized sugar), but I also like pineapple, apple, and ginger. You can buy Pok Pok's Som line of vinegars and others online and even in some markets, and I have included shortcuts to making your own, less expensive, homemade substitutes on page 251. In many cases you could also substitute a good-quality aged balsamico.

Essential Oils

Nothing broadens flavor like these oils, which are made by distilling or pressing ingredients to extract their aromatic flavorful elements. As distinct from extracts, essential oils contain many flavor components. Oils are pure and pressed out of the natural ingredients. Oils of bitter orange, pine needle, bergamot, ginger, rose petal, and others prove so interesting to the palate that less sugar is required to achieve delightful desserts. The best food-grade oils are pricey, but just a single drop can transform a recipe from run-of-the-mill into something new and different. Of all the gustatory experiences, aroma has the most subtlety and variety. Some scientists have devoted their lives to the study of aroma as it applies to food. Retro-nasal gastronomy is the scientific—if unromantic—term for this body of knowledge. Human beings can distinguish millions of aroma combinations.

Be advised: *Use only food-grade essential oils!* And while you are at it, buy the best available; some essential oils are as unpleasant as the exhaust from an outboard motor on a windless day. My favorite—in fact the only brand I find consistently satisfying—is Aftelier. If you are interested in this subject go to International Flavors and Fragrance. The Monell Institute (monell.org) offers even more in-depth science.

Thickeners, Stabilizers, Powders, and Gels

Although thickeners are used on occasion by savory chefs, dessert makers would be lost without them. Pies would spill their juices on our laps, puddings would collapse into a gooey puddle, meringues would deflate in less time than it takes to say "Where did that meringue go?" To add body to desserts, flour, cornstarch, arrowroot, and gelatin are trusted standbys, but at times, especially with some delicate ingredients, they can mute the palate or iron out the wrinkles in texture that make each mouthful more interesting. Fortunately, we've added some new arrows to our thickening quiver in recent years. Molecular cuisine has given us potent thickening agents like xanthan and methylcellulose, which, although they sound like test tube creations are, in fact, completely organic. From the wave-tossed shorelines of the ocean, seaweed has given us the gift of agar, which keeps things nicely gelled at temperatures that would melt common gelatin. Chia seeds, which were unheard of in my apprenticeship, create beautiful texture and are packed with protein and heart-healthy fats, but I can imagine my teachers of long ago saying, "Get those mouse droppings out of my kitchen!"

Other Novel Ingredients *(pictured pages 22 to 23)*

MAIZ MORADO (1): Dried South American sweet corn that pretty much goes with everything. Very balanced in flavor, beautiful deep purple in color.

GOJI BERRIES (2): An immigrant from China—full of antioxidants, similar in taste to dried cherries.

RED BEAN PASTE (3): From Japan, good for fillings all on its own, not overly sweet. High in protein.

FREEZE-DRIED FRUITS: Such as raspberries (4), oranges (6), and grapes (7). Concentrated fruit that's tart, sweet, crunchy, with lots of vitamins and fiber. Freeze-dried fruit powders have proved invaluable in creating recipes for frostings and fillings and they're every bit as fun as butter cream . . . but without the butter! Blackberry powder, which adds flavor and a lovely color, is the one I use most.

RICE WAFER PAPER (5): Much more healthful than the *New York Times*, completely edible.

VERJUS (8): A nonalcoholic syrup made from pressed, unripe grapes. Full of flavor, a good substitute for vinegar. I've loved this forever.

MATCHA (9): Dried freshly harvested green tea leaves. A truly caffeinated herb and an oxidant's worst enemy (it's full of antioxidants).

DRIED HIBISCUS (10): Adds color and tartness. Jamaicans call it sorrel and make tea with it, as do the folks that make Red Zinger. Wonderful for a poaching liquid for fruits.

THAI SCENTED CANDLE (11): Its smoke is used to infuse puddings. Also nice to light and perfume the air as you eat dessert. After you blow it out, it still releases a beautiful aroma.

BEE POLLEN (12): The bees gather it and store it in the hive. The beekeepers help themselves and take it to market. High in protein and vitamins. A true superfood.

CACAO BEANS (13): These beans are the raw material for chocolate. I think they are magic. Crushed, they are called cacao nibs.

POPPED QUINOA (14): Crunchy as Rice Krispies but so much more nutritious. Thank you, Incas.

SAKURA SYRUP (15): A Japanese syrup made from cherry petals—floral and fruity.

TAMARIND PODS AND PASTE (16): Used throughout Asia to flavor chutneys, soups, and sauces. Available fresh, frozen, or as a concentrated extract or paste in many Asian markets. Slightly sour, a little sweet, with notes of caramel.

FENNEL POLLEN (17): High in nutrients, it has lovely and subtle licorice flavor that makes everything seem sweeter.

A FEW HANDY TOOLS

I assume that you have a rolling pin; some kind of standing mixer; pie plates; cake, tart, and springform pans; and a bowl scraper, but in recent years I've come across some useful, less common tools that have made the dessert-making process easier and often better. You don't have to invest in everything on these pages, but the next time you're baking and you say, "Gee, I wish they made a thing that did this," you might find the answer in these next few pages.

NESTING CIRCLE CUTTERS (1): Different desserts want to be different sizes. Instead of using an overturned water tumbler or your aunt Mabel's teacup to trace a circle, you'll be able to make cookies and biscuits with exactly the right diameter.

IMMERSION BLENDER (2): The most convenient type of blender on the market and best of all it's the easiest to clean. Perfect for purees, foams, and fancy Modernist ingredients.

SPRINGERLE MOLDS (3): cookie molds with debossed designs used to make Springerle Cookies (page 186), this "new" tool has been around for eight centuries, but I bet it's new to you.

ZESTING MICROPLANER (4): So much of a citrus fruit's flavor is locked away in the zest. This tool is designed specifically to shave off the oil-rich zest without removing the bitter white pith (or shredding your knuckles).

CARTA FATA PAPER (5): This see-through synthetic is miraculous. You can freeze it or heat it to 400°F and it lets you watch ingredients as they cook. Present them at the table like a florist's bouquet with its shiny wrap.

DIGITAL SCALE (6): Although we use standard volume measurements throughout the book (teaspoons, cups, ounces), for those times when you want to weigh things, these are relatively inexpensive and superaccurate.

TWEEZERS (7): Forget about all those pictures of chefs bent over, nose to the plate, painstakingly arranging teeny-tiny ingredients just so. I have found this tool very practical for those times when I want to peel away baking paper from the side of a pan or remove runaway seeds from fruit juices . . . better than trying to pick them up with press-on nails!

SPHERIFICATION SPOON (8): invented by Ferran Adrià to handle gelled globes (see Fizzicals, page 213). It's basically a slotted spoon with a lot more slots and useful for moving gels and for fishing stray seeds and pits out of liquids.

NOVACART BAKING MOLDS (9): Reusable, easy to clean, and wonderfully nonstick, these paper molds don't require buttering or greasing. Good for a few uses.

FLEXIPAT MOLDS (10): Completely flexible and totally nonstick, they can go from freezer to oven and will increase your repertoire of shapes not available with metal molds. The professional baker's new favorite tool.

RECHARGEABLE WHIPPED CREAM DISPENSER AND NITROUS OXIDE CARTRIDGES (11): makes light and airy whipped creams and delicate fruit foams for frothy and aerated desserts. The more I use it, the more I discover new uses for it.

NEWFANGLED BUNDT PAN (12): Traditional Bundt pans haven't changed their shapes since all great-grandmothers put their hair up in a bun. These computer-designed, laser-cut pans have opened up a whole new world of shapes for bakers. My favorite is made by Nordic Ware.

THREE-INCH PAINT BRUSH (13): When applying a soak to a cake, it's tedious to use a 1-inch brush. It also tends to damage the crumb if you keep going over the cake. This wide brush allows you to do it in one fell swipe.

GRAIN MILL FOR HOMEMADE FLOURS: If you're fanatical about freshly milled heritage grains and nut flours or hate to buy specialty flours online, this is just the thing for you. It's especially practical for milling ingredients such as millet or quinoa when you only need a small quantity. That way you won't end up with partial packages of these perishable flours hanging around the kitchen.

The grain mill attachment for the KitchenAid Stand Mixer is economical and reliable. The Ferrari of home grain mills is made by KoMo (see photo, page 13). It's expensive, but what true zealot lets price stand in their way?

1

PIES

They Call Me Crustmaster

*t*hough pies are uncomplicated recipes, they can be deceptively difficult to master. How do you properly bake (and/or prebake) the bottom crust? How do you get the top to lie down correctly and how do you pinch the top and bottom together? Underneath its golden crust, a pie is a bit of a mystery, a gift to be unwrapped. Just as the ability to make an omelet is the time-honored way of gauging the skills of a chef, a pie is the litmus test for the baker. Though uncomplicated, it is the measure of your mastery of technique and ingredients plus your understanding of what happens in the oven. A successful pie is a contrast of flaky and juicy, sweet and sour, crisp and soft, crusty and fruity, an inside and an outside. It is made from the simplest of ingredients, yet how those ingredients combine is what differentiates a wonderful pie from something that can only be salvaged with a scoop of ice cream on top. It is with a sense of reverence for dessert history that I have used new, or overlooked, ingredients and novel combinations to create pies with fewer sweeteners but with no less contentment for your palate. And if these pies don't get eaten up at dinner, I urge you to indulge come morning . . . pie for breakfast!

Flaky Piecrust • Apple Pie with Caramelized Honey and Tamarind Vinegar
Blueberry Pie with an Orange Accent • Ginger Peachy Pie
Gin Crust Winter Pie • Lemon Curd Pie with Meringue
Kabocha Persimmon Pie • Chocolate Quinoa Kweem Pie

The Perfect Piecrust—Foolproof and Flaky

We make pies because they are a lovely way to capture the flavor of seasonal fruits, but we judge them first and foremost on crispness, crunchiness, and flakiness of their crusts. Scientists have written volumes worthy of the Nobel Prize on the chemistry and physics behind a great crust. To my way of thinking it all comes down to three questions:

What About Flakiness?

After a lifetime at the mixing bowl, I can say with the conviction borne of having baked thousands of pies, that I consistently get the best results with butter. The water content in the butter and the water you add to the dough becomes trapped in the gluten matrix. When you heat the pie dough in the oven, the water turns into steam and inflates the pockets of gluten, producing flakes around each of those steam pockets. Here is a good place to remind you to cut air vents in the top of your crust, since all that steam has to escape somewhere and you don't want it to blow holes in the crust at random.

Why Does Pie Dough Roll out into a Sheet You Can Pick Up Like a Piece of Paper?

Wheat flour contains two proteins—glutenin and gliadin. When you add water, these proteins form gluten: a stretchy network that gives pie dough its structure. This network forms a matrix of linked strands that hold the water and starches together and form a sheet when you roll it out. If gluten is overdeveloped from manipulating the dough too much, it becomes really elastic and resists rolling out. Overworked dough is tough. The gluten strands set up best if they are left alone to relax for at least thirty minutes after rolling.

What Gives Pie Dough Its Golden Color?

The Maillard reaction takes place when amino acids (from the proteins in flour) combine with sugar (from the breakdown of carbohydrates in flour). It is essential for the golden brown color and for thousands of flavor compounds that are created when we heat these elements to 375°F. What starts as a bland dough tasting only of raw flour, butter, and salt becomes an attractive flavor bomb.

With the advent of more precisely milled and less-gritty whole wheat flour I have taken to adding a tablespoon or two of whole wheat as a kind of down-home "seasoning" that I feel goes well with the old-timey feel of pie. It also adds a bit of desirable fiber.

And now, let's do it!

FLAKY PIECRUST

MAKES ONE 9-INCH SINGLE CRUST / DOUBLE FOR A DOUBLE-CRUST PIE

1½ cups unbleached all-purpose flour, plus more for dusting

1 tablespoon whole wheat flour

¼ teaspoon kosher salt

10 tablespoons (1¼ sticks) cold unsalted butter, preferably grass-fed, high fat, cut into ¼-inch pieces

¼ cup plus 1 tablespoon ice water or gin

north, south, east, west

Don't roll in just one direction. This will overdevelop the gluten and you'll begin to feel resistance, as if the dough wants to snap back. Instead, roll north, south, east, west, starting from the center each time and rolling out to the edge.

1 | Combine the flours and salt in the bowl of a food processor and pulse one or two times. Add the butter pieces and pulse until the mixture resembles tiny pebbles. Gradually add the water and pulse *just until the dough comes together*. Dump the dough onto a work surface and flatten into a ½-inch-thick disk. Wrap in plastic and freeze for at least 20 minutes or refrigerate overnight. (If doubling the recipe, divide the dough into two equal portions, then flatten and wrap each portion separately.)

2 | Dust a work surface and a rolling pin with flour. Roll out the dough (north, south, east, and west) into a ¼-inch-thick circle. To prevent sticking, sprinkle a bit of flour on the dough as you work and flip the dough over occasionally. On the last roll, roll it out to ⅛-inch thickness. Lift the dough around the edges to "weigh" it with your hands; it should feel uniform.

3 | Preheat the oven to 400°F.

4 | Transfer the dough to a 9-inch pie plate, rolling it back onto the rolling pin as you would a carpet. Set the pin over the pie plate at the edge nearest you and unroll the dough over and into it. Using your index finger, push the dough into the plate where the bottom meets the sides, pressing into the rim with your opposite thumb. Working around the pie plate, pinch the dough along the rim to make a lip that overhangs by ½ inch *into* the pie plate (this enables you to form a fluted edge), then flute the edges by interlocking your thumbs and index fingers, working your way around the rim. Freeze until the dough is as hard as a rock, 20 minutes to 1 hour (this will prevent the dough from shrinking as it bakes). Fill the crust as directed and bake, with or without a top crust.

(RECIPE CONTINUES)

5 | For a blind-baked pie shell, cover the edge of the crust with an aluminum foil "collar" to prevent it from overbrowning. This piece of foil is the only thing between you and an unsuccessful crust. Press it against the underside of the outside rim of the plate and be sure it is fully covering the edge of the crust. Place the crust in the oven and bake until the crust has a lightly browned edge and the base is still slightly raw but the starches have set, 10 to 15 minutes. Remove from the oven and carefully remove the foil. If the base has puffed up, prick it all over with a fork. Return the crust to the oven and bake until it is lightly browned all over, about 10 minutes more. Remove from the oven and set aside on the counter to cool, sliding a fork underneath the dish to allow airflow.

If you want to mix by hand. Whisk together the flours and salt in a large mixing bowl. Add the butter pieces and, using your hands, alternately press the butter into the flour between your fingers, then squeeze the dough in your fists until it becomes granular. Add the water and mix with your hands just until the dough comes together into a ball. Dump the dough onto a work surface and flatten into a ½-inch-thick disk. Wrap in plastic and freeze for at least 20 minutes or refrigerate overnight. Proceed as above.

conditioning THE DOUGH

Chilled dough is difficult to roll straight out of the refrigerator and may crack or split when you put pressure on it with your rolling pin. After you chill the dough and are ready to proceed with rolling it out, leave it at room temp for 7 to 10 minutes, then gently massage it with your palms and thumbs. By compacting it, you create a dough that is uniformly structured. By massaging it, you repair faults and cracks. Where you see a crack develop, push it back together. Massage for just a few minutes—don't overdo it—then roll as usual.

Blueberry Pie with an Orange Accent, page 38

Ginger Peachy Pie, page 40

Apple Pie with Caramelized Honey and Tamarind Vinegar, opposite

tweaked **FRUIT PIES**

These three basic fruit pies got an attitude adjustment to show how little you need to add to the natural sweetness of fruit and how a few ingredients— just one or two—can transform the flavor and the texture of these old favorites.

APPLE PIE with Caramelized Honey and Tamarind Vinegar

MAKES ONE 9-INCH DOUBLE-CRUST PIE/SERVES 10 • This is a novel approach to the time-honored apple pie. There's no refined sugar in it, only honey and magical sweetened tamarind vinegar (available online or make your own, page 251). It replaces the more traditional lemon juice used in most pies and adds molasses-like depth. Caramelizing the honey develops hundreds of flavor compounds. Instead of adding cornstarch to thicken the filling, I use nutritious chia seeds. These few simple adjustments produce an apple pie with flavor that comes on strong and can stand up to an after-dinner espresso or perhaps some warm Armagnac.

1 double-batch Flaky Piecrust dough (page 31), chilled

¼ cup local honey

¼ cup tamarind vinegar, such as Pok Pok Som (or homemade, page 251)

3 pounds apples (about 9), preferably a mix of Fuji, Granny Smith, Golden Delicious, and Pink Lady, peeled, cored, and cut into ⅛-inch slices

½ teaspoon kosher salt

1 tablespoon black chia seeds

1 large egg

Organic cane sugar, for sprinkling

1 | Preheat the oven to 375°F.

2 | Roll out one disk of the dough to ⅛-inch thickness. Flip a 9-inch pie plate over and place it on the dough. Then, using a sharp knife, cut out a circle with a 2-inch border around the edge of the pie plate. Remove the pie plate and roll out the dough 1 inch more in all directions. Roll the dough back onto the pin, then unroll it like a carpet into the pie plate.

3 | Using your index finger, push the dough into the plate where the bottom meets the sides, pressing into the rim with your opposite thumb. Working around the pie plate, pinch the dough along the rim to leave a lip that overhangs by ¼ inch into the pie plate. Flute the edges by interlocking your thumbs and index fingers, working your way around the rim. Freeze until the dough is as hard as a rock, 20 minutes to 1 hour (this prevents the dough from shrinking as it bakes).

4 | Cover the edge of the crust with an aluminum foil "collar" to prevent it from overbrowning. This piece of foil is the only thing between you and an unsuccessful crust. Press it against the underside of the outside rim of the plate, and be sure it fully covers the edge of the crust. Place in the oven and bake until the crust has a lightly browned edge and the base is still slightly raw but the starches have set, 10 to 15 minutes. Remove from the oven and carefully remove

(RECIPE CONTINUES)

do the math!

A computer survey of the 140 most popular apple pie recipes on the Food Network website shows that they average 366 grams of sugar for a standard apple pie. Our pie calls for 200 grams in the form of honey and tamarind vinegar. Trust me, ours won't fail you on the sweetness vs. satisfaction scale.

the foil. If the base has puffed up, prick it all over with a fork. Return the crust to the oven and bake until it is lightly browned all over, about 10 minutes more. Remove from the oven and set aside on the counter to cool, sliding a fork underneath the dish to allow airflow.

5 | **Make the filling.** In a medium saucepan, bring the honey to a boil over medium-high heat and cook until it begins to bubble and smoke. (The entire surface will be covered in large, foamy bubbles.) Immediately add the vinegar and ¼ cup water to stop the caramelization; if you don't do this right away, the honey will continue to cook, and burn. Add the apples and ¼ teaspoon of the salt. Cook, turning the apples frequently, until some of the juice from the apples starts to release, about 2 minutes. Add the chia seeds and stir to distribute. Cook until the apples have softened (different apples cook at different rates; it's okay if they are not uniformly softened), about 12 minutes. Remove from the heat and let cool completely.

6 | **Make the egg wash.** In a small bowl, whisk together the egg, ¼ cup water, and the remaining salt. Set aside to allow the salt to dissolve.

7 | Preheat the oven to 350°F.

8 | Transfer the cooled filling to the cooled shell. With a spatula, gently compact and shape the filling into a neat mound. Roll out the remaining dough and, using a sharp knife, cut out a circle that overhangs by ½ inch beyond the edges of the pie plate; the dough should be ⅛ inch thick. Brush the edges of the dough with the egg wash. Brush the rim of the baked pie shell with egg wash as well. Gently pick up the dough and lay it over the fruit, egg wash side down. Working around the rim, pinch the dough together with the bottom crust, interlocking your thumbs and index fingers (see page 33). Trim away the excess dough and set aside. Brush the top of the pie all over with the egg wash, then use a sharp knife to make ½-inch slits in the top crust in two concentric circles (12 slits around the rim and 4 in the center), leaving enough room in the center for decoration.

9 | If desired, reroll the dough scraps and cut out shapes either freehand with a sharp knife or with a cookie cutter to decorate the pie. Brush the underside of the cutouts with egg wash, place on the pie, brush the top with the egg wash, and sprinkle a pinch of sugar all over the top of the crust.

10 | Bake until the pie filling begins to bubble out of the vents and the top of the crust is golden brown, about 45 minutes. Remove from the oven and set aside on the counter, sliding a fork underneath the dish to allow airflow. Cool for 1 to 2 hours to let the filling set before serving.

the ALCHEMY *of* CARAMEL

Caramel is a simple miracle whereby sugar is transformed into thousands of new flavor molecules with a variety of flavors and colors. Its boring sweetness becomes a layered flavor that is sweet, bitter, woodsy, floral, and probably two hundred other adjectives. The chemical formula for sucrose is $C_{12}H_{22}O_{11}$, which means each molecule of sugar contains 12 carbon atoms, 22 hydrogen atoms, and 11 oxygen atoms. When sugar cooks in a hot pan it turns from a solid to a liquid and the molecules become energized to the point of breaking apart to form new ones with an astonishing range of flavors that hardly resemble the original ingredient. Sugar in a hot pan caramelizes at 380°F, but it will caramelize at even lower temperatures if the heat is applied slowly, and the resulting flavor is much better. However, slow cooking does require constant supervision because sugar left too long will burst into flame! Another tip: Avoid stirring caramel as it cooks or it may crystallize, which means it forms granular chunks that will not melt. It is better to swirl the pan, a technique that the French call *vanner*.

BLUEBERRY PIE
with an Orange Accent

MAKES ONE 9-INCH DOUBLE-CRUST PIE/SERVES 10 • A classic blueberry pie contains a full cup of sugar. Here I have swapped it for honey, reducing sugar by 75 percent compared to the blueberry pie I used to make. Chia adds a pleasing texture to the thickener. A tiny bit of bergamot essential oil lends a delicate come-hither background note, but you can achieve some of the same effect with orange zest. See photo on page 34.

1 double-batch Flaky Piecrust (page 31)

3 pounds (about 8 cups) fresh (preferably) or frozen blueberries

¼ cup local honey

1 teaspoon vanilla paste

¼ cup cornstarch

1 tablespoon black chia seeds

Zest and juice of 1 orange

2 drops food-grade bergamot essential oil (optional)

1 large egg

¼ teaspoon kosher salt

Organic cane sugar, for sprinkling

1 | Preheat the oven to 375°F.

2 | Roll out one disk of the dough to ⅛-inch thickness. Flip a 9-inch pie plate over and place it on the dough. Then, using a sharp knife, cut out a circle with a 2-inch border around the edge of the pie plate. Remove the pie plate and roll out the dough 1 inch more in all directions. Roll the dough back onto the pin, then unroll it like a carpet into the pie plate.

3 | Using your index finger, push the dough into the plate where the bottom meets the sides, pressing into the rim with your opposite thumb. Working around the pie plate, pinch the dough along the rim to leave a lip that overhangs by ½ inch into the pie plate. Flute the edges by interlocking your thumbs and index fingers, working your way around the rim. Freeze until the dough is as hard as a rock, 20 minutes to 1 hour (this prevents the dough from shrinking as it bakes).

4 | Cover the edge of the crust with an aluminum foil "collar" to prevent it from overbrowning. This piece of foil is the only thing between you and an unsuccessful crust. Press it against the underside of the outside rim of the plate, and be sure it fully covers the edge of the crust. Place in the oven and bake until the crust has a lightly browned edge and the base is still slightly raw but the starches have set, 10 to 15 minutes. Remove from the oven and carefully remove the foil. If the base has puffed up, prick it all over with a fork. Return the crust to the oven and bake until it is lightly browned all over, about 10 minutes more. Remove from the oven and set aside to cool on the counter, sliding a fork underneath the dish to allow airflow.

5 | **Make the filling.** If using fresh blueberries, set aside 1 cup. Combine the remaining blueberries (or all the berries if using frozen) with the honey and vanilla in a heavy saucepan and bring to a boil over medium-high heat, stirring frequently to avoid scorching. Tap the cornstarch through a fine-mesh sieve onto the blueberries, then stir in the chia. In a small bowl, combine the orange juice, zest, and bergamot and add to the saucepan. Return the blueberry mixture to a boil and cook, stirring constantly, until the mixture thickens, about 1 minute. Set the filling aside to cool completely. Once cooled, add the reserved cup of fresh blueberries, if using.

6 | In a small bowl, whisk together the egg, ¼ cup water, and the salt to make an egg wash. Set aside to allow the salt to dissolve.

7 | Preheat the oven to 350°F.

8 | Transfer the cooled filling to the cooled shell. With a spatula, gently compact and shape the filling into a uniform mound. Roll out the remaining dough to ⅛-inch thickness and, using a sharp knife, cut out a circle that overhangs by ½ inch beyond the edges of the pie plate. Brush the edges of the dough with the egg wash. Brush the rim of the baked pie shell with egg wash as well. Gently pick up the dough and flip it over the filling, egg wash side down. (Don't roll the crust onto your rolling pin, as the egg wash will cause it to stick to the pin.) Working around the rim, pinch the dough together with the bottom crust, interlocking your thumbs and index fingers (see page 33). Trim away the excess dough and set aside. Brush the top of the pie all over with the egg wash, then use a sharp knife to make ½-inch slits in the top crust in two concentric circles (12 slits around the rim and 4 in the center), leaving enough room in the center for decoration.

9 | If desired, reroll the dough scraps and cut out shapes either freehand with a sharp knife or with a cookie cutter to decorate the pie. Brush the underside of the cutouts with egg wash, place on the pie, brush with egg wash, and sprinkle a pinch of sugar all over the top crust.

10 | Bake until the filling begins to bubble out of the vents and the top crust is golden brown, about 45 minutes. Remove from the oven and set aside on the counter, sliding a fork underneath the dish to allow airflow. Cool for 1 to 2 hours to let the filling set before serving.

note

Food-grade essential oils are highly concentrated, which can lead to that flavor lingering in one spot in the filling if it's added directly. To evenly distribute such intense flavor, I generally combine it with another liquid (in this case lemon juice) before adding to a mixture.

GINGER PEACHY PIE

MAKES ONE 9-INCH DOUBLE-CRUST PIE/SERVES 10 • Sometimes simply adding one ingredient—in this case, fresh grated ginger—broadens the range of flavor in a dessert so much that you don't miss all the sweetener that's left out. Ginger adds a bit of spicy heat that wakes up the palate and a floral note that pairs perfectly with peaches. It seems like such a minor addition to the canonical peach pie, yet I can't think of a clearer expression of the Sweet Spot philosophy: *Less sweetener + more flavor = a better dessert.* See photo on page 34.

1 double-batch Flaky Piecrust Dough (page 31)

3 pounds peaches, peeled, pitted, and cut into ⅛-inch-thick slices

¼ cup local honey

1 tablespoon peeled, grated fresh ginger

¼ cup cornstarch

1 tablespoon black chia seeds

1 large egg

¼ teaspoon kosher salt

Organic cane sugar, for sprinkling

1 | Preheat the oven to 375°F.

2 | Roll out one disk of the dough to ⅛-inch thickness. Flip a 9-inch pie plate over and place it on the dough. Then, using a sharp knife, cut out a circle with a 2-inch border around the edge of the pie plate. Remove the pie plate and roll out the dough 1 inch more in all directions. Roll the dough back onto the pin, then unroll it like a carpet into the pie plate.

3 | Using your index finger, push the dough into the plate where the bottom meets the sides, pressing into the rim with your opposite thumb. Working around the pie plate, pinch the dough along the rim to leave a lip that overhangs by ½ inch into the pie plate. Flute the edges by interlocking your thumbs and index fingers, working your way around the rim. Freeze until the dough is as hard as a rock, 20 minutes to 1 hour (this prevents the dough from shrinking as it bakes).

4 | Cover the edge of the crust with an aluminum foil "collar" to prevent it from overbrowning. This piece of foil is the only thing between you and an unsuccessful crust. Press it against the underside of the outside rim of the plate, and be sure it fully covers the edge of the crust. Place in the oven and bake until the crust has a lightly browned edge and the base is still slightly raw but the starches have set, 10 to 15 minutes. Remove from the oven and carefully remove the foil. If the base has puffed up, prick it all over with a fork. Return the crust to the oven and bake until it is lightly browned all over, about 10 minutes more. Remove from the oven and set aside to cool on the counter, sliding a fork underneath the dish to allow airflow.

5 | **Make the filling.** Combine the peaches with the honey and ginger in a heavy saucepan and bring to a boil over medium-high heat, stirring frequently to avoid scorching. Tap the cornstarch through a fine-mesh sieve onto the peaches, then stir in the chia. Return the mixture to a boil and cook, stirring constantly, until the mixture thickens, about 1 minute. Set the filling aside to cool completely.

6 | In a small bowl, whisk together the egg, ¼ cup water, and the salt to make an egg wash. Set aside to allow the salt to dissolve.

7 | Preheat the oven to 350°F.

8 | Transfer the cooled filling to the cooled shell. With a spatula, gently compact and shape the filling into a uniform mound. Roll out the remaining dough to about ¼-inch thickness and, using a sharp knife, cut out a circle that overhangs by ½ inch beyond the edges of the pie plate. Brush the edges of the dough with the egg wash. Brush the rim of the baked pie shell with egg wash as well. Gently pick up the dough and flip it over the filling, egg wash side down. Working around the rim, pinch the two crusts together, interlocking your thumbs and index fingers (see page 33). Trim away the excess dough and set aside. Brush the top of the pie all over with the egg wash, then use a sharp knife to make ½-inch slits in the top crust in two concentric circles (12 slits around the rim and 4 in the center), leaving enough room in the center for decoration.

9 | If desired, reroll the dough scraps and cut out shapes either freehand with a sharp knife or with a cookie cutter to decorate the pie. Brush the underside of the cutouts with egg wash, place on the pie, brush with egg wash, and sprinkle a pinch of sugar all over the top of the crust.

10 | Bake until the pie filling begins to bubble out of the vents and the top of the crust is golden brown, about 45 minutes. Remove from the oven and set aside on the counter, sliding a fork underneath the dish to allow airflow. Cool for 1 to 2 hours to let the filling set before serving.

GIN CRUST WINTER PIE

MAKES ONE 9-INCH DOUBLE-CRUST PIE/SERVES 10 • If you want to use nothing but seasonal local fruit in your winter baking, move to Chile. While there is a lot of fresh fruit in our stores year-round, it rarely rivals the deliciousness of in-season peak-flavor fruits. Dried fruits—and a mix of nuts—are a good understudy. If you are one of those cooks who has a bunch of dried fruit around after you've made your holiday fruitcake, here's a way to use them without waiting until next Christmas. I add a fresh pear to this recipe for juiciness and soft texture; without it the dried fruits are too leathery. Orange blossom water brings out a fleeting floral note. A splash of gin adds a subtle mix of aromatic spice to the crust while its alcohol inhibits the development of gluten in the dough.

When nuts are mixed into a dough they never reach a temperature hot enough during the baking process to release their flavorful oils. Toasting beforehand maximizes flavor and I recommend it in every instance they are called for in a crust.

1 double-batch Flaky Piecrust dough (page 31), made with gin

Vegetable oil cooking spray, for the pie plate

3½ cups dried mixed fruit (currants, apricots, strawberries, blueberries, dates, cherries), roughly chopped into raisin-size pieces

3 tablespoons unbleached all-purpose flour

½ cup pistachios, lightly toasted

¼ cup pecan halves, lightly toasted

2 tablespoons local honey

Grated zest and juice of 2 limes

Pinch of kosher salt

¼ teaspoon orange blossom water

1 tablespoon gin (optional)

1 ripe pear, peeled, cored, and cut into ¼-inch pieces

FOR THE EGG WASH

1 large egg

Pinch of kosher salt

Organic cane sugar, for sprinkling

1 | Preheat the oven to 400°F. Lightly spray a 9-inch pie plate with vegetable oil cooking spray. Place the chilled dough on the countertop as you prepare the filling.

2 | Combine the dried fruits in a large bowl. Tap the flour through a sieve over the fruits and toss to coat. Add the nuts and toss once more to combine. Set aside.

3 | In a large saucepan, combine 2 cups water with the honey, lime zest and juice, and salt and bring to a boil over medium-high heat. Add the dried-fruit mixture and stir with a wooden spoon to incorporate. Add the orange blossom water and gin, if using, and cook, stirring occasionally, until the fruits have softened and melded with each other a bit; the mixture should have the texture of thickened oatmeal. Add the pear and continue to cook until the mixture returns to a boil. Set aside to cool.

4 | Roll out one disk of the dough to ⅛-inch thickness. Flip a 9-inch pie plate over and place it on the dough. Then, using a sharp knife, cut out a circle with a 2-inch border around the edge of the pie plate. Remove the pie plate and roll out the dough 1 inch more in all directions. Roll the dough back onto the pin, then unroll it like a carpet into the pie plate.

5 | Using your index finger, push the dough into the plate where the bottom meets the sides, pressing into the rim with your opposite thumb. Working around the pie plate, pinch the dough along the rim to leave a lip that overhangs by ½ inch into the pie plate. Flute the

edges by interlocking your thumbs and index fingers, working your way around the rim. Freeze until the dough is as hard as a rock, 20 minutes to 1 hour (this prevents the dough from shrinking as it bakes).

6 | Cover the edge of the crust with an aluminum foil "collar" to prevent it from overbrowning. This piece of foil is the only thing between you and an unsuccessful crust. Press it against the underside of the outside rim of the plate, and be sure it fully covers the edge of the crust. Place in the oven and bake until the crust has a lightly browned edge and the base is still slightly raw but the starches have set, 10 to 15 minutes. Remove from the oven and carefully remove the foil. If the base has puffed up, prick it all over with a fork. Return the crust to the oven and bake until it is lightly browned all over, about 10 minutes more. Remove from the oven and set aside on the counter to cool, sliding a fork underneath the dish to allow airflow.

7 | In a small bowl, whisk together the egg, 1 tablespoon water, and salt to make the egg wash. Set aside to allow the salt to dissolve.

8 | Preheat the oven to 350°F.

9 | Transfer the filling to the shell. Roll out the remaining dough to about ⅛-inch thickness and, using a sharp knife, cut out a circle that overhangs by ½ inch beyond the edges of the pie plate. Brush the edges of the dough with the egg wash. Brush the rim of the baked pie shell with the egg wash as well. Gently pick up the dough and lay it over the filling, egg wash side down. Working around the rim, pinch the two crusts together, interlocking your thumbs and index fingers (see page 33). Trim away the excess dough and set aside. Brush the top of the pie all over with the egg wash, then use a sharp knife to make ½-inch slits in the top crust in two concentric circles (12 around the rim and 4 in the center), leaving enough room in the center for decoration.

10 | If desired, reroll the dough scraps and cut out shapes either freehand with a sharp knife or with a cookie cutter to decorate the pie. Brush the underside of the cutouts with egg wash, place on the pie, brush with egg wash, and sprinkle a pinch of sugar all over the top of the crust.

11 | Bake until the crust is golden brown, about 45 minutes. Remove from the oven and set aside on the counter, sliding a fork underneath the dish to allow airflow. Cool for 1 to 2 hours.

note

Dried fruits tend to weep as they bake. The liquid that is released then caramelizes and can cause the crust to stick to the pie plate, which is why I apply a very thin layer of vegetable oil cooking spray to the dish before pressing the pie dough into it.

LEMON CURD PIE with Meringue

MAKES ONE 9-INCH SINGLE-CRUST PIE/SERVES 10 • Lemon meringue pie was very popular at the White House, one of the few things that reached across the aisle and united partisans of both parties. The filling is normally very heavy on butter, but my version is based on yogurt, with just a bit of butter for richness. Although a great meringue must be made with some sugar (in order to allow the air to be captured by the egg whites), this recipe has only about one third as much sweetener as the traditional pie, while remaining a supremely luscious dessert.

1 batch Flaky Piecrust (page 31), blind baked

FOR THE FILLING

⅓ cup plain, full-fat Greek yogurt

3 large eggs

2¼ teaspoons (1 envelope) gelatin

¼ cup local honey

¾ cup lemon juice

4 tablespoons (½ stick) cold unsalted high-fat European-style butter

FOR THE MERINGUE

4 large egg whites

Pinch of cream of tartar

¼ cup organic cane sugar

2 tablespoons coarsely chopped almonds

1 | **Prepare the filling while the piecrust bakes.** In a medium bowl, whisk together the yogurt and eggs and set aside. In a small bowl, combine the gelatin with ¼ cup cold water and set aside to bloom.

2 | Combine the honey and lemon juice in a stainless steel saucepan and bring to a boil over medium-high heat. Slowly drizzle the honey mixture over the yogurt mixture, whisking briskly so as not to curdle the eggs. Off the heat, transfer the mixture back to the saucepan, using a rubber spatula to thoroughly scrape out the mixing bowl. Reduce the heat to medium. Return the saucepan to the heat and cook, stirring constantly, until the mixture comes to a gurgling boil. Pour through a sieve set over a medium bowl. Whisk in the butter and bloomed gelatin and mix thoroughly with an immersion blender or handheld mixer. Pour the filling into the prepared pie shell and set aside.

3 | **Make the meringue.** Preheat the oven to 450°F. In the bowl of a standing mixer fitted with the whisk attachment, combine the egg whites, cream of tartar, and a pinch of the sugar. (Make sure the bowl is very clean or the whites won't whip properly.) Whisk on medium-high until the tines of the whisk are visible in the whites. Slowly add the remaining sugar and continue whisking until stiff peaks form.

4 | Using a serving spoon, scoop large dollops of the meringue from the bowl and, using a second spoon, scrape it out of the serving spoon and onto the curd. Sprinkle with the chopped almonds. Bake the pie until the meringue is just golden, 3 to 5 minutes (do not leave the room). Let the pie cool to room temperature. Refrigerate for 2 to 3 hours to allow the curd to set before serving. Use a wet knife to cut the pie into wedges and serve.

the
MAGIC
of
MERINGUES

Meringue is a network of clingy egg white molecules that stick together. Egg whites are 90 percent water and 10 percent protein. Proteins are tightly folded chains of amino acids folded in on themselves, and unless you do something disruptive to them—like beat them—these chains are quite happy to remain separate. When we beat the egg whites, the proteins unfold and connect to one another to form a matrix, or network. The scientific term for what we have done to the protein is *denaturing*. Adding sugar draws out and traps the water in the egg whites. When heated, the water steams away and the egg white matrix stiffens, trapping the air left behind to produce airy baked meringue.

note I prefer pointy-bottomed Hachiya persimmons, but they must be very ripe; they should feel almost like a water balloon. Squat fuyus, the other type of persimmon commonly found in markets, don't need to be as fully ripe as Hachiyas. A quince, like a melon, should feel heavy in the hand, which means it is full of juice.

KABOCHA PERSIMMON PIE

MAKES ONE 9-INCH SINGLE-CRUST PIE/SERVES 10 • I first made this pie on a trip to Uzbekistan when the State Department sent a number of chefs to far-flung countries as goodwill ambassadors. This Central Asian "stan" is a bountiful garden country with a variety of fruits and vegetables that would make a Whole Foods shopper salivate. And what an array of squashes! I thought of doing a pumpkin pie, but for me that old Thanksgiving warhorse is a real case of "been there, done that." I was seduced, though, by the kabocha squash in the market. Its deep orange flesh continues to ripen after it is picked, developing its own natural sweetness, yet it is lower in calories than pumpkin or butternut squash. I sealed the deal by adding persimmon, a too-often-overlooked fruit that is as creamy as a mango and adds a honey-like flavor as well as bright floral notes. Grated fresh ginger and clementine juice really wake it up. The soy milk adds earthiness to the mix. The Uzbeks were delighted and it has become a holiday staple for me.

1 batch Flaky Piecrust (page 31), blind baked

3 pounds kabocha, butternut, or acorn squash (enough to yield about 2 cups roasted flesh), quartered lengthwise, seeds removed

2 medium very ripe Hachiya persimmons, root and stem end removed and flesh scooped out (about ½ cup)

1 large egg

Grated zest and juice of 1 clementine

½ cup soy milk

2 tablespoons local honey

1 tablespoon grade B maple syrup

1 teaspoon peeled, grated fresh ginger

½ teaspoon kosher salt

2 tablespoons roasted pumpkin seeds, for garnish

Maple Whipped Cream (page 241), for serving

1 | Preheat the oven to 400°F.

2 | Place the squash on a sheet pan and roast until a fork easily pierces the flesh. Alternatively, prick the squash all over with a fork and microwave until the flesh is tender, about 10 minutes. When cool enough to handle, scrape out the flesh and discard the skin.

3 | Reduce the oven temperature to 300°F.

4 | Combine the squash, persimmons, egg, clementine zest and juice, soy milk, honey, maple syrup, ginger, and salt in a blender and blend on medium speed until the ingredients are thoroughly incorporated and the mixture is smooth.

5 | Pour the squash mixture into the prepared piecrust and set on a rimmed baking sheet. Slide the baking sheet into the oven and pour enough water to reach within ¼ inch of the pan's rim. Bake until the filling is set, about 45 minutes; it should not ripple when gently nudged. Transfer the pie to a rack and let cool for 1 to 2 hours to allow the filling to set. Sprinkle the roasted pumpkin seeds on top and serve with the Maple Whipped Cream.

CHOCOLATE QUINOA KWEEM PIE

MAKES ONE 9-INCH SINGLE-CRUST PIE/SERVES 10 • Crumb crusts don't only come in graham cracker flavor, as this recipe demonstrates. It's no-bake, and there's only ¼ cup added sugar in the whole shebang. I originally called this Chocolate Quinoa Cream, but try saying that five times—it really wants an Elmer Fudd pronunciation. But the flavor is no joke: Once you taste this ultra-chocolaty pie, you may be surprised to learn that it has no cream and no egg yolks. Sesame oil adds a funky and deep nuttiness that enhances the layered flavors. The flour, used for thickener, is ground whole quinoa, one of the very few plant foods that provide complete protein.

FOR THE CRUST

30 savory rosemary crackers (about 7 ounces) (Raincoast brand is especially nice), crumbled

3 ounces dark (70%) chocolate, at room temperature

2 tablespoons toasted sesame oil

FOR THE FILLING

1 tablespoon quinoa flour, purchased or home-milled

2 tablespoons unsweetened cocoa

¼ teaspoon kosher salt

1¾ cups whole milk

¼ cup organic cane sugar

4 ounces dark (70%) chocolate, finely chopped

1 | Spray a 9-inch pie plate with vegetable oil cooking spray.

2 | **Make the crust.** Pulse the crackers in the bowl of a food processor until finely ground. Add the chocolate, oil, and 1 tablespoon water and process until the crumbs are uniformly fine and the mixture comes together (the friction of the blade will warm the oils in the chocolate to achieve this). Transfer the crumbs to the pie plate and press onto the bottom and up the sides in an even layer. Use the bottom of a small saucepan, flat-bottomed coffee mug, or a measuring cup to tamp down the crust. Chill in the refrigerator for 30 minutes.

3 | **Make the filling.** Combine the quinoa flour, cocoa, and salt in a fine-mesh sieve set on a piece of parchment and tap through to sift. Set aside.

4 | In a large, deep saucepan (larger than you think—the quinoa will cause the liquid to foam up and triple in volume), combine the milk and sugar and bring to a boil over medium-high heat. Sprinkle the quinoa mixture into the pan, whisking constantly, and return to a boil. Cook until the mixture is thick and bubbling, about 3 minutes.

5 | Remove from the heat and add the chocolate, stirring until it is completely melted and smooth. Strain the mixture through a fine-mesh sieve into the prepared crust. Tap the pie plate on the counter a few times to release any air pockets. Chill in the refrigerator until set, about 4 hours. Remove from the refrigerator 10 to 15 minutes before serving. Cut into wedges and serve.

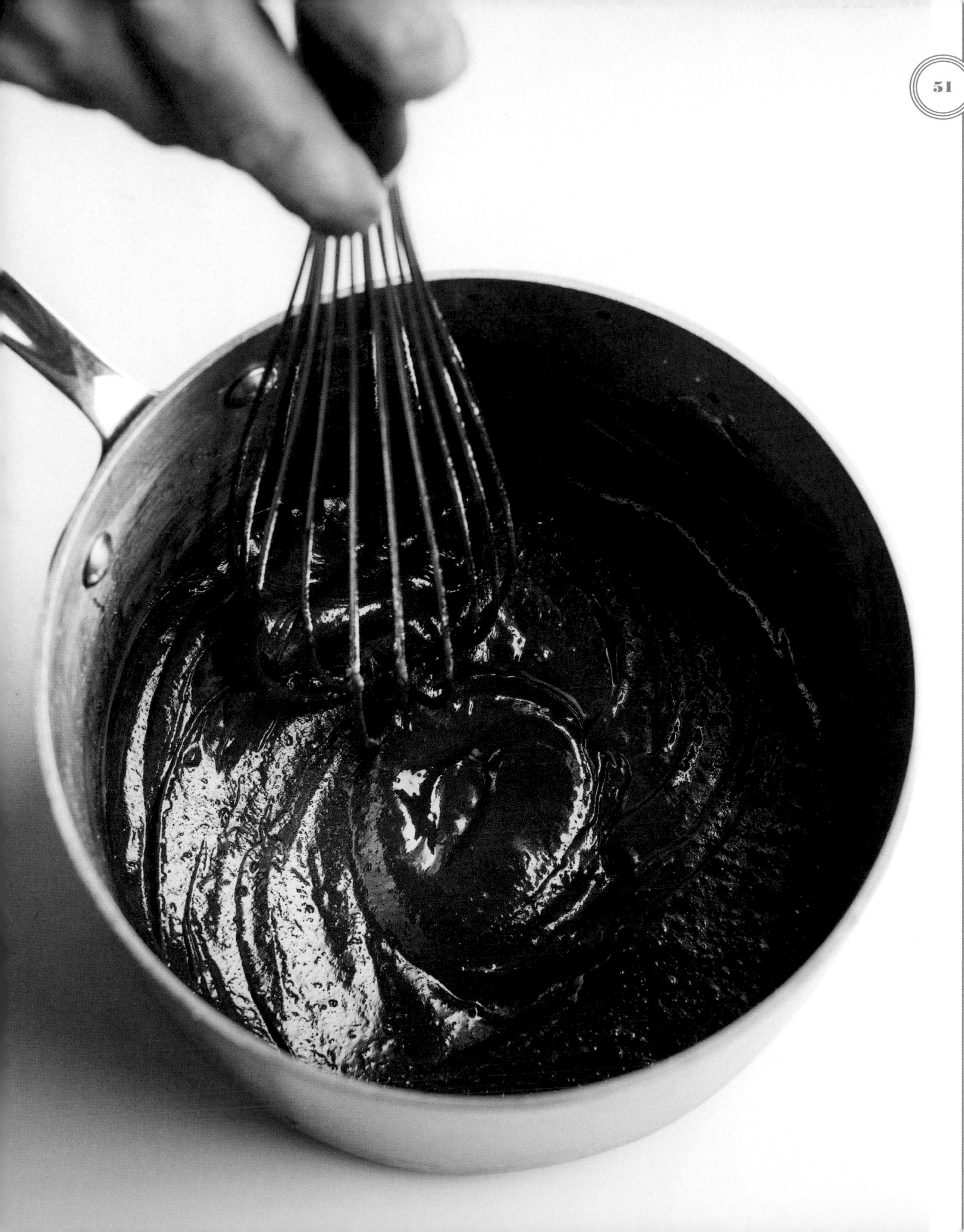

 **2** | **TARTS**

*a*lthough bipartisanship is in short supply in our nation's capital, it is worth noting that George W. Bush, Barack Obama, and every member of their families all agreed that you're never wrong when you offer a tart fresh from the oven. It's as American as apple tart. Think of the crust of a tart as an artist's canvas; you can fill it with just about every ingredient in the dessert larder. A tart is basically a fruit filling on top of a cookie crust. Compared to a piecrust, the added sweetness in tart dough (even though it is reduced in the following recipes) gives you a crunchy crust. The dough is also more forgiving: It doesn't toughen as easily as pie dough and you can easily "patch" mistakes. Though they are simple to make, tarts are complex in flavor and texture. I often call for nut flours in my shells, both for their roasty, toasty depth of flavor and the brittle texture that you get when you bake with them.

• — — — — •

Maple Apple Tarte Tatin • **Candied Grapefruit and Ricotta Tart**
Blackberry Almond Linzer Torte • **Provençale Tart with Figs and Black Olives**
Pignoli Tart with Nectarines and Rosemary • **Chocolate Raspberry Tart**
A Tart for Nuts • **Freeform Stone Fruit Galette**

MAPLE APPLE TARTE TATIN

MAKES ONE 9-INCH TART/SERVES 10 • There's no arguing with centuries of French diners—but to my taste, the flavor of the apples in the standard brasserie tarte tatin is overpowered by sugar and butter. Cutting down on those two ingredients makes the apples more assertive and brings their inherent sweetness forward. I also substituted maple syrup (grade B, the deep dark kind) for some of the sugar, a natural combination, since apple trees and maple trees often thrive on the same Vermont hillsides. The French tarte tatin is made with Reinette apples. The closest to those in America are Golden Delicious, which, like the Reinette, maintain their structure while baking and are able to absorb flavor. One of the great delights in baking is that moment when you flip the tarte tatin out of the skillet to behold the dark golden color of apples and to breathe in the seductive aroma.

1 tablespoon turbinado sugar

2 tablespoons unsalted high-fat European-style butter

1 tablespoon grade B maple syrup

8 Golden Delicious apples, peeled, cored, and quartered

1 batch Flaky Piecrust dough (page 31)

Maple Whipped Cream (page 241), for serving

note

This recipe must be made in a cast-iron pan. If you don't have one, *fuhgeddaboutit*. You are doomed to failure!

1 | Preheat the oven to 375°F.

2 | Combine the sugar and 1 tablespoon water in a 9-inch cast-iron skillet and cook over medium heat, swirling the mixture in the pan until the sugar is dissolved; it will immediately begin to bubble and caramelize around the rim of the pan. Cook until the liquid is mahogany in color and has reduced by half. When it begins to smoke and turns deep dark brown, remove the pan from the heat and carefully add the butter and maple syrup. Swirl it around to coat the bottom of the skillet.

3 | Arrange about half the apples in the skillet, flat side down, in concentric circles, packing them tightly. Arrange the remaining apples on top in a second layer, tucking them in tightly (you need at least two layers of apples because they shrink). Place the skillet over medium heat and bring the syrup mixture to a boil. Leave the pan on the heat until the apples begin to release their juices and get a head start cooking, about 7 minutes more. Remove the pan from the heat.

(RECIPE CONTINUES)

4 | Roll out the dough to ⅛-inch thickness and 2 inches larger than the diameter of the cast-iron pan. Roll the dough back onto the rolling pin like a carpet. Unroll the dough over the apples in the skillet. Carefully tuck the edges of the dough in between the apples and the edge of the skillet. Transfer to the oven and bake for 30 minutes. (The kitchen should be smelling pretty good by then.) Reduce the heat to 350°F and bake 30 minutes more. Insert a toothpick into the tarte through an apple slice; if it slides in easily, the tarte is done.

5 | Remove from the oven and set aside on the counter, sliding a fork underneath the skillet to allow airflow. Let cool for 10 minutes. Run a sharp knife around the rim of the tarte, then, wearing oven mitts (the molten caramel can burn you if it escapes), top the skillet with an overturned rimmed plate and flip it over. Remove the skillet. Serve warm with a dollop of Maple Whipped Cream.

CANDIED GRAPEFRUIT AND RICOTTA TART

MAKES ONE 9-INCH TART/SERVES 10 • Too often in our pursuit of desserts, we cater to a child's palate and forget that bitter notes can add elegance and complexity. Think of the way bitter and sweet work together in Campari: decidedly sweet but with a bitter component that keeps the palate lively. Grapefruit falls into that category as well. For this recipe, the peel is poached, candied with honey, and spiced with anise. Ricotta cheese has natural sweetness and it volumizes when you whip it, so you get a pleasant creaminess and texture while adding loft—which means less fat and calories per forkful. A bit of white wine in the crust adds a hint of fruitiness that ties into the fruit of the filling.

3 grapefruits, peel and pith removed and the peel of 1 grapefruit reserved

2 tablespoons local honey

1 star anise

10 tablespoons (1½ sticks) cold unsalted high-fat European-style butter, plus more for greasing the tart pan

¼ cup organic cane sugar

2 cups plus a heaping ¼ cup unbleached all-purpose flour, plus more for dusting

Pinch of kosher salt

¼ cup buttery Chardonnay, Riesling, or Gewürztraminer

5 large eggs

15 ounces full-fat ricotta cheese

1 | Bring a medium pot of water to a simmer. Cut the reserved grapefruit peel into yarn-like strips and blanch by adding it to the pot and bringing the water to a rolling boil. Drain the strips of peel and repeat the process two more times, refilling the pot with fresh water each time. Drain the pot one last time and refill it with a quart of water. Put the peels back in and add 1 tablespoon of the honey and the star anise. Bring to a boil. Reduce the heat and cook until the liquid is reduced by two thirds, about 20 minutes. Using a slotted spoon, transfer the peels to a plate and discard the liquid.

2 | While the peels candy, use a sharp knife to section the grapefruits, working over a bowl to catch the juices. Squeeze the juice from the membranes into the bowl and discard the membrane. Using an immersion blender, puree the grapefruit sections into the juice. Set aside.

3 | **Make the crust.** Cut the butter into ¼-inch-thick pieces and combine it with the sugar in the bowl of a standing mixer fitted with the paddle attachment. Mix on medium speed until the butter loosens and lightens in color, 3 to 4 minutes, occasionally scraping down the sides of the bowl. Add one third of the flour and the salt and mix just until crumbly. Add the remaining flour and mix just until partially combined. Do not overmix. Add the wine by pouring it around the perimeter of the mixture (instead of pouring it in one spot, the liquid should be evenly dispersed to avoid wet spots) and mix just until the dough comes together.

(RECIPE CONTINUES)

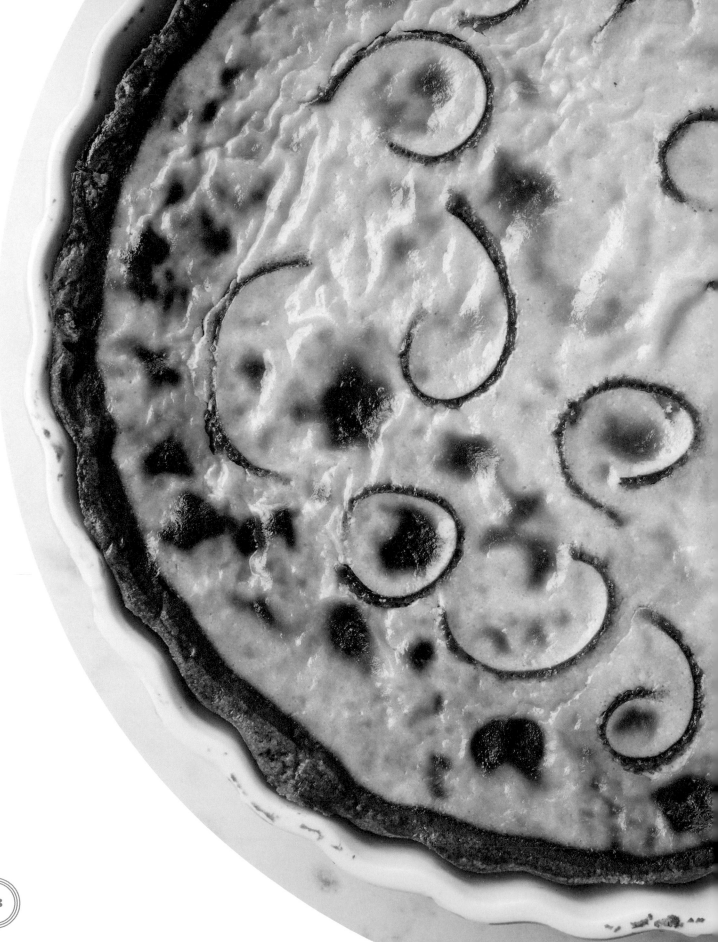

THE SWEET SPOT | *candied grapefruit and ricotta tart*

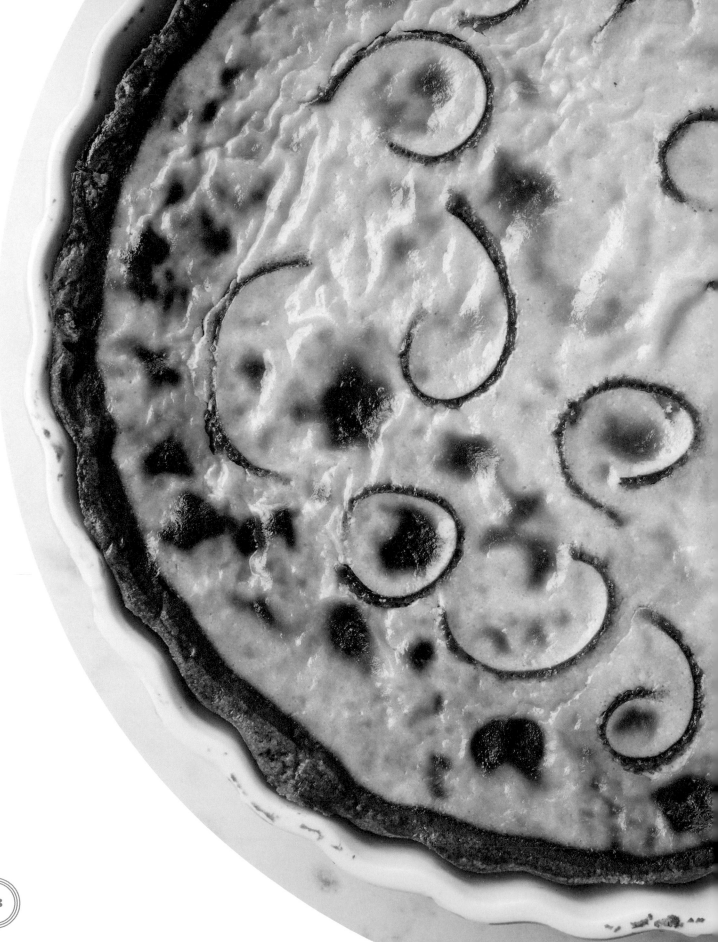

4 | Place the dough into a resealable gallon-size plastic bag and with your hands press it into a ½-inch-thick disk. Freeze for 20 minutes or refrigerate overnight.

5 | Thoroughly butter a 9-inch tart pan with a removable bottom.

6 | Place the dough on the counter and let it soften just until pressing your thumb into it makes an impression. Lightly dust a clean work surface and a rolling pin with flour and roll out the dough to ⅜-inch thickness. Roll the dough back onto the pin like a carpet and unroll it out into the tart pan. Press the dough into the pan, using your index finger to push it into the crease where the base meets the sides. Push the excess dough into a ½-inch lip overhanging the interior of the tart shell. Working around the pan, pull the lip back up along the sides and press firmly against the edge of the pan so that it slightly overshoots the height of the tart pan. Make sure the crust is of even thickness around the rim of the tart; use extra dough if necessary to patch thinner areas.

7 | Press a sheet of aluminum foil into the shell and up the sides, leaving the top edge of the crust exposed. Place in the freezer for 15 minutes.

8 | Preheat the oven to 350°F. Whisk together 1 egg with a pinch of salt and 2 tablespoons water to make an egg wash. Remove the foil from the crust and brush the crust all over with the egg mixture. Bake for 5 minutes to seal the crust. Slide a fork under the pan to allow airflow. Let cool.

9 | **Make the filling.** Combine the ricotta, remaining 1 tablespoon honey, the remaining 4 eggs, and the grapefruit puree in a deep medium bowl. Using an immersion blender, blend until the mixture is smooth and the large lumps of ricotta are broken up. Using a rubber spatula, scrape the filling into the tart shell and gently spread it evenly to the edges of the tart. Sprinkle the candied grapefruit threads over the top.

10 | Bake until the filling just begins to pull away from the crust, about 35 minutes. Remove from the oven and set aside on the counter, sliding a fork under the pan to allow airflow. Cool for 1 hour to let the filling set before serving. This tart will keep at room temperature up to 24 hours. To store any leftovers, tightly cover with plastic wrap and refrigerate. Bring the tart to room temperature 1 hour before serving.

BLACKBERRY ALMOND LINZER TORTE

MAKES ONE 9-INCH TART/SERVES 10 • This dessert is guaranteed to have you leaping in your lederhosen. Austrian pastries are acknowledged by all to be glorious, but they are often so complicated that they could drive many home cooks into psychoanalysis (not uncoincidentally another Austrian invention). Doing away with the demanding lattice of the classic torte and greatly reducing the butter and sugar simplifies the preparation and makes it far less cloying than the original. I further cut down on refined sugar by filling the torte with cooked and strained blackberries instead of the standard red currant jam. In place of cinnamon and cloves—frankly, I think dessert recipes default to those spices too often—I opted for cardamom; it rings through brilliantly, as it sharpens and defines the full flavors of the crust and fruit.

10 tablespoons (1½ sticks) unsalted high-fat European-style butter, at room temperature

¼ cup organic cane sugar

2 large egg yolks

¾ cup roasted salted almonds, very finely ground in a food processor

1 teaspoon ground cardamom

Grated zest of 1 small orange

1 cup unbleached all-purpose flour, plus more for dusting

5 to 6 cups fresh blackberries, 10 berries reserved for decoration

2 tablespoons cornstarch

3 tablespoons black chia seeds

1 large egg, whisked

12 hazelnuts, coarsely chopped

1 | In the bowl of a standing mixer fitted with the paddle attachment, mix the butter and sugar on medium speed until the butter is smooth and fluffy. Add the egg yolks, almonds, cardamom, and orange zest and mix until thoroughly combined. Reduce the speed to low and add the flour, scraping down the sides of the bowl, and mix until just incorporated. Turn the dough onto a work surface, press into a ½-inch-thick disk, wrap tightly in plastic wrap, and refrigerate for 2 hours or overnight.

2 | Prepare a 9-inch tart pan with a removable bottom with vegetable oil cooking spray.

3 | Heat the blackberries in a saucepan over medium heat. Tap the cornstarch through a small fine-mesh sieve into the saucepan and cook, stirring occasionally, until the berries have softened, released their juices, and thickened, about 5 minutes. Set aside to cool.

4 | Set the dough on the counter and let sit at room temperature until a mark appears when you press your thumb into it, about 5 minutes. Place the dough between two large sheets of plastic wrap and roll as close to a ¼-inch-thick circle as possible, working quickly so that the dough remains chilled. When it is a few inches larger than your tart pan, remove the plastic wrap and roll the dough onto the rolling pin,

(RECIPE CONTINUES)

then unroll into the tart shell. Press the dough into place, using your index finger to push it into the crease where the base meets the sides. Push the excess dough into a ½-inch lip overhanging the interior of the tart shell. Working around the pan, pull the lip back up along the sides and press firmly against the edges of the pan so that it slightly overshoots the height of the tart pan. Make sure the crust is of even thickness around the rim of the tart; use additional dough if necessary to patch thinner areas. Refrigerate. Gather up the scraps and press them into a 1-inch-thick disk for use as decoration for the top. Wrap the disk in plastic wrap and refrigerate for 1 hour.

5 Liberally dust a work surface and rolling pin with flour. Roll out the remaining dough to ¼-inch thickness. To make decorations for the tart, first dip a cookie cutter in flour, then cut out enough shapes to cover the surface of the tart.

6 Preheat the oven to 350°F. Remove the tart crust from the refrigerator. Use any leftover dough to reinforce the sides of the tart. It's a very flaky, crumbly dough and this will add strength. If it's too thin, it will fall apart.

7 Using a rubber spatula or bowl scraper, push the cooled filling through a sieve to strain out the blackberry seeds. Stir in the chia seeds. Spread the mixture evenly in the tart shell and smooth with an offset spatula. Arrange the cutouts on top, packing them rather tightly. Brush each with the whisked egg. Tuck the reserved whole blackberries in the spaces in between the cutouts, then sprinkle the hazelnuts all over.

8 Bake until the fruit is bubbling and the crust is well browned and the edges are crisp, about 30 minutes. Remove from the oven and set aside on the counter, sliding a fork underneath the pan to allow airflow. Cool for 1 hour to let the filling set. Remove the tart pan and, using a very sharp knife, cut into wedges, wiping the knife clean between each cut.

handy tool

When you want to get every last bit of your wonderful ingredients out of the mixing bowl or smushed through a sieve, an inexpensive plastic bowl scraper will be your new best friend.

PROVENÇALE TART
with Figs and Black Olives

MAKES ONE 9-INCH TART/SERVES 10 • Tapenade in a dessert tart? It's unusual, to be sure, but I wanted this dessert to capture the essence of Provence: terraced olive trees climbing the hillside and fig trees clustered around a stone farmhouse. Cured black olives have such a strong savory flavor that you would think they'd fight the figs, but like the anchovies that Julia Child used to put on her leg of lamb, the oliveness of the tapenade disappears into a savory undertone that provides a tart and salty complement to the lushly soft and sweet fig.

FOR THE CRUST

7 tablespoons unsalted high-fat European-style butter, at room temperature

½ cup confectioners' sugar

1 large egg yolk

2 cups unbleached all-purpose flour

Pinch of kosher salt

FOR THE FILLING

⅔ cup almond flour, purchased or home-milled

1 tablespoon unbleached all-purpose flour

6 tablespoons unsalted high-fat European-style butter, at room temperature

1 tablespoon local honey

2 large eggs

2 tablespoons black olive tapenade (without garlic)

8 to 24 fresh figs (or enough to cover the top of the tart), halved lengthwise

1 | **Make the crust.** In the bowl of a standing mixer fitted with the paddle attachment, beat together the butter and sugar on medium speed until the mixture is light and fluffy. Add the egg yolk and beat until incorporated. Reduce the speed to low and gradually add the flour and salt and mix until the dough comes together. Scrape the dough out of the bowl and onto a sheet of plastic wrap. Shape the dough into a ½-inch-thick disk, wrap tightly, and refrigerate for 20 minutes.

2 | Lightly dust a clean work surface with flour. Roll out the dough to a ⅛-inch-thick circle about 12 inches in diameter.

3 | Roll the dough back onto the rolling pin and unroll over a 9-inch tart pan with a removable bottom. Gently ease the dough into the pan by using your fingers to tuck it into the crease where the base meets the sides. Press the excess dough into a ½-inch lip overhanging the interior of the tart shell. Working around the pan, pull the lip back up along the sides and press firmly against the edges of the pan so that it slightly overshoots the height of the tart pan. Make sure the crust is of even thickness around the rim of the tart; use extra dough if necessary to patch thinner areas. Place the tart shell in the freezer for 1 hour to firm up.

4 | **Make the almond cream filling.** Combine the flours in a fine-mesh sieve set over parchment and tap through to sift. In the bowl of

(RECIPE CONTINUES)

a standing mixer fitted with the whisk attachment, whisk together the butter and honey on medium-high speed until the mixture is soft and creamy. Add the eggs, one at a time, beating thoroughly after each addition. Reduce the speed to low and gradually add the flour mixture. Whisk until thoroughly incorporated.

5 | Preheat the oven to 350°F.

6 | Spread the tapenade in a thin layer over the bottom of the chilled crust. Spread the almond cream over the tapenade, then arrange the figs over the almond cream. Bake until the crust is golden brown and the fruits have softened and begun to release their juices, 30 to 35 minutes. Remove from the oven and place on the counter, sliding a fork underneath the pan to allow airflow. Cool for about 1 hour to allow the filling to set before serving. Don't refrigerate this tart; it will lose its appealing flakiness. Make it and eat it the same day.

note

Make sure your tapenade doesn't include garlic or, to be certain, chop your own olives. While I'm all for including nontraditional ingredients in my dessert club, garlic, I am bound to report, will never be a member.

PIGNOLI TART
with Nectarines and Rosemary

MAKES ONE 9-INCH TART/SERVES 10 • Roger Vergé, whose spirit must have lent an inspiring hand to the creation of this cake, was one of the giants of nouvelle cuisine. From his Provençale restaurant, Moulin de Mougins, he created the Cuisine of the Sun; it was much less heavy than the Parisian style that had ruled the restaurant world for generations. He made liberal use of the herbs, vegetables, and olive oil that were the hallmarks of Mediterranean cuisine. Still, he was a French chef, so he never swore off butter. It was with him in mind that I added healthful almond and pistachio flours and pine nuts to this recipe and paired nectarines with that most Mediterranean of herbs: rosemary. Instead of the typical mascarpone cheese, I opted for the benign fat of a New World ingredient: the avocado.

FOR THE CRUST

2¾ cups cake flour, plus more for dusting

⅓ cup almond flour, purchased or home-milled

Pinch of kosher salt

10 tablespoons (1½ sticks) cold unsalted high-fat European-style butter, cut into small pieces

½ cup confectioners' sugar

1 large egg yolk

1 | Combine the cake flour, almond flour, and salt in a sieve set over parchment and tap through to sift. Set aside. In the bowl of a standing mixer fitted with the paddle attachment, mix together the butter and sugar on medium speed for 1 minute, scraping down the sides of the bowl one or two times. Reduce the speed to low and add the egg yolk. With the mixer running, gradually add half the flour mixture to the bowl and mix, scraping down the sides, until it is just incorporated. Add the remaining flour and mix just until the dough comes together. The dough will be soft.

2 | Scrape the dough out of the bowl and onto a sheet of plastic wrap. Shape the dough into a ½-inch-thick disk and wrap tightly twice with plastic wrap. Refrigerate at least 3 hours or overnight.

3 | Lightly dust a clean work surface with flour. Roll out the dough to a ⅛-inch-thick circle that is about 2 inches larger than the tart pan. If the dough is rock-hard, hold it between the palms of your hands to warm a bit before rolling. If the dough breaks apart as you roll it, rejoin it with the palms of your hands and reroll. Sprinkle with a little flour if it becomes too sticky. Work quickly so that the dough does not become too soft; flip it over often.

4 | Roll the dough back onto the rolling pin and unroll over a 9-inch tart pan. Ease the dough into the pan gently by using your fingers to tuck it into the crease where the base meets the sides. Press some of

FOR THE FILLING

1 medium avocado (about 4 ounces), pitted, peeled, and passed through a sieve

½ cup local honey

1 teaspoon kosher salt

1 large egg

½ cup heavy cream

2 teaspoons finely chopped fresh rosemary

Grated zest and juice of 1 orange

3 nectarines, pitted and coarsely chopped

1 tablespoon pistachio flour, purchased or home-milled

1 cup pine nuts, lightly toasted

the excess dough around the sides into the fluted edges of the pan, then trim away the excess. Place the tart shell in the freezer for 1 hour to firm it up.

5 | Preheat the oven to 350°F. Remove the tart shell from the freezer and prick the bottom all over with a fork. Line the shell along the bottom and sides with aluminum foil to prevent the sides from sliding. Bake until the edges are golden brown, about 20 minutes. Remove from the oven and remove the foil, then return to the oven and bake 10 minutes more to brown the bottom. Remove from the oven and set aside on the counter to cool, sliding a fork underneath the pan to allow airflow.

6 | **Make the filling.** In the bowl of a food processor, puree the avocado until smooth. Add the honey and salt and puree until thoroughly incorporated and smooth. Add the egg and the cream and pulse until incorporated. Add the rosemary, orange zest, and juice and pulse a few times more. Stir in the nectarines and the pistachio flour. Pour the mixture into the prepared tart shell and scatter the pine nuts over the entire surface. Bake until the custard sets, about 10 minutes. Remove from the oven and set aside on the counter, sliding a fork underneath the pan to allow airflow. Cool for 1 hour to let the filling set before serving.

righteous **ROASTING**

I fell into the habit of always roasting nuts before adding them to a recipe when I started making pecan pralines at the White House. I now recommend lightly roasting nuts whenever you use them in a recipe because toasted nuts have a deeper, more complex flavor than raw. When you use raw nuts in a cake batter they are surrounded by eggs, sugar, and wheat flour in the batter and rarely cook through in the process of baking. Why walk away from the flavor potential of nuts when just a little roasting will add so much to the finished dessert?

CHOCOLATE RASPBERRY TART

MAKES ONE 9-INCH TART/SERVES 10 • In another time, in another book, this recipe could have been a high-calorie, fat-filled mega bomb. It has four components: a crust, a layer of caramel, a fresh-fruit gel, and chocolate to top it off. The caramel layer is the thinnest layer, not the normal gooey mouthful. Why use caramel at all, you might ask? Because the process of caramelization produces hundreds of flavor compounds impossible to achieve in any other way—it's all a matter of proportion. Take it away and it's like serving a steak without salt. Ripe raspberries in the filling reinforce the berry notes characteristic of the high-quality strains of cacao (Criollo and Trinitario) in the ganache. It's noteworthy that chocolate—which is the product of fermenting cacao—develops flavors that evoke fresh fruits, just like another fermented product: wine. Almond flour adds a layer of flavor and completes the time-honored marriage of chocolate and almonds; they bring out the best in each other.

FOR THE ALMOND CRUST

⅔ cup (1⅓ sticks) unsalted high-fat European-style butter, at room temperature, plus more for the pan

¼ cup local honey

⅓ cup almond flour, purchased or home-milled

1 large egg

1 cup plus 1 tablespoon pastry flour, plus more for dusting

Pinch of kosher salt

FOR THE CARAMEL LAYER

⅓ cup organic cane sugar

3 tablespoons heavy cream

FOR THE RASPBERRY GELÉE

½ teaspoon gelatin

¾ teaspoon agar powder or 3 teaspoons agar flakes

½ cup fresh raspberries, pushed through a fine-mesh sieve

1 | **Make the crust.** In the bowl of a standing mixer fitted with the paddle attachment, mix together the butter, honey, and almond flour on medium-high speed until thoroughly combined. Add the egg and mix until incorporated. Add one third of the pastry flour and mix until incorporated, then add the remainder with the salt and mix again.

2 | Place the dough in a gallon-size resealable plastic bag and, using your hands, flatten it into a ½-inch-thick disk. Place in the freezer for 20 minutes or refrigerate overnight. When ready to use, place the dough on the counter and allow it to soften just until pressing your thumb into it makes an impression.

3 | Thoroughly butter a 9-inch tart pan with a removable bottom. Lightly dust a clean work surface and a rolling pin with flour. Roll out the dough to a ⅛-inch-thick circle with an 11-inch diameter. Roll the dough back onto the pin like a carpet and unroll it out into the tart pan. Press the dough into the pan, using your index finger to push it into the crease where the base meets the sides. Push the excess dough into a ½-inch lip overhanging the interior of the tart shell. Working around the pan, pull the lip back up along the sides and press firmly against the edges of the pan so that it slightly overshoots the height of the tart pan. Cut away the excess dough and set aside. Make sure the crust is of even thickness around the rim of the tart; if necessary, use the dough trimmings to patch thinner areas.

(RECIPE CONTINUES)

FOR THE GANACHE LAYER

¾ cup half-and-half

4 ounces dark (70%) chocolate, chopped into dime-size pieces

FOR THE TOPPING

Chocolate shavings from block chocolate, scraped with a vegetable peeler

Large salt flakes, such as Maldon

4 | Press a sheet of aluminum foil into the base of the shell and up the sides, leaving the top edge of the crust exposed. Place in the freezer for 15 minutes. Meanwhile, preheat the oven to 350°F.

5 | Bake the tart shell until lightly golden, about 25 minutes. Remove from the oven and set aside on the counter to cool, sliding a fork underneath the pan to allow airflow.

6 | **Make the caramel.** Spread the sugar in a thin layer in a heavy saucepan and set over medium-high heat. As the sugar begins to liquefy, swirl it around in the pan by moving the pan (do not stir). When the liquid turns dark amber, carefully and slowly stir in the cream and return the mixture to a boil.

7 | Working quickly, strain the liquid through a fine-mesh sieve into the blind-baked tart shell and refrigerate to allow the caramel to set. (If the caramel is too firm to spread in the shell, slide the coated tart shell into a 350°F oven for a few minutes to loosen.) Place the caramel-filled tart shell in the freezer to set until firm, about 10 minutes. This will prevent the raspberry layer from bleeding into the caramel layer.

8 | **Make the raspberry gelée.** In a small bowl, combine the gelatin with 1 tablespoon cold water and set aside to bloom. Fill a saucepan with 1 cup water. Place the agar in a paper cup (I use a Dixie cup because the lightweight paper responds well to tapping!) and tap half of it over the water in the saucepan, as if you were feeding fish, to cover the surface and avoid clumping. Using a wire whisk, mix to help the agar absorb the water. Tap the remaining agar into the water. Bring to a boil over medium-high heat and boil for a full 2 minutes. Whisk in the raspberry puree and return to a boil. Continue boiling for 1 minute more, whisking frequently to prevent the agar from sticking to the bottom. Bubbles will begin to form—not to worry.

9 | In a small bowl, combine the bloomed gelatin with ½ cup of the gelée and whisk until smooth. Add the mixture to the saucepan and whisk until incorporated. Pour the raspberry gelée over the caramel layer in the tart and refrigerate until it sets, about 5 minutes. Do not freeze; it will turn into a sandy mess!

10 │ **Make the ganache.** In a medium saucepan, bring the cream to a boil over medium-high heat. Place the chocolate in a medium heatproof bowl and pour half the hot cream over it. Whisk the chocolate and cream together, starting from the center and pulling in the cream from the edges. Add the remaining cream and continue to whisk, pulling the remaining liquid from the edges to the center, until smooth and thoroughly incorporated. Hold a fine-mesh sieve over the tart and strain the chocolate directly onto the raspberry gelée. Tilt the tart to evenly distribute. Refrigerate until the ganache has set, at least 15 minutes.

11 │ Remove the tart from the refrigerator 1 hour before serving. Scatter chocolate shavings all over the tart, then sprinkle with the salt and serve.

note

To give fruit gelée body, both agar and gelatin are necessary. Agar without gelatin produces a brittle result and gelatin without agar is rubbery. The combination produces an agreeably smooth and creamy texture.

A TART FOR NUTS

MAKES ONE 4 × 14-INCH TART/SERVES 10 • I have been making versions of this tart since I tasted it on my first trip to Provence to celebrate my fortieth birthday. It's inspired by Elizabeth Bourgeois, the resolutely *ferme-à-table* chef of restaurant *Le Mas Tourteron* just outside the village of Gordes. Elizabeth is known for her modern treatment of traditional recipes and she won my heart with a generously laden dessert buffet: sponge cakes, floating islands, and the airiest chocolate mousse. My healthified version of her simple yet magnificent almond tart calls for a mix of nuts and pecan (or walnut) oil instead of butter. Maple sugar in the filling adds caramel undertones—the perfect supporting cast for nuts.

FOR THE CRUST

3 tablespoons plus 1 teaspoon unsalted high-fat European-style butter, at room temperature

3 tablespoons almond flour, purchased or home-milled

2 tablespoons local honey

2 large eggs

1¼ cups pastry flour, plus more for dusting

Pinch of kosher salt

FOR THE FILLING

¼ cup grade B maple syrup

2 tablespoons nut oil, such as pecan or walnut

¾ cup whole milk

1 teaspoon vanilla paste

2 cups mixed unsalted nuts (blanched almonds, pecans, blanched hazelnuts, cashews, walnuts), lightly toasted

½ teaspoon kosher salt

1 | **Make the crust.** In the bowl of a standing mixer fitted with the paddle attachment, mix together the butter, almond flour, and honey on medium speed until well blended, about 3 minutes. Add the eggs, one at a time, and mix until incorporated. Add one third of the pastry flour and mix to combine. Add the remaining pastry flour and the salt and mix until thoroughly combined. Scrape the dough out of the bowl and onto a sheet of plastic wrap. Shape the dough into a ½-inch-thick disk and wrap tightly with plastic wrap. Place in the freezer for 20 minutes or refrigerate overnight. When ready to use, place the dough on the counter and allow it to soften just until pressing your thumb into it makes an impression.

2 | Spray a 4 × 14-inch tart pan with vegetable oil cooking spray. Lightly dust a clean work surface and a rolling pin with pastry flour and roll out the dough into a rectangle 2 inches wider than your tart mold on all sides, about ¼ inch thick. Roll the dough back onto the pin like a carpet and unroll it into the tart shell. Press the dough into the pan, using your index finger to push it into the crease where the base meets the sides. Press the excess dough into a ½-inch lip overhanging the interior of the tart shell. Working around the pan, pull the lip back up along the sides and press firmly against the edges of the pan so that it slightly overshoots the height of the tart pan. Cut away the excess dough and set aside. Make sure the crust is of even thickness around the rim of the tart; if necessary, use the dough trimmings to patch thinner areas.

(RECIPE CONTINUES)

3 Press a sheet of aluminum foil into the base of the shell and up the sides, leaving the top edge of the crust exposed. Place in the freezer for 15 minutes. Meanwhile, preheat the oven to 350°F.

4 Bake until lightly golden, about 25 minutes. Remove from the oven and set aside on the counter, sliding a fork underneath the pan to allow airflow. Remove the foil and let cool. Raise the oven temperature to 375°F.

5 **Make the filling.** Combine the maple syrup, oil, milk, and vanilla in a 2-quart saucepan and bring to a boil over medium-high heat. Cook until the mixture becomes foamy and turns lightly golden brown, about 2 minutes. Add the nuts and salt and cook for 2 minutes more, stirring gently, until the liquid becomes a pale caramel color. Pour the almond mixture into the crust and spread into an even layer. Bake until golden brown, about 12 minutes. Remove from the oven and set aside on the counter, sliding a fork underneath the pan to allow airflow. Let cool for 1 hour before serving.

note I usually choose vanilla paste over vanilla extract. I find the paste has a more pleasing and natural vanilla flavor.

FREEFORM STONE FRUIT GALETTE

SERVES 8 • I think of a great fruit galette as happy chaos in a kitchen; I'd almost say the sloppier the better as long as you remember to call it "rustic." Really it's a less artfully constructed tart. It's just the thing to make in a vacation rental kitchen where you don't have much in the way of baking equipment. When I was turning out thirty pies at a time in the White House I discovered that precooking the fruits and thickener gives much more dependable results because every fruit releases different amounts of moisture and pectin when it is baked. If you are wondering what stone fruit to use, I don't mean to leave you hanging. Any and all work when ripe, sweet, and in season.

1 cup (2 sticks) cold unsalted high-fat European-style butter, cut into pieces

1 tablespoon organic cane sugar

2 cups unbleached all-purpose flour, plus more for dusting

¼ cup corn flour, purchased or home-milled

Pinch of kosher salt

4 nectarines, halved, pitted, and cut into ¼- to ⅜-inch-thick slices

3 cups Rainier or Queen Anne cherries, pitted (see page 141 for pitting technique)

1 tablespoon local honey

2 tablespoons black chia seeds

Pinch of ground white pepper

1 | Preheat the oven to 375°F.

2 | In the bowl of a standing mixer fitted with the paddle attachment, mix the butter on medium speed until softened. Add the sugar and continue to mix until the butter becomes loose and smooth.

3 | Combine the all-purpose flour, corn flour, and salt in a fine-mesh sieve set over parchment and tap through to sift. Add one third of the flour mixture to the bowl and mix on medium speed until incorporated. Add half the remaining flour and mix, scraping down the sides of the bowl, until incorporated. Add the remaining flour and mix until incorporated. With the mixer running, add 1 tablespoon cold water and continue mixing until the dough comes together, about 30 seconds. Turn the dough out onto a sheet of plastic wrap and, using the palm of your hand, press into a ½-inch-thick disk and wrap tightly. Refrigerate for 15 minutes.

4 | Meanwhile, combine the nectarines, cherries, honey, and 1 tablespoon of water in a saucepan over medium-high heat. Add the chia seeds and cook, stirring occasionally with a wooden spoon, until the fruits are shiny and somewhat softened but have not collapsed, 8 to 10 minutes. Do not mash. Set aside.

5 | Place the dough on a lightly floured surface. Knead with the palms of your hands until it becomes soft and malleable, periodically dusting

(RECIPE CONTINUES)

with flour. The dough will be somewhat crumbly. Roll it out into a ¼-inch-thick disk, smoothing the ragged edges with your hand. Place an overturned 12-inch dinner plate on the dough and, using a sharp knife, trace around the plate. Set aside the excess dough. Gently roll the circle of dough back onto the rolling pin and unroll it onto a cookie sheet. Pinch the edges of the dough into a 1½-inch-high rim. Crimp the edge, then place the crust in the freezer to firm, about 20 minutes.

6 | Spoon the fruit and half the juices onto the tart shell and sprinkle with the pepper. Reserve the remaining fruit juice. Bake until the crust is golden brown, about 30 to 40 minutes. Remove from the oven and set aside on the counter, sliding a fork underneath the pan to allow airflow. Let cool for 30 minutes. Just before serving, bring the reserved juices to a boil and immediately remove from the heat. Using a pastry brush, brush the liquid onto the tart. Cut into wedges and serve.

PRECOOKING *pie fillings* | By precooking before filling meets dough, you know exactly what the consistency of the filling will be. Will it be goopy? Will it be too thick? It should look like jam or a fruit preserve; scoop a spoonful onto a plate and allow it to cool to determine how thick it will be. You also ensure that all the fruit will cook evenly.

CRUNCH

Crisps, a Cobbler, and a Pavlova

i f you want to make sure that everyone tries your dessert and likes it, a cobbler (or crisp) is my go-to. They are especially suited to casual dinner parties or picnics. The fillings are similar to a pie, and there is little fussing required for a flawless crust (you really have to work at it to make a bad topping!). The pay-off is watching your guests scraped up every semi-burnt, but delicious, bit of fruit and topping. Crisps and cobblers were big favorites of the Obamas'. These simple desserts are all about the intense taste of bright, preferably seasonal fruit, and the way the crunchy-to-crumbly textures of the topping contrast with the soft interior. The same is true of a pavlova. I often leave the skin on the fruit for extra flavor. I have included a pavlova in this chapter because the combination of baked meringue and a simple layer of fruit produces a similar effect to a crisp or a cobbler: a crunchy top and sweet bottom.

—————————•—————————

Crinkly Phyllo Cherry Crisp • **Fruit Crisps with Nut Toppings**
Extra-Crumbly Plum Cobbler • **Pavlova with Blackened Stone Fruit**

CRINKLY PHYLLO CHERRY CRISP

MAKES ONE 9-INCH CRISP/SERVES 10 • Many phyllo desserts are made with so much butter and sugar that those flavors overwhelm everything else. I use neither. Instead, I baste the phyllo leaves with egg white and oil rather than butter and add bread crumbs between the layers to replace the sugar. The phyllo still curls and crinkles on top and looks very pastry shop-y, but the overall effect is a lot less cloying. Pomegranate juice and red wine vinegar lend a bracingly tart as well as sweet note to the cherry filling. Please note: If you want a caramelized crust with a lacquer finish, there is no way around sprinkling a tablespoon of sugar on top. Nice, but not necessary.

2 tablespoons walnut oil, plus more for the pie plate

4 cups fresh cherries, preferably a mix of sweet and tart, pitted

½ cup dried tart cherries

2 tablespoons local honey

2 tablespoons plus 1 teaspoon cornstarch

2 teaspoons freshly grated lemon zest

1 tablespoon pomegranate juice

1 tablespoon red wine vinegar

1 large egg white

Six 16 × 12-inch sheets phyllo dough, thawed in the refrigerator overnight if frozen

4 teaspoons fine dry unflavored bread crumbs

1 tablespoon organic cane sugar

Cherry Licorice Sauce (page 240), for serving

note • I like mixing dried and fresh fruits, in this case cherries. The dried fruit intensifies the natural flavor of the fruit without resorting to artificial extracts (but take note, some dried fruits such as cranberries and cherries are sweetened with concentrated fruit juice) or added sugar. It also adds chewiness to the fruit filling.

1 | Preheat the oven to 400°F. Prepare a 9-inch pie plate with walnut oil.

2 | In a large bowl, combine the fresh and dried cherries, honey, cornstarch, lemon zest, pomegranate juice, and vinegar and toss to thoroughly coat the fruit. Set aside.

3 | In a small bowl, briskly whisk together the oil and egg white for 1½ to 2 minutes, until loosely blended. Arrange a sheet of phyllo in the pie plate and brush all over with the egg white mixture. Sprinkle with 1 teaspoon of the bread crumbs and top with a second sheet of phyllo. Repeat, using 4 sheets of phyllo and ending with the egg mixture and bread crumbs. Spoon the fruit mixture into the pie plate, scraping down the bowl to catch all the juices and zest. Turn any phyllo that overhangs the plate back onto itself to form a rim.

4 | To make the decorative top, cut the remaining two pieces of phyllo into thirds, crosswise. Working with one piece at a time, brush one side with the egg white mixture. Holding it with the egg-washed side up, pinch the center of the phyllo from the underside and gather it up to create a flower bloom. Give the gathered part a twist to form a "stem." Set the flower onto the pie and repeat with remaining sheets of phyllo. Sprinkle the sugar evenly over the flowers. Bake for 10 minutes, then reduce the heat to 350°F and rotate the crisp 180 degrees. Bake until the pastry is golden and the fruit mixture is bubbling, 40 to 50 minutes. Remove from the oven and set aside on the counter to cool slightly, sliding a fork underneath the plate to allow airflow. Serve warm with the Cherry Licorice Sauce.

FRUIT CRISPS
with Nut Toppings

MAKES ENOUGH NUT TOPPING FOR TWELVE 5-OUNCE RAMEKINS OR TWO 9-INCH CRISPS,
MAKES ENOUGH FILLING FOR SIX 5-OUNCE RAMEKINS OR ONE 9-INCH CRISP • Definitely not my grandma's crisps, but I know she would have appreciated the elegance that oils and vinegars add to these rustic down-home desserts. By adding sweet and tart drinking vinegars to the fruit filling and the perfumed notes of essential oils to the toppings, I achieve a much wider palate of flavors than normally found in these old-timey desserts, and the extra flavor compensates for how much sugar we are losing. The specialty oils and vinegars are not absolutely necessary, but I give you the option and guarantee that you will find the result is more complex and nuanced. You can't cut down on butter in the toppings, because they become powdery rather than crunchy. Finally, instead of serving with a scoop of ice cream, I reduce fat and calories with a dollop of Maple Whipped Cream.

The recipe below yields enough filling for one crisp, but the topping recipe will make enough for two crisps. Why did I do that? Because the proportions of ingredients for the topping bake best that way and it's always nice to have extra topping in the freezer when you need to throw together a quick dessert.

This is a basic fruit and nut recipe followed by a number of suggested pairings—ones that I tried and liked. Don't be limited. If you have an inclination to try other pairings, have at it!

FOR THE NUT TOPPING

- 1 cup (2 sticks) unsalted high-fat European-style butter, at room temperature
- ¾ cup muscovado or light brown sugar
- 2 drops food-grade essential oil (fir balsam, bergamot, bitter orange, lavender, or rose; optional)
- 1½ cups unbleached all-purpose flour
- ½ cup old-fashioned rolled oats
- 1 cup coarsely chopped nuts
- 1 tablespoon finely chopped fresh thyme

1 | Preheat the oven to 350°F. Line two rimmed baking sheets with parchment.

2 | **Make the topping.** In the bowl of a standing mixer fitted with the paddle attachment, mix together the butter and sugar on medium-high speed until smooth, about 3 minutes. Add the essential oil and mix to incorporate. Reduce the speed to low, add half the flour, and mix until incorporated, then add the remaining flour and mix until combined. Add the oats, nuts, and thyme and mix until just combined. Do not overmix. The mixture will resemble chunky paste. Spread in thin layers on the prepared baking sheets and bake until golden, about 15 minutes. Let cool, then break into marble-size pieces.

3 | **Make the filling.** In a small bowl, whisk together the sugar, chia seeds, cinnamon, cardamom, and salt. In a separate medium bowl, combine the fruit, lemon zest and juice, and drinking vinegar, if using

(RECIPE CONTINUES)

FOR THE FILLING

⅓ cup organic cane sugar

3 tablespoons black chia seeds

½ teaspoon cinnamon

¼ teaspoon ground cardamom

Pinch of kosher salt

2½ pounds fresh fruit, pitted and/or peeled and cut into 2-inch pieces, if applicable

Zest and juice of 1 lemon

2 tablespoons drinking vinegar

Maple Whipped Cream (page 241), for serving

(see Topping combinations below) and toss. Add the dry mixture to the fruit mixture and toss together with your hands until the fruit is coated all over. Spoon the fruit into six individual ramekins or into a 9-inch oven-safe dish. Press the fruit down to make room for the topping, if necessary. Divide the crumble evenly over the fruit. Bake until the fruit bubbles, about 30 minutes. Remove from the oven and set aside to cool for 30 minutes. Serve with the Maple Whipped Cream.

TOPPING *combinations*

For the adventuresome, I have included some optional vinegar and essential oil combos. You don't *need* to use them, but we don't need symphonies or Broadway musicals either—and they sure are nice.

○ **CHERRY PECAN** (with 1 tablespoon apple cider vinegar and 2 drops food-grade rose essential oil)

○ **PLUM ALMOND** (with 1 tablespoon cherry vinegar and 2 drops food-grade petit grain essential oil)

○ **APPLE HAZELNUT** (with 1 tablespoon verjus and 2 drops food-grade sweet wild orange essential oil)

○ **HUCKLEBERRY WALNUT** (with 2 drops food-grade bergamot essential oil)

○ **PEACH CASHEW** (with 1 tablespoon tamarind vinegar and 2 drops food-grade bergamot essential oil)

○ **FIG WALNUT** (with 1 tablespoon white wine vinegar and cinnamon)

○ **PLUM-NECTARINE MACADAMIA NUT** (with shredded unsweetened coconut)

Cherry Pecan

Apple Hazelnut

Huckleberry
Walnut

Plum
Peach
Almond

85

Extra-Crumbly PLUM COBBLER

MAKES SIX 3-INCH INDIVIDUAL COBBLERS OR ONE 8-INCH COBBLER • We often made cobblers at the White House at the request of the First Family. In fact, I think First Families all the way back to George Washington ate them while in office. Instead of saying something is "as American as apple pie," you could make a case for calling a dessert "as American as a fruit cobbler." The secret to the crumbly crust here is a hard-boiled egg yolk mixed into the dough. Because cooked yolk has less moisture than the raw yolks called for in standard cobbler recipes, there is less tendency for gluten to develop in the dough. This keeps the crust from turning pasty and makes it more crumbly, which is definitely your goal for all cobblers; that way, the crust breaks easily into bite-size mouthfuls as you dig down and pull up fruit filling.

2 cups unbleached all-purpose flour, plus more for dusting

1 teaspoon baking powder

Pinch of kosher salt

¾ cup plus 2 tablespoons full-fat sour cream

3 tablespoons cold unsalted high-fat European-style butter, cut into ¼-inch pieces

2 large egg yolks, hard-boiled

2½ pounds plums, pitted and cut into quarters or eighths depending on their size

⅓ cup organic cane sugar

½ teaspoon ground cinnamon

¼ teaspoon ground cardamom

Grated zest and juice of 1 lemon

2 tablespoons cornstarch

Maple Whipped Cream (page 241), for serving

1 | Spray six 5-ounce ramekins or one 8-inch round baking dish with vegetable oil cooking spray.

2 | In the bowl of a standing mixer fitted with the paddle attachment, mix together the flour, baking powder, salt, sour cream, and butter. Remove the bowl from the mixer and push the egg yolks through a fine-mesh sieve into the bowl. Return the bowl to the mixer and mix on medium speed, just until the ingredients come together into a rough paste. Do not overmix. Spoon the dough into a gallon-size resealable plastic bag. There will be visible specks of egg yolk. Press the dough into a ½-inch-thick disk and refrigerate for 20 minutes. (Do not freeze; the liquid in the dough will harden.)

3 | Combine the plums, sugar, cinnamon, cardamom, lemon zest, and juice in a saucepan over medium-high heat. Tap the cornstarch through a fine-mesh sieve over the plums. Cook, stirring occasionally to avoid scorching, until the juices released from the plums begin to thicken, 8 to 10 minutes.

4 | Preheat the oven to 350°F.

5 | Divide the fruit among the six ramekins or spoon into the baking dish and press with the back of a fork to make it compact.

6 | Leave the dough in the plastic bag and roll it out to a ¼-inch-thick disk. Dust a clean work surface with flour. Remove the dough from the bag (use scissors if necessary) and place on the work surface.

7 | Using a water glass or biscuit cutter that is just slightly smaller in diameter than the ramekins, cut out six circles of dough. (Gather up the scraps, if necessary, and reroll to cut out.) Place one over each filled ramekin. Alternatively, use a sharp knife to cut out a single circle with an 8-inch diameter. Roll it back onto the rolling pin and place over the baking dish. Unroll the dough onto the fruit like a carpet and trim away any excess. If desired, reroll the dough scraps and cut out shapes either freehand with a sharp knife or with a cookie cutter to decorate the cobbler.

8 | Heat the honey in a small saucepan over medium heat or in the microwave until it is spreadable. Using a pastry brush, brush the cobbler(s) with the honey. Place the decorations on top, if using, and brush honey on them as well. Place the ramekins on a sheet pan or slide the baking dish directly onto the oven rack and bake until the top is deep golden brown, about 35 minutes for small cobblers to 45 minutes for a large cobbler. Remove from the oven and set aside on the counter, sliding a fork underneath the dish(es) to allow airflow. Let cool for 15 minutes. Serve with Maple Whipped Cream.

note

A quick reminder how to make hard-boiled eggs without turning the yolks green and that are easy to peel: Place the eggs at the bottom of a saucepan on high heat and bring the water to a boil. Turn off the heat, cover, and let sit for 13 minutes. Then plunge the eggs into ice water and peel immediately.

PAVLOVA with Blackened Stone Fruit

MAKES 6 • A pavlova—a baked meringue usually served with some kind of fruit on top—is basically egg white, sugar, and lots of air. The time-honored pavlova recipe calls for three times the amount of sugar by weight as egg white. When I took the sugar down by two thirds I had to compensate with something else to create the kind of structure sugar achieves. Not only does yogurt powder fit the bill, it adds creaminess and tang, too. It's also gluten-free. Although you can top a pavlova with many different fruits and berries, I find that stone fruits are particularly good because when you blacken them, the nearly-burnt edges develop tremendous complexity of flavor.

FOR THE PAVLOVA

3 large egg whites

¼ cup organic cane sugar

Pinch of cream of tartar

1 tablespoon yogurt powder or nonfat powdered milk

FOR THE FRUIT TOPPING

3 tablespoons local honey

2 bay leaves

3 peaches, plums, or apricots, halved and pitted

1 teaspoon peeled, grated fresh ginger

2 cups farmers' or quark cheese, drained

1 | Preheat the oven to 220°F. Line a rimmed baking sheet with parchment paper.

2 | **Make the pavlova.** Combine the egg whites, 1 tablespoon of the sugar, and the cream of tartar in the bowl of a standing mixer fitted with the whisk attachment and whisk on medium-high speed until stiff peaks form. Gradually add the remaining sugar and mix on high speed to obtain maximum volume, 5 to 6 minutes. Remove the bowl from the mixer and tap the yogurt powder through a fine-mesh sieve into the mixture. Fold in with a rubber spatula.

3 | Using a large spoon (a serving spoon works nicely), scoop the meringue from the bowl and drop onto the parchment in six equal portions. Bake for 2 hours, then turn off the oven and leave the meringues in the oven until crisp, dry, and cool, about 1 hour more.

4 | **Make the fruit topping.** In a large, heavy skillet set over high heat, combine the honey and bay leaves and cook until the honey is lightly caramelized. Arrange the fruit, cut sides down, over the darkened honey and cook until the pieces are blackened but not thoroughly burnt. Transfer the fruit to a plate and carefully stir ½ cup water into the juices in the skillet, taking care not to allow the hot caramel to splatter. Add the ginger. Using a rubber spatula, scrape up all the sticky bits and cook the liquid down until it is the thickness of syrup. Strain into a small bowl.

5 | To serve, arrange a blackened peach half on each meringue, drizzle some syrup over, and top with a generous dollop of the cheese.

note For a quick and easy dessert, serve the blackened fruits over ice cream.

HALF-POUND CAKES

(Or Less)

hen you want to serve a home-baked cake without a tremendous investment of time, these cakes come together quickly, with little collateral damage by way of filling your sink with a lot of bowls and utensils to wash. Many modern casual restaurants take this approach to desserts: In other words, make them quick and satisfying, with some surprising new flavors. I started this chapter with pound cakes in mind, and then, as is my habit, let my inner pastry chef wander. If there is a recipe simpler than a pound cake, I haven't come across it: just a pound of sugar, a pound of eggs, a pound of butter, and a pound of flour. My update is equally simple, but you won't find anything close to a pound of anything in the recipes that follow. From green tea to lavender honey to bitter orange essential oil (or grated zest), I have reached for exotic subplots to build drama into the following recipes. These are cakes that will stimulate the most jaded palate or, in the words of my favorite poet, William Butler Yeats, "would keep a drowsy emperor awake."

Plum-Side-Up Cake • Chocolate Pear Cake • Banana Flip Cake

Semolina Cake with Cherry Licorice Sauce • A Big Brown Butter Financier • Almond Cake

Pistachio Sponge Cake with Kumquat Compote • Cashew Cake • Blackberry Walnut Cake

Coffee Walnut Cream Cake • Pistachio Mango Cake

Hazelnut Sponge Cake with Cherry Compote and Whipped Coconut Cream

Tunisian Blood Orange Tea Cake • Green Tea Loaf • Black Cherry–Chocolate Pain D'epice

Lavender Honey Castella • Hazelnut Mocha Loaf • Coffeed Cake

note

Not every pie or cake has to be the same size. It's nice to throw a few changeups into your repertoire. Making this in a smaller pan allows for a taller dessert. If you don't have a 6-inch cake pan, a 6-inch cast-iron pan works just as well.

PLUM-SIDE-UP CAKE

MAKES ONE 6-INCH CAKE/SERVES 6 TO 8 • The idea of baking a cake by putting fruit in the pan and then cake batter on top no doubt came from not wanting to dirty more than one pot or pan. Maybe that's why you rarely see upside-down cakes (or, as I often think of them, fruit-side-up cakes) in restaurants where chefs, traditionally, could not care less how many pots, pans, plates, and utensils they use. During baking, the juices of ripe, fragrant, and naturally sweet summer plums infuse the batter. Avocado oil replaces butter here quite well and adds a haunting, lightly floral note.

3 tablespoons local honey

3 to 5 plums, depending on size (greengage, dinosaur, damson, Italian), halved and pitted

1 cup cake flour

1 teaspoon baking powder

1 teaspoon kosher salt

4 large eggs

¾ cup (packed) light brown sugar

2 tablespoons avocado oil

Maple Whipped Cream (page 241), for serving

1 | Preheat the oven to 350°F. Coat a 6-inch cake pan with vegetable oil cooking spray and line with parchment (see page 125). Spray the parchment with the cooking spray, too.

2 | Heat the honey in a heavy saucepan over medium-high heat until it turns golden and it bubbles and caramelizes. The distinct aroma of caramelized honey will permeate the kitchen. Add 3 tablespoons water and swirl in the pan. Take care; the caramel will splatter. Set the plums in the honey, cut side down, gently pressing them into place. Reduce the heat to low. Cook without disturbing them until they have darkened, about 2 minutes. Using a spatula, transfer the plums to the cake pan, arranging them cut side down. Set aside.

3 | Combine the flour, baking powder, and salt in a fine-mesh sieve set over parchment and tap through to sift. In the bowl of a standing mixer fitted with the whisk attachment, whisk together the eggs and sugar on medium-high speed until the mixture is pale and fluffy, about 8 minutes. Remove the bowl from the mixer and fold in the flour mixture in three batches. Add the oil and fold in gently. Pour the batter over the plums and swirl the pan to evenly distribute. Bake until a toothpick inserted in the center comes out clean, about 45 minutes. Let cool on a rack for 5 minutes. To unmold, run a knife around the edges of the cake pan to release it. Set an overturned plate on the pan and flip it over. Serve warm with the Maple Whipped Cream.

CHOCOLATE PEAR CAKE

MAKES ONE 9-INCH SINGLE-LAYER CAKE/SERVES 10 • This cake represents much of the philosophy that I have attempted to put on the plate to create new, more healthful desserts. Sugar is reduced by nearly half, and fermented kefir adds silky creaminess, structure, and a touch of tanginess. Honey-glazed pears with anise pulled it all together.

FOR THE PEARS

4 tablespoons local honey

1 star anise

4 pears (Comice, Bosc, or Bartlett), halved lengthwise, seeds and stem removed

FOR THE CAKE

1 cup unbleached all-purpose flour

⅔ cup organic cane sugar

⅓ cup unsweetened cocoa powder

2 tablespoons quinoa flour, purchased or home-milled

1 teaspoon baking powder

Pinch of kosher salt

½ cup kefir

⅓ cup canola oil

2 tablespoons almond oil

2 large eggs

Plain unsweetened full-fat Greek yogurt, for serving

1 | Preheat the oven to 375°F. Prepare a 9-inch springform pan with vegetable oil cooking spray and wrap the bottom with aluminum foil.

2 | **Prepare the pears.** Combine the honey and star anise in a medium saucepan and bring to a boil over medium-high heat. Cook until the honey is reduced to a thick, bubbly glaze. It will begin to caramelize and a distinct honey caramel aroma will permeate the air. Continue to cook until the honey is a dark amber. Immediately add ¼ cup water to stop the cooking and, using a slotted spoon, remove the star anise. Remove the pan from the heat and stir. Return the pan to the heat and return the mixture to a boil. Pour into the springform pan, scraping the saucepan clean with a rubber spatula. Using the back of a spoon, spread the caramelized honey evenly over the bottom of the pan. Arrange the pears, cut side down, over the honey and set aside.

3 | **Make the cake.** Combine the flour, sugar, cocoa powder, quinoa flour, baking powder, and salt in a large fine-mesh sieve set over parchment and tap through to sift. Repeat, sifting into a large mixing bowl. (Sifting twice helps to evenly distribute the baking powder; since it's the only leavener, you want it well dispersed.)

4 | In another large mixing bowl, combine the kefir, canola oil, almond oil, and eggs and vigorously whisk to break up the eggs. Pour the egg mixture into the flour mixture and whisk until well blended. Pour the batter over the pears. Bake until a toothpick inserted in the center comes out clean, about 60 minutes. Remove from the oven and set aside on the counter, sliding a fork underneath the pan to allow airflow. Let cool for 15 minutes. Serve at room temperature with a dollop of the yogurt.

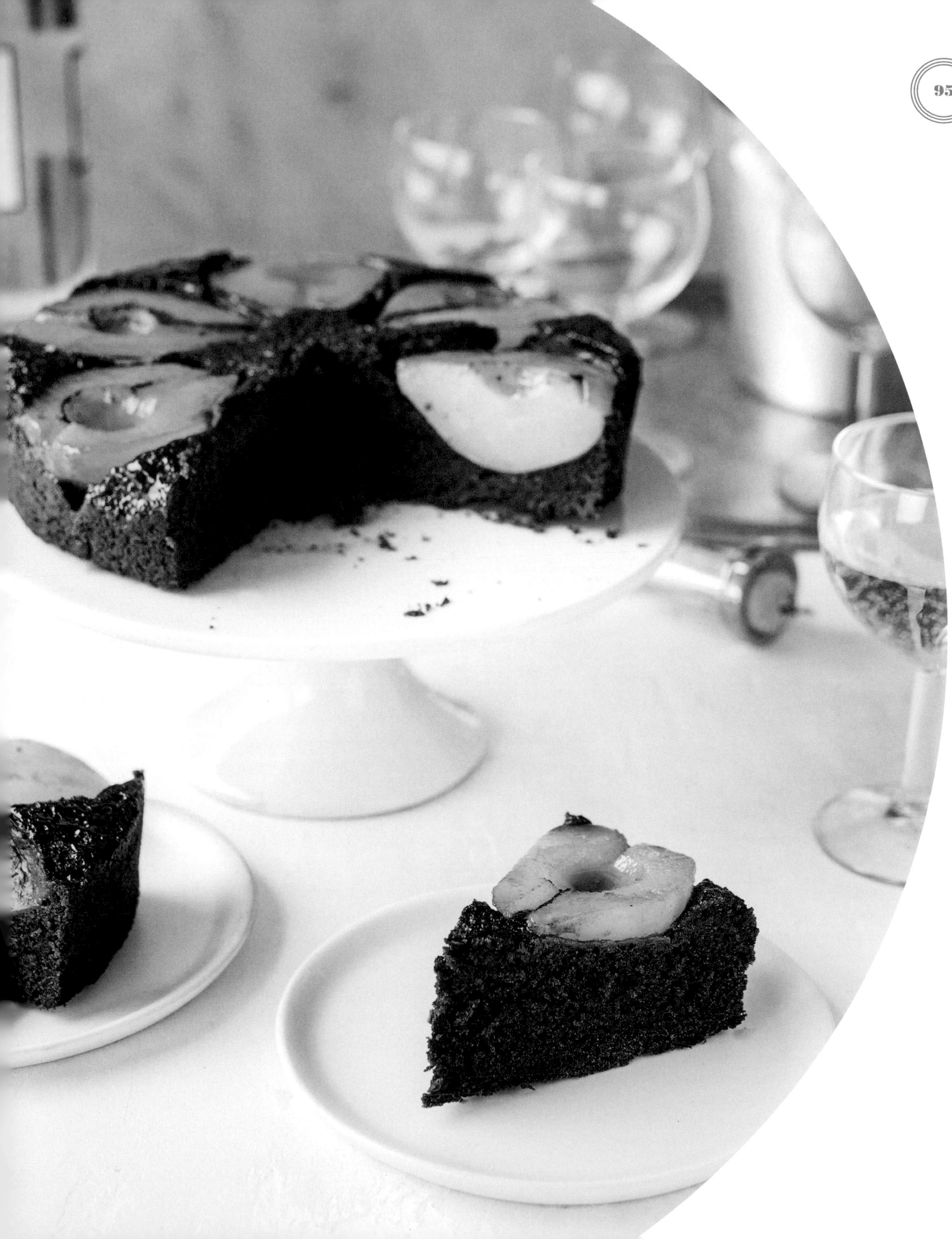

BANANA FLIP CAKE

MAKES ONE 10-INCH SINGLE-LAYER CAKE/SERVES 8 TO 10 • Years ago when I was the pastry chef at Montrachet in Tribeca, I set myself the task of refining the classic banana quick bread, giving it the down-home title: Banana Flip Cake. It was wildly popular. It was also wildly off the scale when it came to the amount of sugar it delivered per serving. Fortunately, I found it was still plenty sweet after I cut the sugar in the caramel down by two thirds and the sugar in the cake by half.

FOR THE CARAMEL

4 tablespoons (½ stick) unsalted high-fat European-style butter

½ cup turbinado or light brown sugar

3 ripe yet firm bananas, sliced

FOR THE CAKE

1 cup unbleached all-purpose flour

1½ teaspoons baking powder

¼ teaspoon kosher salt

4 tablespoons (½ stick) unsalted high-fat European-style butter, at room temperature

¼ cup organic cane sugar

1 teaspoon vanilla paste

1 large egg

½ cup whole milk

Maple Whipped Cream (page 241), for serving

note • When you paddle butter and sugar together, the sugar crystals cut their way through the butter and open up air pockets. This happens because the water content of butter is relatively low, so sugar dissolves slowly during paddling, opening little chambers for air to enter and expand during baking. The extra aeration adds volume to a cake and lightens the texture. It takes a good ten minutes in a standing mixer to get the proper airiness.

1 | Preheat the oven to 350°F.

2 | **Make the caramel.** Combine the butter, sugar, and 2 tablespoons water in a 10-inch cast-iron pan over medium heat. Using a wooden spoon, stir and swirl constantly until the sugar dissolves and the mixture turns to dark amber; watch carefully as this can happen in a split second. Swirl the caramel in the pan so that it coats the bottom entirely. Remove from the heat and arrange the banana slices over the caramel. Set aside.

3 | **Make the cake.** Combine the flour, baking powder, and salt in a fine-mesh sieve set over parchment and tap through to sift. Set aside. In the bowl of a standing mixer fitted with the paddle attachment, beat together the butter and sugar on medium-high speed until light and fluffy, about 5 minutes. Add the vanilla and the egg and beat until smooth. Reduce the speed to low and alternately add the flour mixture and the milk in three portions, mixing until incorporated.

4 | Carefully spoon the batter over the banana layer, using an offset spatula to distribute it evenly and push it out to the edges. Bake until golden brown and a toothpick inserted in the center comes out clean, 50 to 60 minutes. Remove from the oven and set aside on the counter, sliding a fork underneath the pan to allow airflow. Let the caramel set for at least 5 minutes. While the cake is still warm, set an overturned plate over the skillet and, using oven mitts and dish towels draped over your wrists and forearms (the caramel is still hot enough to hurt), invert the skillet to release the cake onto the plate. Serve (warm is nice, but not necessary) with the Maple Whipped Cream.

SEMOLINA CAKE
with Cherry Licorice Sauce

MAKES ONE 9-INCH SINGLE-LAYER CAKE • Semolina flour produces a grainier but no less pleasing texture than regular all-purpose or cake flour. In this recipe the semolina batter is cooked with milk on the stovetop before being poured into a cake pan. The result of this twice-cooked process is somewhere between a flan and a cake, kind of like the ancient New England stalwart Indian pudding (which is made with cornmeal). It's a blank tablet of texture that can accept a creative mix of strong flavors. Normally, a baker would use six tablespoons of sugar to make caramel for a recipe this size. I'm going with just two here—enough to season the cake with the flavor compounds that caramelization produces, but without drowning out every other nuance with intense sweetness. Serve with Cherry Licorice Sauce, which explodes on the palate.

½ cup plus 2 tablespoons muscovado or light brown sugar

3 large eggs

Grated zest and juice of 1 orange (about ⅓ cup of juice)

4 cups whole milk

1 vanilla bean, split and scraped

Pinch of kosher salt

¾ cup plus 1 tablespoon semolina flour

½ teaspoon ground cardamom

½ cup currants

Cherry Licorice Sauce (page 240)

1 | Preheat the oven to 350°F. Prepare a 9-inch springform pan with vegetable oil cooking spray, then line with parchment (see page 125).

2 | Place 2 tablespoons of the sugar in a small saucepan over medium heat and cook until it liquefies, tilting the pan every now and then, and turns mahogany brown. Do not stir! Once the liquid sugar begins to smoke, carefully add 3 tablespoons water to the pan. (Stand back from the stove because it will splatter.) Swirl the water around in the pan to blend with the sugar, then pour the hot sugar into the prepared cake pan and spread it on the parchment.

3 | In a small bowl, whisk together the eggs and orange zest and juice.

4 | Combine the milk, vanilla, and salt in a medium saucepan and bring to a boil. Gradually whisk in the semolina and the cardamom until fully incorporated and return to a boil. Add the currants and cook, whisking constantly, until the mixture begins to bubble, 8 to 10 minutes. Whisk in the egg mixture until thoroughly incorporated. Remove the pan from the heat and transfer the batter to the pan in giant spoonfuls. Smooth the top with an offset spatula.

5 | Bake until a toothpick inserted in the center comes out clean, about 50 minutes. Transfer to a rack to cool in the pan for about 5 minutes. Remove the cake from the pan and let cool on the rack to room temperature. Serve with the Cherry Licorice Sauce.

A BIG BROWN BUTTER FINANCIER

MAKES ONE 9-INCH SINGLE-LAYER CAKE/SERVES 8 TO 10 • As a hedge against last-minute guests, it's useful to have a repertoire of ready-to-bake batters and doughs in the fridge or freezer that you can pop in the oven and serve to the hungry multitudes in minutes. The financier, usually made as bite-size cookies, is so called, they say, because it looks like a bar of gold. I decided to use the batter as the base for a cake. It's a rich-tasting alternative to a brownie or pound cake. I covered it with fresh raspberries, though any fresh berry will do the trick. Optional lavender buds add a luxurious perfume and always pair well with honey.

6 tablespoons (¾ stick) unsalted high-fat European-style butter, at room temperature

⅔ cup unbleached all-purpose flour

¾ teaspoon baking powder

¾ cup confectioners' sugar

¾ cup almond flour, purchased or home-milled

5 large egg whites

½ teaspoon vanilla paste

3 drops food-grade wild bitter orange essential oil (or grated zest of 1 orange)

2 teaspoons local honey

4 cups fresh raspberries

Pinch of dried lavender buds

1 | Melt the butter in a small skillet over medium heat, then continue to cook, swirling it in the pan, until it is browned and fragrant. Set aside to cool. Meanwhile, combine the all-purpose flour and baking powder in a sieve set over parchment and tap through to sift.

2 | In the bowl of a standing mixer fitted with the paddle attachment, beat together the confectioners' sugar and almond flour until thoroughly combined.. Reduce the speed to low and let the paddle turn a few times. Add the egg whites, vanilla, and browned butter and mix while gradually adding the flour mixture. Mix until thoroughly incorporated. Remove the bowl from the mixer. Add the essential oil and stir thoroughly by hand to evenly distribute. Cover the bowl with plastic wrap and refrigerate for at least 3 hours or overnight.

3 | Preheat the oven to 350°F. Coat a 9-inch springform pan with vegetable oil cooking spray and line the bottom with parchment (see page 125). Transfer the batter to the pan and, using an offset spatula, smooth the top while pushing the batter out to the edges to prevent a mountain forming in the center of the cake. Bake until a toothpick inserted in the center comes out clean, about 40 minutes. Remove from the oven and set aside on the counter, sliding a fork underneath the pan to allow airflow. Let cool for about 15 minutes (it is very fragile when hot). Turn the cake out onto a cake plate to cool for 1 hour more.

4 | In a small saucepan over medium heat, stir together the honey with 2 tablespoons water, until just warmed through. Brush the honey mixture all over the top of the cake and arrange the berries on top. Sprinkle the lavender buds all over and serve warm.

note

While you can make this from scratch to serve on the same day, French bakers have always recommended storing the batter overnight in the fridge. In the same way that a stew's flavors meld when it's made the day before serving, so do many batters.

NUT
cakes

One of the most pleasing discoveries in writing this book is the way nuts deliver exquisite flavor that more than compensates for lowering sugar. When compared to many other ingredients, the flavor of nuts is more subtle on your palate. Less sweetener allows the essence of their flavors to come forward. Nuts and their nutritious oils also produce the kind of moist crumb that is desirable in any cake and lends a bit more heft to the texture. A side benefit of working with nuts is that you will inevitably munch on a few and this is the kind of healthy snacking that I recommend instead of, say, peanut M&M's.

ALMOND CAKE

MAKES ONE 9-INCH SINGLE-LAYER CAKE/SERVES 8 • Almond flour, though quite common in French baking, is used less often in American desserts. Combining almond flour with good almond paste is the best way to get the texture and gentle flavor of almonds with an accent on its essential taste. I use almond oil as well as almond extract to suffuse the crumb and to make this cake even more almondy. Although I have greatly reduced the sugar, this is still a pleasantly sweet, citrus-accented cake with a moist crumb and fewer starchy carbs. It's gluten-free, too!

6 large eggs, separated

½ cup superfine sugar

Grated zest of 1 lemon

Grated zest of 1 orange

4 drops pure almond extract,
   such as Nielsen-Massey

1¾ cups almond flour, purchased
   or home milled

2 tablespoons almond or canola oil

Elderflower Cream (page 243)

note • Before the egg whites are folded in, the batter will be quite thick. Don't be timid. Put some oomph in your folding; I promise the batter will loosen.

1 | Preheat the oven to 350°F. Coat a 9-inch round cake pan with vegetable oil cooking spray and line the bottom with parchment (see page 125).

2 | In the bowl of a standing mixer fitted with the whisk attachment, whisk together the egg yolks and sugar on medium-high speed until the mixture is pale and thick ribbons fall into the bowl when the paddle is lifted, about 8 minutes. Add the zests and almond extract and beat until incorporated. Add the almond flour and mix until thoroughly incorporated. Transfer the mixture to a large mixing bowl.

3 | Thoroughly clean the whisk and bowl of the standing mixer and beat the egg whites on medium-high speed until stiff peaks form. Fold the egg whites into the almond mixture (the mixture will be very thick; you will need to turn it over quite a bit to incorporate the whites). Transfer ½ cup of the mixture to a small bowl. Whisk in the oil. Return this mixture to the large mixing bowl and gently fold in.

4 | Transfer the mixture to the prepared pan and bake until a toothpick inserted in the center comes out clean, about 40 minutes. Remove from the oven and set aside on the counter, sliding a fork underneath the pan to allow airflow. Let cool for 10 minutes. Run a knife around the rim of the pan and turn the cake out onto a cake plate. Serve warm with the Elderflower Cream.

PISTACHIO SPONGE CAKE
with Kumquat Compote

MAKES ONE 9-INCH SINGLE-LAYER CAKE/SERVES 8 • Why is common store-bought pistachio paste green when ground pistachios are more blond in color? Quite often food coloring—which I don't use—is the answer. Still, if you chew a pistachio all on its own, when you breathe out through your nose there is the mild aroma of a green herb. I like to serve Kumquat Compote here because kumquats and pistachios both grow in the Mediterranean, where long tradition has found a way to combine tamer-tasting ingredients, such as pistachios, with astringent, powerfully flavored ingredients—in this case, kumquats.

4 large eggs, separated

¼ cup plus 2½ tablespoons organic cane sugar

2 cups pistachio flour, purchased or home-milled

3 tablespoons cake flour

Pinch of kosher salt

Kumquat Compote (page 237)

1 | Preheat the oven to 350°F. Coat a 9-inch springform pan with vegetable oil cooking spray and line the bottom with parchment (see page 125).

2 | In the bowl of a standing mixer fitted with the whisk attachment, whisk together the egg yolks and ¼ cup of the sugar on medium-high speed until the mixture is pale yellow and fluffy, about 10 minutes.

3 | Transfer to a large mixing bowl. Thoroughly wash and dry the whisk and bowl of the standing mixer and mix the egg whites and half the remaining 2½ tablespoons of sugar on medium-high speed until the tines of the whisk appear in the whites. Add the remaining sugar and whisk until stiff peaks form.

4 | Combine the flours and salt in a fine-mesh sieve set over parchment and tap through to sift.

5 | Fold the egg whites into the egg yolks until there is no trace of whites in the batter. Sprinkle the flour mixture into the batter with a light touch (avoid dumping it in all at once and in one place), and thoroughly fold it in.

6 | Pour the batter into the prepared pan and bake until faintly golden and a toothpick inserted in the center comes out clean, 30 to 40 minutes. Remove from the oven and set aside on the counter, sliding a fork underneath the pan to allow airflow. Let cool for about 5 minutes. Run a knife around the rim of the pan and turn the cake out onto a cake plate. Serve warm with the Kumquat Compote.

CASHEW CAKE

MAKES ONE 9-INCH SINGLE-LAYER CAKE/SERVES 8 • When you are snacking on mixed nuts, how often do you pick out the cashews first? I find myself going back for just a few more, and then a few more after that. It seems our bodies are telling us that cashews are irresistible, yet they are not commonly used in traditional cake making. Perhaps that's because their powerful flavor would compete with milder ingredients. I implore the baking world to reconsider the noble cashew. Make this cake and you will agree with me that their time has come! The silky texture of my Miracle Ganache Frosting is a foil to the denser crumb of the cake.

9 large egg whites

½ cup turbinado or light brown sugar

¾ cup raw, unsalted cashews, lightly toasted

10 tablespoons (1¼ sticks) unsalted high-fat European-style butter, at room temperature

1 teaspoon kosher salt

2 tablespoons unsweetened cocoa powder

1½ cups cashew flour, purchased or home-milled

Miracle Ganache Frosting (page 244)

1 │ Preheat the oven to 350°F. Coat a 9-inch springform pan with vegetable oil cooking spray and line with parchment (see page 125).

2 │ In the bowl of a standing mixer fitted with the whisk attachment, whisk ¾ cup of the egg whites on medium-high speed until the tines of the whisk appear in the whites. Add 1 tablespoon of the sugar to the bowl and continue whisking until soft peaks form. Add 2 tablespoons more of the sugar and beat until stiff peaks form. Set aside.

3 │ Place the cashews in the bowl of a food processor and pulse until they resemble Grape-Nuts. Add the butter, remaining 5 tablespoons of sugar, and the salt and pulse, scraping down the sides. Add the remaining egg whites and process until thoroughly combined. Add the cocoa powder and pulse until incorporated. The mixture will appear broken but will come back together when the flour is added. Transfer the mixture to a large steel bowl and stir in the cashew flour until thoroughly incorporated. Fold in the egg whites.

4 │ Pour the batter into the prepared cake pan, set the pan on a baking sheet, and bake until the cake is firm to the touch, about 40 minutes. Transfer to a rack to cool in the pan for about 5 minutes. It will puff up and deflate slightly as it cools. Slide a fork underneath the pan to allow airflow and let the cake cool completely. Serve with a spoonful of the Miracle Ganache Frosting.

BLACKBERRY WALNUT CAKE

MAKES ONE 9-INCH SINGLE-LAYER CAKE/SERVES 8 • Imagine that the moon was made out of cake batter and flecked with blackberry meteorites—that's the mental tableau I had in mind when I created this dessert. Why marry blackberries and walnuts in a cake? The best answer I can give is that I did what all chefs do (and that includes home chefs): I am always looking to try new taste combinations and it seemed like a nice idea. In this case I wondered how one can use blackberries other than throw some cobbler topping on them and leave it at that. Here the berries fill beautiful purplish/blue craters that are much more pleasant tasting than your average celestial object. Serve with Maiz Morado Cream, smooth as purple velvet.

13 tablespoons (1⅝ sticks) unsalted high-fat European-style butter, at room temperature, plus more for the pan

2 tablespoons walnut oil

½ cup organic cane sugar

1½ cups almond flour, purchased or home-milled

4 large eggs

¾ cup unbleached all-purpose flour

½ teaspoon kosher salt

1½ cups finely ground toasted walnuts

Grated zest of 1 lemon

1 cup fresh blackberries

Maiz Morado Cream (page 244) or plain whipped cream

1 | Preheat the oven to 375°F. Line a 9-inch springform pan with parchment paper and lightly butter the paper (see page 125).

2 | Combine the butter, oil, sugar, and almond flour in the bowl of a standing mixer fitted with the paddle attachment and beat on medium-high speed until the mixture is light and fluffy. Add the eggs, one at a time, beating after each addition until incorporated. Beat until the mixture is pale yellow and thick ribbons fall into the bowl when the paddle is lifted, about 10 minutes.

3 | Combine the all-purpose flour and salt in a fine-mesh sieve set over parchment and tap through to sift. With the mixer running on low speed, gradually add the flour until thoroughly incorporated. Remove the bowl from the mixer and fold in the ground walnuts and the lemon zest. Pour the batter into the prepared pan and use an offset spatula to smooth the top.

4 | Arrange the blackberries all over the top of the cake, pushing them into the batter slightly and arranging them all the way out to the edges. Bake until a toothpick inserted in the center comes out clean, 60 to 70 minutes. Transfer the cake to a rack to cool in the pan for about 5 minutes. Run a knife around the rim of the cake and turn it out onto the rack to cool completely. Serve with the Maiz Morado Cream.

COFFEE WALNUT CREAM CAKE

MAKES ONE 9-INCH SINGLE-LAYER CAKE/SERVES 8 • This recipe celebrates the complex flavors of walnut oil, walnut flour, and chopped walnuts. Coffee pairs well, perhaps because coffee beans take on nutlike characteristics when roasted. I double down on coffee by lacing the mascarpone cream filling with it.

FOR THE CAKE

3 large eggs

½ cup organic cane sugar

1 tablespoon instant coffee crystals

1⅓ cups unbleached all-purpose flour

1 cup walnut flour, purchased or home-milled

2 teaspoons baking powder

½ teaspoon ground cinnamon

¼ teaspoon baking soda

¼ teaspoon kosher salt

¼ cup walnut oil

½ teaspoon vanilla paste

FOR THE COFFEE-MASCARPONE CREAM

1 cup heavy cream

¾ cup walnuts, toasted and finely chopped

½ cup mascarpone

½ cup confectioners' sugar

4½ teaspoons instant coffee crystals

½ teaspoon vanilla paste

Pinch of kosher salt

1 teaspoon gelatin

1 │ Preheat the oven to 350°F. Coat a 9-inch cake pan with vegetable cooking spray, then line the bottom with parchment (see page 125).

2 │ Combine the flours, baking powder, cinnamon, baking soda, and salt in a fine-mesh sieve set over parchment and tap through to sift.

3 │ **Make the cake.** In the bowl of a standing mixer fitted with the whisk attachment, whisk the eggs, sugar, and coffee on medium-high speed until frothy, about 5 minutes. Remove the bowl from the mixer and gradually fold in the flour mixture, a third at a time. Fold in the walnut oil and vanilla and pour into the cake pan. Bake until a toothpick inserted in the center comes out clean, about 40 minutes. Transfer to a rack to cool in the pan for about 5 minutes. Run a knife around the rim of the pan and turn the cake out onto the rack to cool completely.

4 │ **Make the coffee-mascarpone cream.** Chill the bowl of a standing mixer in the refrigerator. Using the whisk attachment, whisk the cream in the chilled bowl until soft peaks form. Set aside.

5 │ In a medium bowl, combine the walnuts, mascarpone, sugar, coffee, vanilla, and salt and mix until thoroughly incorporated. In a small saucepan, combine the gelatin with 3 tablespoons cold water and set aside to bloom, 3 to 5 minutes. Set the pan over low heat to melt the bloomed gelatin. Pour it into the mascarpone mixture and immediately whisk until thoroughly incorporated. Fold one third of the whipped cream into the mascarpone mixture, then fold in the remaining whipped cream. Note the frosting will set quickly.

6 │ Working quickly, before the gelatin in the frosting causes it to set, slice the cake in half horizontally using a serrated knife. Spoon half the cream onto the bottom half of the cake and spread it out to the edges. Replace the top half of the cake and spoon the remaining cream on top. Spread all over the top (leave the sides unfrosted) and serve.

PISTACHIO MANGO CAKE

MAKES ONE 9-INCH SINGLE-LAYER CAKE/SERVES 8 • We didn't have a lot of mangoes where I grew up in Toledo, Ohio, although now you can easily find them in markets far from the nearest palm tree. I am fond of using mangoes because they keep their cheerful bright color and texture after baking. Another plus: Reasonably nice mangoes are available in the winter, a time when there aren't many good fresh fruits to be had. Using nut oils rather than butter not only carries the benefit of healthful fats, but it infuses the crumb of the cake with a strong undertone of nut flavor. Although this cake is quite nice all by itself, a topping of Clementine Coconut Mango Compote is a sensuous and rock 'em, sock 'em finishing touch.

2 large eggs

¼ cup organic cane sugar

1 tablespoon local honey

½ cup whole milk

½ cup pistachio or other nut oil

¾ cup unbleached all-purpose flour

2½ teaspoons baking powder

2 mangoes, peeled and pitted, 1 chopped into small dice and the other thinly sliced

Clementine Coconut Mango Compote (page 236), for serving

note This cake needs to rest for a good 4 hours, or overnight, before it's cut into wedges.

1 | Preheat the oven to 350°F. Coat a 9-inch springform pan with vegetable oil cooking spray and line with parchment (see page 125).

2 | In the bowl of a standing mixer fitted with the whisk attachment, whisk together the eggs, sugar, and honey on medium-high speed until the mixture is light and fluffy, about 10 minutes.

3 | In a small bowl, whisk together the milk and oil. Set aside. Combine the flour and baking powder in a fine-mesh sieve set over parchment and tap through to sift.

4 | Remove the bowl from the mixer and fold in one third of the milk mixture followed by one third of the flour mixture, alternating until the wet and dry ingredients are thoroughly folded into the egg mixture.

5 | Transfer ¾ cup of the batter to a small bowl and fold in the chopped mangoes. Add the mixture back to the batter and fold until it is just mixed in. Avoid overmixing. Pour the batter into the prepared pan and, using an offset spatula, spread it evenly to the edges of the pan. Arrange the sliced mangoes on top (they will sink into the cake as it bakes). Bake for 30 minutes, then rotate the pan 180 degrees. Bake until a toothpick inserted in the center comes out clean, about 10 minutes more.

6 | Remove from the oven and set aside on the counter, sliding a fork underneath the pan to allow airflow. Let cool for 30 minutes. Remove the cake from the pan, cover in plastic wrap, and let rest. Serve with the Clementine Coconut Mango Compote.

Hazelnut
Sponge Cake,
opposite

Hazelnut Mocha Loaf,
page 117

HAZELNUT SPONGE CAKE
with Cherry Compote and Whipped Coconut Cream

MAKES ONE 9 × 5-LOAF/SERVES 6 TO 8 • The airiness of a sponge cake is well suited to coaxing out the maximum delicate hazelnut flavor and it soaks up a truly luscious topping of Cherry Compote and Whipped Coconut Cream. The result is that the combination of hazelnuts, cherries, and coconut play together in a beautiful *ménage à trois*. They give a rounded, tart, and balanced result that is slightly exotic yet instantly satisfying.

1¾ cups hazelnut flour, purchased or home-milled

⅓ cup cake flour

Pinch of kosher salt

4 large eggs, separated

⅔ cup organic cane sugar

¼ teaspoon cream of tartar

Cherry Compote (page 238)

Whipped Coconut Cream (page 242)

1 | Preheat the oven to 350°F. Coat a 9 × 5-inch loaf pan with vegetable oil cooking spray and line with parchment (see page 116).

2 | Combine the hazelnut flour, cake flour, and salt in a fine-mesh sieve set over parchment and tap through to sift. Set aside.

3 | In the bowl of a standing mixer fitted with the whisk attachment, whisk together the egg yolks and ⅓ cup of the sugar on medium speed until thick, pale yellow ribbons form, 7 to 8 minutes. Transfer to a large mixing bowl.

4 | Thoroughly wash and dry the whisk and bowl of the standing mixer and mix the egg whites and cream of tartar on medium-high speed. When the tines of the whisk begin to appear in the whites, add the remaining ⅓ cup of sugar and beat until stiff peaks form.

5 | Fold the whites into the yolk mixture until no traces of the whites show. Fold in the flour mixture until thoroughly incorporated. Pour the batter into the pan and tap lightly on the counter to release the air bubbles.

6 | Bake until a toothpick inserted in the center comes out clean, 35 to 40 minutes. Remove from the oven and set aside on the counter, sliding a fork underneath the pan to allow airflow. Let cool for about 5 minutes. Transfer the cake from the pan onto a work surface or a plate and let cool completely. Serve with the Cherry Compote and Whipped Coconut Cream.

TUNISIAN BLOOD ORANGE TEA CAKE

MAKES ONE 9 × 5-INCH LOAF/SERVES 6 TO 8 • I could have called this Moroccan or Corsican or Straight-Outta-Malta Tea Cake because the ingredients are very Mediterranean, particularly blood oranges, honey, and bergamot. I settled on Tunisia because it was one of my early exotic travel experiences. When I worked as a sales rep for Air France I fell in love with Tunisia and would take every chance to escape the Twentieth century (actually more like the eighth through twentieth centuries) with trips to an ancient oasis in the Sahara.

2 cups unbleached all-purpose flour, plus more for the pan

1 tablespoon baking powder

Pinch of kosher salt

3 large eggs

1 cup confectioners' sugar

1 cup extra-virgin olive oil, plus more for drizzling

½ cup whole milk

Grated zest and juice of 3 blood oranges (about ½ cup juice)

3 drops food-grade bergamot essential oil

Kumquat Compote (page 237)

1 Preheat the oven to 325°F. Coat a 9 × 5-inch loaf pan with vegetable oil cooking spray and line with parchment (see page 116).

2 Combine the flour, baking powder, baking soda, and salt in a fine-mesh sieve set over parchment and tap through to sift. Repeat. Set aside.

3 In the bowl of a standing mixer fitted with the whisk attachment, mix together the eggs and confectioners' sugar on medium-high speed until the batter reaches three quarters of the way up the bowl. Remove the bowl from the mixer and gradually fold in the olive oil, milk, and zest and juice. Then fold in the flour mixture, adding it in thirds. Add the essential oil and stir thoroughly to evenly distribute.

4 Pour the batter into the prepared loaf pan and bake until a toothpick inserted in the center comes out clean, about 65 minutes. Remove from the oven and set aside on the counter, sliding a fork underneath the pan to allow airflow. Let cool for about 1 hour. Turn out onto a serving plate and serve warm with the Kumquat Compote.

note

Like many denser cakes made with honey, this one wants a strong balancing topping. I created a Kumquat Compote especially for this cake and found that it works with many of the honey cakes in this book.

GREEN TEA LOAF

MAKES ONE 9 × 5-INCH LOAF/SERVES 8 • A few years ago Chef Dan Barber hosted a meeting of the Basque Culinary Council at his celebrated farm-to-table (actually, make that table-to-farm) restaurant, Blue Hill at Stone Barns. It's an idyllic setting in the rolling Pocantico Hills, twenty miles north of Manhattan with hundreds of acres for grazing livestock, bountiful gardens, and a gargantuan greenhouse. Ferran Adrià, Michel Bras, and Alex Atala were among the world-famous chefs attending. I was asked to do the desserts. "K-I-S-B [Keep It Simple, Bill!]," I told myself and, listening to the better angels of my nature, devised a cake with restrained amounts of sweeteners, no butter, and a dose of matcha green tea for its beneficial antioxidants. Instead of the usual confectioners' sugar glaze, I served it with a tangy curd flavored with yuzu, a tart Japanese citrus fruit. The chefs scarfed it up, once again proving my belief that big-shot chefs really appreciate simple. Hope you do, too.

1½ cups unbleached all-purpose flour

2 tablespoons matcha powder

2 teaspoons baking powder

1 teaspoon ground nutmeg

1 teaspoon kosher salt

½ teaspoon baking soda

½ teaspoon roughly chopped black peppercorns

2 large eggs

¼ cup local honey

¼ cup agave syrup

½ cup orange juice concentrate, softened

1 cup good-quality extra-virgin olive oil

Yuzu Curd (page 249)

1 | Preheat the oven to 350°F. Coat a 9 × 5-inch loaf pan with vegetable oil cooking spray and line the bottom and sides with parchment (see page 116).

2 | Combine the flour, matcha, baking powder, nutmeg, salt, and baking soda in a fine-mesh sieve set over parchment and tap through to sift. Add the peppercorns and set aside.

3 | In the bowl of a standing mixer fitted with the whisk attachment, mix together the eggs, honey, and agave on medium-high speed until thick ribbons fall into the bowl when the whisk is pulled from the mixture, 5 to 8 minutes. Add the orange juice concentrate and mix until thoroughly combined.

4 | Reduce the speed to low and gradually add the flour mixture, mixing until combined. Transfer ½ cup of the cake batter to a small bowl and whisk in the oil until thoroughly combined. Using a rubber spatula, fold the mixture back into the batter.

5 | Transfer the batter to the loaf pan and bake for 10 minutes. Using a sharp knife, score the loaf down the middle (this prevents it from cracking in the wrong places during baking). Bake until a toothpick inserted in the center comes out clean, about 50 minutes more. Remove from the oven and set aside on the counter, sliding a fork underneath the pan to allow airflow. Let cool for about 1 hour. Serve with the Yuzu Curd.

BLACK CHERRY–CHOCOLATE PAIN D'EPICE

MAKES ONE 9 × 5-INCH LOAF OR ONE 9-INCH ROUND SINGLE-LAYER CAKE/SERVES 8 • You might translate this as spice cake, but to me, that evokes too many childhood Christmases featuring cakes so full of dried fruit and sugar that simply taking one out of the box made my fillings vibrate. In France this cake is traditionally made with rye flour and not much sugar. Rye has its own dark undertones, the flavor equivalent of a bass note. For the fruit, instead of resorting to the standard go-to of candied fruits that are super high in sugar, I opted for dried cherries. This pain d'epice really wants a topping, and you can choose a number of them from chapter 10. I love it with Plum Compote. As a finishing touch, you can never go wrong with whipped cream. This pain d'epice stands on its own, but you can also incorporate it into other desserts, cubed and toasted as croutons, such as a soufflé or a parfait.

1 cup dried cherries

1 cup unbleached all-purpose flour, plus more for the pan

½ cup rye flour, purchased or home-milled

2 teaspoons baking soda

½ cup extra-virgin olive oil

⅓ cup muscovado or dark brown sugar

1 tablespoon unsulphured molasses

2 level tablespoons unsweetened cocoa powder

1 teaspoon ground cinnamon

½ teaspoon ground cloves

½ teaspoon ground allspice

½ teaspoon kosher salt

Plum Compote (page 237), for serving

1 | Coat a 9 × 5-inch loaf pan or a 9-inch round cake pan with vegetable oil cooking spray, then dust with flour and tap out the excess. Bring 2 cups of water to a boil.

2 | Place the dried cherries in a medium bowl and pour the boiling water over them. Set aside to cool. Preheat the oven to 300°F. Combine the flours and the baking soda in a fine-mesh sieve set over parchment and tap through to sift. Set aside.

3 | Drain the cherries, reserving 1½ cups of the water. Spread the cherries on a baking sheet and dry in the oven for 10 minutes. Remove from the oven and set aside. Raise the heat to 350°F.

4 | In a large saucepan, bring the reserved soaking water to a boil over medium-high heat then add the oil, sugar, molasses, cocoa powder, cinnamon, cloves, allspice, and salt. Whisk to thoroughly combine. Remove from the heat and set aside until the mixture is cool enough to touch. Using a rubber spatula, stir in the flour mixture, then fold in the cherries.

5 | Spoon the batter into the prepared pan and bake until the top springs back when tapped, about 40 minutes. Remove from the oven and set aside on the counter, sliding a fork underneath the pan to allow airflow. Let cool for about 1 hour, then turn the cake out of the pan and onto a serving plate. Serve warm with the Plum Compote.

note

Start at a high heat to brown the top of the Castella before lowering the heat to finish the baking. This is mostly for looks. After a couple hundred thousand years of cooking, we humans have learned to associate this kind of browning with deliciousness.

LAVENDER HONEY CASTELLA

MAKES ONE 9 × 5-INCH LOAF/SERVES 8 • Riding the tides of history in the Age of Exploration—the Portuguese bestowed the cake known as Castella on the Japanese, who embraced it as their own. Every bakery in Japan has its own version of the Castella, and aficionados debate the fine points of their favorite shop the way Americans champion the virtues of different pizzas. A Japanese Castella is already light in sugar and honey, but I cut back even further. Aerating the egg yolks as much as possible makes each mouthful lighter with a more delicate crumb.

6 large eggs

½ cup plus 2 tablespoons lavender honey

2 tablespoons organic cane sugar

¾ cup unbleached all-purpose flour

¼ teaspoon kosher salt

2 tablespoons canola oil

Autumn Fruit Packet (page 230), for serving

1 | Preheat the oven to 400°F. Line a 9 × 5-inch loaf pan with parchment (see page 116), then rub all over with butter.

2 | Fill a medium saucepan with 2 inches of water and bring to a gentle simmer over medium heat. Combine the eggs, ½ cup of the honey, and the sugar in the bowl of a standing mixer. Set the bowl over the saucepan and heat, whisking constantly to avoid scrambling the eggs, until the mixture is hot to the touch, 131°F.

3 | Return the mixing bowl to the standing mixer fitted with a whisk attachment and whisk on medium-high speed until the eggs reach three quarters of the way up the bowl, about 10 minutes. Meanwhile, combine the flour and salt in a fine-mesh sieve set over parchment and tap through to sift. Reduce the mixer speed to low, gradually add the flour mixture, and mix for 15 seconds or until the batter resembles pancake batter.

4 | Transfer ¼ cup of the batter to a small bowl and whisk together with the canola oil. Add it back to the batter and gently fold it in by hand. Pour the batter into the prepared cake pan and tap the bottom of the pan against the counter several times to release the air bubbles. Set on a sheet pan and bake for 5 minutes. Reduce the heat to 350°F, rotate the pan, and invert a second loaf pan over it (like a cap). Bake until a toothpick inserted in the center comes out clean, 20 to 30 minutes. Remove from the oven and set aside on the counter, sliding a fork underneath the pan to allow airflow. Let cool for 10 minutes.

(RECIPE CONTINUES)

5 | Run a knife around the rim of the cake to loosen it from the pan. Lay a piece of plastic wrap on a work surface and turn the cake out onto it, leaving the parchment attached to it. While warm, double wrap the cake and parchment tightly in plastic wrap and refrigerate overnight. This captures the humidity as the cake cools and reintegrates it into the spongy center.

6 | Remove the cake from the refrigerator and remove the plastic and parchment. Combine the remaining 2 tablespoons honey with 1 tablespoon water in a small saucepan and bring to a boil for 45 seconds. Note when the honey is bubbling and the mixture begins to smell like burnt honey. It will bubble all over on the surface. Remove the pan from the heat (the honey will continue to cook) and place on a damp cloth or in a bowl of cold water. Using a pastry brush, brush the entire surface of the cake with the honey. Once the glaze has set (it will be shiny, not sticky) and the cake reaches room temperature, cut into 1-inch-thick slices. Serve a slice with the Autumn Fruit Packet.

LINING A LOAF PAN
with parchment paper

HAZELNUT MOCHA LOAF

MAKES ONE 9 × 5-INCH LOAF/SERVES 6 TO 8 • Hazelnuts are among the most versatile nuts, yet do not, in my opinion, star enough in America. They are very delicate in flavor. Nutella, a well-known spread, combines hazelnuts and cocoa powder but has so much sugar and palm oil that I would serve it only to cloven-hooved devils. Classic dessert masters in France resort to high-sugar hazelnut paste. Much better, I think, to use the real thing—whole nuts, dark chocolate, and less sugar. (See photo, page 108.)

1½ cups blanched hazelnuts, lightly toasted and skins removed

1½ cups unbleached all-purpose flour

1 teaspoon baking powder

¼ teaspoon kosher salt

6 tablespoons (¾ stick) unsalted high-fat European-style butter, at room temperature

¾ cup organic cane sugar

3 large eggs

1 tablespoon extra-virgin olive oil

½ teaspoon grated orange zest

2 teaspoons instant coffee crystals

1 cup whole milk

2 ounces dark chocolate (70%), chopped into small pieces

Blackberry Chia Sauce (optional, page 240)

1 │ Preheat the oven to 350°F. Coat a 9 × 5-inch loaf pan with vegetable oil cooking spray and cut out a piece of parchment to line the bottom (page 116).

2 │ Place the hazelnuts in the bowl of a food processor and pulse until the nuts resemble chunky peanut butter. Set aside. Combine the flour, baking powder, and salt in a fine-mesh sieve set over parchment and tap through to sift. Set aside.

3 │ In the bowl of a standing mixer fitted with the paddle attachment, beat together the butter and sugar on medium-high speed until the mixture is pale yellow and smooth. Add the eggs, one at a time, beating well after each addition. Add the olive oil, zest, and coffee and beat until thoroughly incorporated. Reduce the speed to low and gradually add the flour mixture and the milk, alternating between them and occasionally scraping down the sides of the bowl. Remove the bowl from the mixer. Using a rubber spatula, fold in the hazelnut paste and chocolate.

4 │ Pour the batter into the prepared pan and bake until a toothpick inserted in the center comes out clean, about 45 minutes. Remove from the oven and set aside on the counter, sliding a fork underneath the pan to allow airflow. Let the loaf cool in the pan for 5 minutes, then run a knife around the rim of the pan, turn the loaf out onto a plate, and let cool completely. Serve with the Blackberry Chia Sauce, if using. The loaf will keep, tightly wrapped, for up to 4 days.

COFFEED CAKE

SERVES 10 TO 12 • Calling something coffee cake is usually shorthand for a very sweet pound cake with a thick topping of brown sugar and cinnamon. It's not really up to the level of contemporary coffee connoisseurs. Instead of serving great coffee with a cake that could have come out of a 1950s supermarket, I wanted my cake to step up its game, too. I've removed a half cup of sugar from the amount typically used to make traditional coffee cake and added rye, which broadens the toasty grain-like flavor. Kefir's sweetly sour taste contributes another flavor-balancing element. As for the all-important crumble on top—I've replaced a lot of the brown sugar with roasted walnuts. Following through on the coffee theme, top with Hazelnut, Maple, and Coffee Whipped Cream if you like.

1 cup Nut Topping (with walnuts, page 81)

1 cup cake flour

½ cup rye flour, purchased or home-milled

1 teaspoon baking powder

1 teaspoon kosher salt

1 tablespoon instant coffee crystals

½ cup (1 stick) unsalted high-fat European-style butter, at room temperature

½ cup muscovado sugar

2 large eggs

¼ cup local honey

1 cup plain kefir

Hazelnut, Maple & Coffee Whipped Cream, optional (page 242)

1 | Preheat the oven to 350°F. Coat a Bundt pan with vegetable oil cooking spray. Scatter the Nut Topping on the bottom of the pan.

2 | Combine the cake flour, rye flour, baking powder, and salt in a fine-mesh sieve set over parchment and tap through to sift. Add the coffee to the mixture and set aside.

3 | In the bowl of a standing mixer fitted with the paddle attachment, mix together the butter and sugar on medium-high speed until the mixture is pale and fluffy. Add the eggs, one at a time, and mix thoroughly after each addition. Add the honey and kefir and mix well, occasionally scraping down the sides of the bowl. Reduce the speed to low and gradually add the flour mixture, mixing until just incorporated. Remove the bowl from the mixer and use a rubber spatula to thoroughly mix.

4 | Pour the batter into the pan and bake until a toothpick inserted in the center comes out clean, 30 to 40 minutes. Remove from the oven and set aside on the counter, sliding a fork underneath the pan to allow airflow. Let cool until the cake separates from the sides of the pan. If necessary, use a fork to release the cake from the sides of the pan. Tap the cake on its side to ensure it is loosened and place an overturned serving plate over it. Flip over onto the plate. Serve warm or at room temperature with the Hazelnut, Maple & Coffee Whipped Cream, if desired.

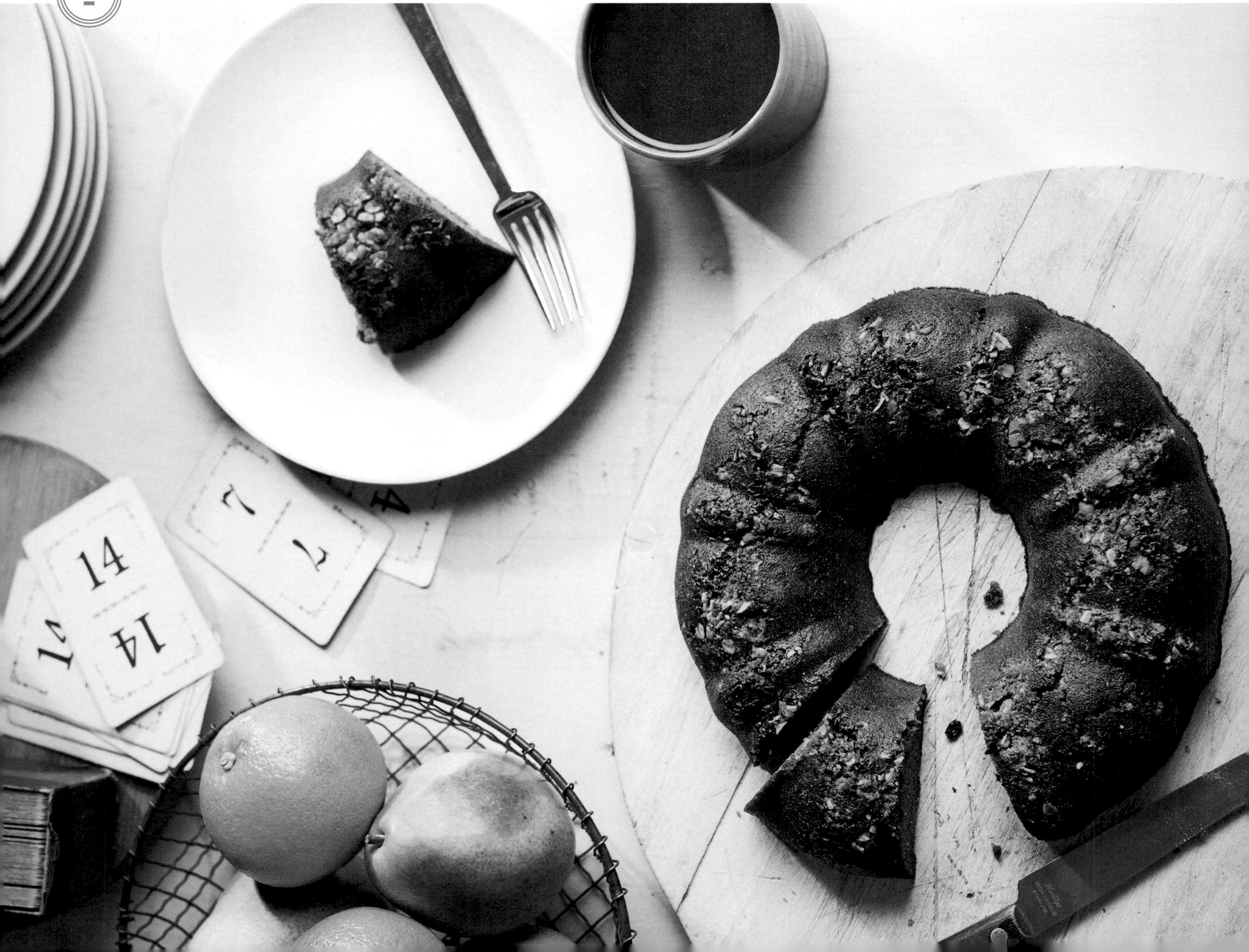

5 HAPPY CAKES
(Layered and Unlayered)

 think of these as happy cakes, not because they are more smiley than other desserts but because I think they go well at special occasions. Happy Birthday, comes to mind, Happy Anniversary/Divorce, Graduation, or even Happy Saturday Night. They'll make you look like a virtuoso baker. Over the last thirty years of making and serving desserts, I have seen people become less interested in the frosting and fillings than they are in the "cakey" part of cakes, technically called the crumb. This poses a challenge if you want your desserts to be healthier, because fat and sugar are essential for a beautiful crumb. But by using alternative sweeteners, nut flours, and a variety of whole grains, you can still create wonderful cakes. Adding herbs, spices, and essential oils puts a greater emphasis on elegant but forceful flavors.

Now that I am more mindful of the healthfulness of a dessert I tend to shy away from multilayer cakes that resemble a Renaissance painting of the Tower of Babel. They look great on the covers of dessert books, but one great layer with a delicious frosting, glaze, topping, or garnish will satisfy with fewer calories, less fat, less sugar. However, if you are a dyed-in-the-wool layer lover, there are a few recipes here that benefit from more than one layer.

Sheba from Queens Cake • **Cake for a Wake** • **Very Fresh Green Cake**

The Lady M • **Honeyed Babas with Blood Orange and Vanilla**

Jellyless Nut Roll • **Matcha Green Tea Roll with Blackberry Pastry Cream**

SHEBA FROM QUEENS CAKE

MAKES ONE 9-INCH SINGLE-LAYER CAKE/SERVES 10 • This is my healthed-up, thoroughly modernized take on the Queen of Sheba cake that Julia Child introduced to TV audiences. I think you will find that mine is nothing short of a revelation. After tinkering with this recipe through five rounds of testing, I achieved a Queen of Sheba cake with 75 percent less added sugar and absolutely no butter! Instead, the smoothness and body comes from avocado. Why was the original called Queen of Sheba? Perhaps because the biblical queen—one of King Solomon's favorite playmates—was said to be dark, voluptuous, and sensual, just like this cake. Why do I call mine Sheba from Queens? Because I first made my version in my test kitchen in Long Island City in the borough of Queens. It was a pun just begging to be eaten.

4 large eggs, separated

½ cup organic cane sugar

½ cup canola or other neutral oil

8 ounces dark (70%) chocolate, melted

½ cup mashed avocado, pressed through a fine-mesh sieve

¼ teaspoon cream of tartar

¼ cup unsweetened cocoa powder, for garnish

Blackberry Whipped Cream (page 241), for serving

1 | Preheat the oven to 350°F. Prepare a 9-inch round cake pan with vegetable oil cooking spray, then line with parchment (see page 125).

2 | Combine the egg yolks and ¼ cup of the sugar in the bowl of a standing mixer fitted with the whisk attachment. Whisk on medium-high speed until the yolks are pale yellow and ribbons form, about 10 minutes.

3 | Meanwhile, combine the oil and chocolate in the top of a double boiler or in a heatproof bowl set over a saucepan of boiling water over medium-high heat. Melt the chocolate, stirring, until smooth and silken. Turn off the heat but leave the pan on the stove to keep the chocolate warm.

4 | With the mixer running on medium speed, add the avocado to the egg and sugar mixture and whisk until smooth and thoroughly incorporated. Remove the bowl from the mixer and add the chocolate. Use a hand whisk to mix until thoroughly incorporated. Transfer to a large mixing bowl.

5 | Thoroughly clean the bowl and whisk of the standing mixer and whisk the egg whites and cream of tartar on medium-high speed. When the tines of the whisk begin to show in the whites, add the remaining ¼ cup sugar and whisk until stiff peaks form.

(RECIPE CONTINUES)

6 | Transfer half the whites to the chocolate mixture and, using a rubber spatula, gently fold them in until smoothly incorporated and no white patches appear. Fold in the remaining whites. Pour the batter into the prepared pan and set on a rimmed baking sheet. Place in the oven, then pour hot water into the baking sheet to just below the rim to create a hot water bath. Bake until a toothpick inserted in the center of the cake comes out clean, about 45 minutes. Remove from the oven and set aside on the counter, sliding a fork underneath the pan to allow airflow. Let cool for 15 minutes. Remove from the pan to a cake plate and let cool for 1 hour more. Place the cocoa in a fine-mesh sieve and tap through over the top of the cake. Serve warm or at room temperature with the Blackberry Whipped Cream.

CUT *to fit* | To cut parchment to fit a round pan or bowl, fold a rectangular sheet of parchment in quarters and then into quarters again, as if making a paper snowflake. Cut the folded wedge to a length equal to the radius of your pan (half the diameter), them trim the open end into a curved shape. Unfold the parchment and place in the pan or directly on the mixture as instructed.

CAKE FOR A WAKE

MAKES ONE 9-INCH DOUBLE-LAYER CAKE/SERVES 10 TO 12 • Like the wardrobes of many fashion-conscious Manhattanites—and folks in mourning everywhere else in the world—this cake is a study in black and gray, a rarity in the candy-colored world of desserts. The flavors, though, are anything but sad.

Black sesame seeds worked their way into my catalog of favorite flavors when I baked in a Japanese pastry shop specializing in American-style desserts in the city of Nagoya. I could not help but admire the craft and marketing savvy of a baker there named Yasui, whose signature offering was New York–style cheesecake! People would line up at the appointed hour and he would sell out right away . . . every day! I gladly shared my knowledge of the Western pastry kitchen and, in return, I came away from that experience with an appreciation of Japanese ingredients. Black sesame seeds are powerfully earthy, nutty, and savory. They more than compensate for reduced sweetener. You may find the unusual taste takes some getting used to, but if you are like me, you may love it right off the bat.

FOR THE CAKE

1 cup unbleached all-purpose flour

1 cup whole wheat flour

¾ cup black sesame powder

2 teaspoons baking powder

½ teaspoon baking soda

½ teaspoon kosher salt

¾ cup (1½ sticks) unsalted high-fat European-style butter, at room temperature

1 cup organic cane sugar

2 large eggs, at room temperature

⅓ cup black sesame paste

1¼ cups unsweetened soy milk

3 tablespoons safflower or grapeseed oil

FOR THE FROSTING

½ teaspoon gelatin

2 cups heavy cream

2 tablespoons black sesame powder, plus more for garnish

2 tablespoons confectioners' sugar

¼ cup crystallized (candied) ginger

1 | Preheat the oven to 350°F. Spray two 9-inch round cake pans with vegetable oil cooking spray and line with parchment paper (see page 125).

2 | **Make the cake.** In a medium bowl, whisk together the flours, black sesame powder, baking powder, baking soda, and salt. Set aside.

3 | In the bowl of a standing mixer fitted with the paddle attachment, beat the butter on medium speed until it has loosened. Add the sugar and beat until smooth and fluffy, occasionally scraping down the bowl. Add the eggs and black sesame paste and beat until well incorporated. Reduce the speed to low and add the soy milk and flour mixture to the bowl, alternating in 3 additions. Scrape down the bowl. Add the oil and mix until thoroughly incorporated.

4 | Divide the batter between the prepared cake pans. Bake until a toothpick inserted in the center of each cake comes out clean, 35 to 40 minutes. Remove from the oven and set aside on the counter, sliding a fork underneath the pans to allow airflow for 5 minutes. Turn the cakes out of the pans and let cool to room temperature.

(RECIPE CONTINUES)

HAPPY CAKES (LAYERED AND UNLAYERED) | *cake for a wake*

note

A serrated knife is essential for slicing a cake in half horizontally; a kitchen knife will tear the cake rather than produce a clean cut. Use the serrated knife as you might a saw. Use a gentle back-and-forth motion to slice into the cake in 1-inch cuts, rotating the cake as you go until the knife reaches the middle and the cake is completely sliced in half.

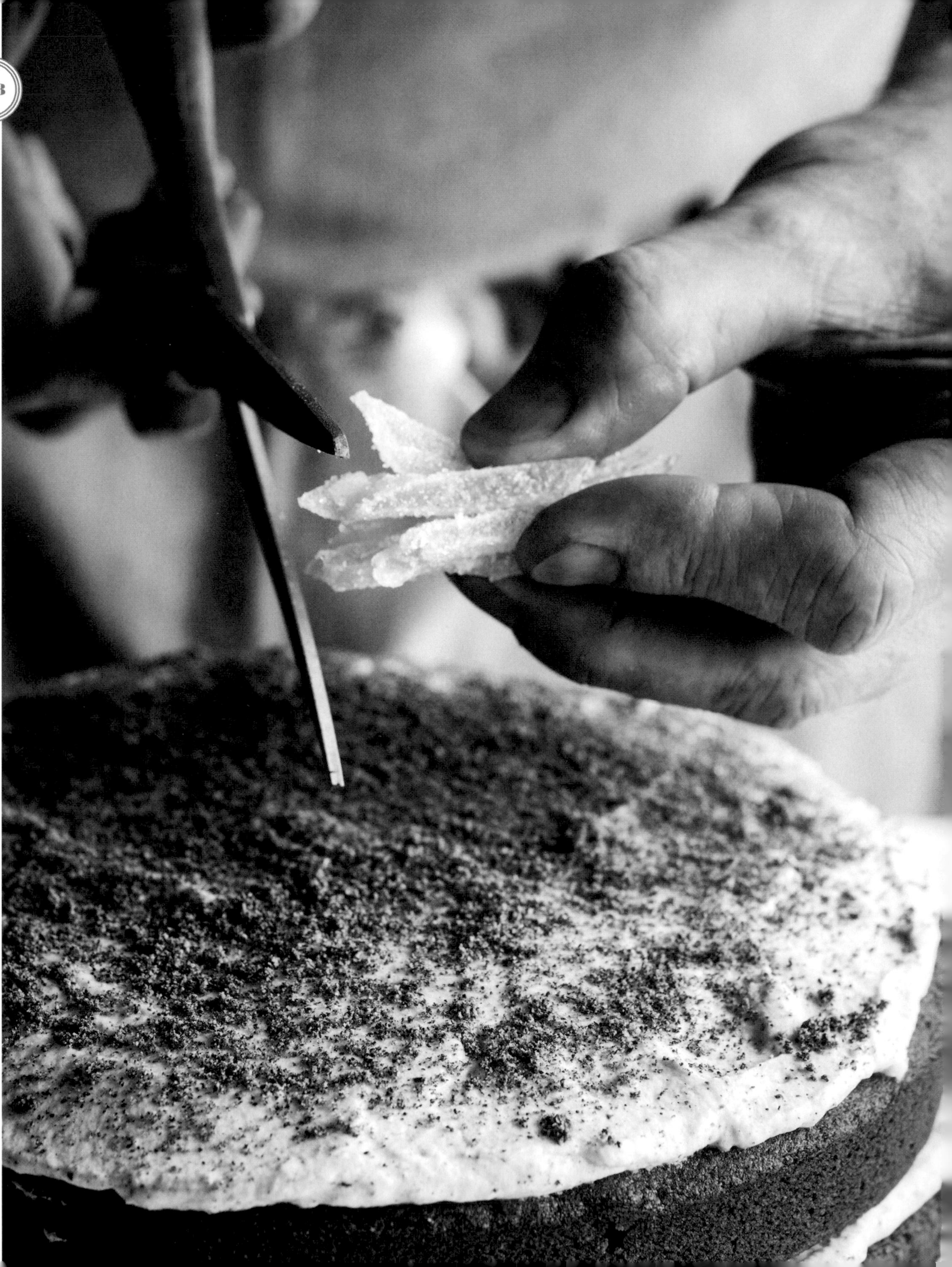

5 | **Make the frosting.** In a small bowl, combine the gelatin with 2 tablespoons of cold water. Set aside to bloom.

6 | Chill the bowl of a standing mixer in the refrigerator. Fit a standing mixer with the whisk attachment and whip the heavy cream in the chilled bowl on medium-high speed until soft peaks form. Reduce the speed to low, add the black sesame powder and confectioners' sugar and mix until thoroughly incorporated.

7 | Heat the gelatin mixture in a small saucepan (or in a microwave) until it melts. Add 2 tablespoons of the cream mixture to the saucepan and whisk to incorporate (this dilutes the gelatin so that it won't seize when added to the larger amount of heavy cream).

8 | Remove the bowl from the standing mixer and, using a hand whisk, rapidly mix the gelatin mixture into the cream mixture until thoroughly incorporated.

9 | To assemble the cake, use a serrated knife to trim the edges and the tops of both cakes so that they are even and horizontal. Place one layer on a cake platter and spread with the black sesame cream. Top with the second layer and spread the remaining frosting just on top of the cake. Sprinkle with black sesame powder. Using sharp scissors, snip the ginger into small pieces over the cake and serve.

note | Because sesame seeds are so tiny, I recommend buying them in powder form rather than grinding them yourself. Both the powder and the black sesame paste—actually tahini made from black seeds—are available in many Asian markets.

VERY FRESH GREEN CAKE

MAKES ONE 9-INCH DOUBLE-LAYER CAKE/SERVES 10 TO 12 • Once upon a time many chefs used food coloring to make a green cake like this for St. Patrick's Day. But since developing the recipes in this book I have become a recovering food coloring abuser. Real and natural are what I'm about now . . . or at least trying to be. I learned I can achieve refreshing greenness with the natural chlorophyll in some common salad herbs. The addition of these clean, bright flavors encouraged me to take a new look at how much—or rather how little—sweetness is required to balance the grassiness of the herbs. I like to think of the result as *chlorophylltastic*.

And what about those cake trimmings that normally go in the trash (or in your mouth)? Perish the thought! See the recipe that follows for an Emerald Parfait.

2 cups (packed) fresh mint leaves

2 cups fresh parsley leaves

1 cup tender watercress (tough stems discarded)

1 cup fresh basil leaves

3 cups unbleached all-purpose flour

2 teaspoons baking powder

1 teaspoon kosher salt

11 tablespoons (1⅜ sticks) unsalted high-fat European-style butter, at room temperature

½ cup organic cane sugar

⅓ cups local honey

6 large eggs

1⅔ cups heavy cream

⅓ cup sour cream

Blackberry Whipped Cream (page 241)

1 | Preheat the oven to 325°F. Spray two 9-inch round cake pans with vegetable oil cooking spray and line them with parchment cut into a circle to fit the bottom of the pans (see page 125).

2 | Bring a large pot of water to a boil. Fill a large bowl with water and ice. Remove the boiling water from the heat and submerge the mint, parsley, watercress, and basil into the water for 10 seconds. Using a slotted spoon, transfer the greens to the ice water to stop the cooking. Squeeze the water from the greens with your hands and set them on paper towels.

3 | Combine the flour, baking powder, and salt in a fine-mesh sieve and tap through onto a piece of parchment. Set aside.

4 | In the bowl of a standing mixer fitted with the paddle attachment, combine the butter and sugar and mix on medium-high speed until the mixture is almost white, about 10 minutes.

5 | Meanwhile, combine the honey, eggs, and the greens in a blender and blend on high speed until completely smooth and airy, about 5 minutes. With the standing mixer on medium speed, gradually add the greens mixture to the butter mixture, scraping down the sides of the bowl frequently. Reduce the speed to low and gradually add the flour mixture, running the machine until it is thoroughly combined. Add the heavy cream and sour cream and mix just until incorporated.

(RECIPE CONTINUES)

6 | Pour the batter into the prepared cake pans, dividing it evenly between them. Set the cakes on a rimmed baking sheet and bake, rotating the cake pans halfway through, until a toothpick inserted in the center comes out clean, about 35 minutes. Remove from the oven and set on a wire rack to cool for 1 hour. Run a knife around the rim of the pans and turn the cakes out onto a cooling rack. Using a serrated knife, trim away the browned edges (a good half inch) and the top of each cake to achieve clean, level surfaces. Save the larger trimmings to make Emerald Parfaits (see Variation). Crumble the smaller pieces in your hands, spread on a baking sheet, and bake for 5 minutes in a 350°F oven to make a topping for the cake.

7 | To assemble the cake, place one layer on a cake plate or stand and spread with half the Blackberry Whipped Cream. Top with the second layer and spread the remaining whipped cream on the top of the cake, leaving the sides unfrosted. Place the toasted trimmings in a fine-mesh sieve, hold it over the cake, and push through to garnish the top.

variation: EMERALD PARFAIT

Cut the reserved large trimmings of the Very Fresh Green Cake into cubes. In a bowl, combine sliced blood oranges, raspberries, blueberries, and any other juicy fruits you like. Mash gently to release the juices. Layer the cake cubes with the Blackberry Whipped Cream, fruits, and their juices in a trifle bowl or individual parfait glasses.

THANK YOU, *chlorophyll!*

We owe chlorophyll a lot, namely life on earth, because it is the key element in photosynthesis, which produces virtually all the oxygen on our planet. Chlorophyll is the green substance in plants that allows them to absorb light energy from the sun (photons) and turn carbon dioxide (CO_2) into sugars, providing us humans with energy in a usable form. You may have noticed an odd thing about chlorophyll: During cooking, gases are released so we see the bright green chlorophyll. The effect is short-lived, as other chemical reactions oxidize the green color, turning it brown. The reason chlorophyll is green is because green is the one wavelength in the electromagnetic spectrum that plants do not use. Red and blue wavelengths are what chlorophyll craves and it absorbs them, leaving only the green to be rejected and sent back to our retina.
Big takeaway: Green plants aren't green!

THE LADY M

MAKES 20 TO 24 CREPES/SERVES 10 TO 12 • The inspiration for this cake comes from New York City's magnificent Lady M Cake Boutique on 77th Street. In my homage, tofu, which is definitely not a traditional crepe ingredient, works beautifully with the chestnut filling of the original to create just the right texture. Orange zest, perhaps because of its volatile oils, amplifies the effect of sweetness. It's not that it makes the crepes any sweeter; it just makes you think that they are. I call for wheat starch here, which is found in Asian markets. It makes the batter looser so that it flows onto the crepe pan with a super-thin consistency. If you can't find it, all-purpose flour is an acceptable substitute.

36 fresh chestnuts or packaged peeled chestnuts

2 cups wheat starch

6 large eggs

¼ cup almond or walnut oil, plus more for the pan

Grated zest and juice of 2 oranges (about ¼ cup juice)

4 cups whole milk

Two 15.5-ounce cans unsweetened chestnut puree

6 tablespoons orange blossom or chestnut honey

1 pound (2 cups) silken tofu

2 cups heavy cream

1 | Preheat the oven to 350°F.

2 | If using fresh chestnuts, score the shells before roasting. Hold the chestnut down on a work surface, flat side up, with one hand. Pierce the flat side with the tip of a kitchen knife. Remove the steadying hand and plunge the knife into the chestnut. Pull the chestnut off the knife and repeat at a 90-degree angle to make an X in the shell. Place the chestnuts on a rimmed baking sheet and toast until the scored part of the shell curls back on itself, about 20 minutes. Let cool, then peel away the shell and remove the meat with a fork. Let cool completely, then finely chop.

3 | Tap the wheat starch through a fine-mesh sieve into a large mixing bowl. Set aside.

4 | In a medium bowl, whisk together the eggs and oil. Whisk in the zest and juice. Pour the mixture into the bowl of wheat starch and give it two stirs with the whisk. Add the milk and whisk until completely smooth.

5 | Lightly coat a nonstick crepe pan or a low-sided 10-inch skillet with a little canola oil. Use a paper towel to spread it evenly onto the bottom of the pan. Heat over medium heat until a drop of water sizzles in the pan. Pour ½ cup of the batter into the hot pan, just off center, while picking up the pan and tilting it so that the batter covers the bottom entirely. As you tilt, pour a bit more batter in the bare spots. Once the bottom of the pan is covered, set it back down on the heat and cook until the edges are slightly browned and the surface of

(RECIPE CONTINUES)

the crepe is matte and dry, 30 to 60 seconds. Using a spatula and your free hand, lift up the crepe and flip it over. Cook for 30 seconds more.

6 Transfer the cooked crepe to a plate and repeat with the remaining batter, stacking the crepes on top of one another if you plan to use them immediately. (Cooked crepes can be stored in a resealable plastic bag, each one separated by a piece of wax paper, and frozen for up to 5 days.)

7 In the bowl of a standing mixer fitted with a paddle attachment, whip the chestnut puree on medium speed until it is light and fluffy. Add the honey and mix until incorporated. Add the tofu and mix until the mixture is fluffy, 8 minutes more. Add the chopped nuts and mix until just incorporated.

8 Chill the bowl of a standing mixer in the refrigerator. Pour the heavy cream into it and whip, using the whisk attachment, until soft peaks form. Fold the whipped cream into the chestnut puree in three additions.

9 To assemble the cake, arrange a crepe on a cake stand or plate. Spread a thin layer of the chestnut mixture over it. Repeat with the remaining crepes, ending with a crepe on top. Using a very sharp knife, cut the cake into wedges and serve. Serve within 4 hours or make a day in advance, cover, and refrigerate. (Many cakes, including this one, benefit from 24 hours of "curing" to blend the flavors.)

note

If you want a tidier, less rustic appearance for your cake, use scissors to trim away any ragged edges from the crepes, creating uniform sides. It's delicious either way.

HONEYED BABAS
with Blood Orange and Vanilla

MAKES 18 • A baba is a yeasted bread, something like a brioche, that is soaked in a flavorful infusion, in this case the bitter and sweet juice of blood oranges. Babas, like donuts and bagels, have had a revival lately. And like those formerly sensibly proportioned foods, they have become super extra-large in recent years. You'll find that mine are impressive—but daintier—bites.

FOR THE BABAS

2 teaspoons active dry yeast

2¼ cups unbleached all-purpose flour

2 tablespoons organic cane sugar

Pinch of kosher salt

4 large eggs

½ cup (1 stick) unsalted high-fat European-style butter, cut into pieces, at room temperature

FOR THE INFUSION

12 blood oranges, 10 juiced and 2 thinly sliced, seeds removed

1 vanilla bean, split lengthwise and seeds scraped out

3 tablespoons local honey

1 tablespoon dark rum

Whipped cream, for serving

1 | **Make the babas.** In the bowl of a standing mixer fitted with the hook attachment, combine the yeast and 2 tablespoons of warm water. Cover with the flour, then place the sugar and salt on top and set aside for 15 minutes (this gives the yeast a chance to come alive).

2 | In a medium bowl, whisk the eggs. Turn the mixer on low speed and pour the eggs into the bowl in small increments (about 1 tablespoon at a time). Let the mixer run for about 15 minutes, or until the dough climbs up the hook. Add the butter, distributing the pieces evenly in the dough as the dough hook turns. The dough will slide off the hook and the butter will eventually fully incorporate itself into the dough, about 12 minutes.

3 | When the dough is shiny and pulls away from the sides of the bowl and back onto the dough hook, stop the mixer and remove the bowl, peeling the dough off the dough hook. Cover the bowl with a damp cloth and set in a warm place for 30 to 45 minutes. The dough will double in volume.

4 | Spray two 12-hole baba molds, Flexipat molds, or muffin tins with vegetable oil cooking spray. Transfer the dough onto a clean work surface dusted with flour. Push out the air bubbles and knead the dough into a round ball. Using scissors, cut the dough into rounds the size of Ping-Pong balls and place in the prepared molds. Cover with plastic wrap and place in a warm dark place to proof for 30 to 45 minutes.

(RECIPE CONTINUES)

5 | Preheat the oven to 400°F.

6 | Bake the babas until golden brown, about 15 minutes. They will feel firm but spongy. Remove from the oven and set aside on the counter, sliding a fork underneath the pan to allow airflow. Let cool for 10 minutes. Turn the babas out onto a work surface or platter.

7 | **Make the infusion.** Bring the orange juice to a boil in a large, heavy saucepan set over medium-high heat. Add the vanilla bean, seeds, and honey and reduce the heat to a simmer. Add the orange slices and continue to simmer for 15 minutes more. Remove from the heat. Add the rum and swirl the pan.

8 | Submerge the babas in the liquid for 15 minutes. To prevent them from bobbing up and out of the liquid, place a circle of parchment cut to fit the pan (see page 125) over them. Transfer to a platter, cover with plastic wrap, and set aside for 3 hours. Arrange a baba in a shallow rimmed bowl and spoon a liberal amount of the blood orange infusion over it. Top with whipped cream and serve.

note | The best of the blood oranges is called the Moro. They're available from December to May, so this dessert has a pretty long season. An added benefit, these have no seeds! The red color is due to anthocyanins, which are also found in red cabbage, beets, raspberries, and pomegranates. It is no accident that these are all called "superfoods" due to their anti-inflammatory and antioxidant qualities.

JELLYLESS NUT ROLL

SERVES 8 TO 10 • Long rolls—the French call them roulades—are a simple way to serve dessert in neat individual portions: much more so than the wedge-shaped servings of a pie or cake. This is especially helpful—as I discovered at the White House—when you are feeding a large party; you simply slice, plate, and serve. You quickly get into an assembly-line rhythm. Here we have my healthed-up version of a 1950s American classic, the jelly roll, only without the jelly.

Beating the egg yolks and whites separately makes the cake pleasantly light and airy, and, most importantly, it's flexible when you roll it up.

1 tablespoon almond oil

½ cup roasted unsalted almonds

½ cup roasted unsalted cashews

½ cup whole walnuts

½ cup dried tart cherries

5 tablespoons plus ½ teaspoon organic cane sugar

Grated zest and juice of 1 blood orange

5 extra-large eggs, separated

¼ teaspoon cream of tartar, salt, or lemon juice

½ cup unbleached all-purpose flour

1 cup fresh Bing cherries, pitted (see opposite for pitting technique)

1 teaspoon unsweetened cocoa powder

1 | Preheat the oven to 400°F. Line a rimmed baking sheet with parchment and spray with vegetable oil cooking spray.

2 | Combine the almond oil, almonds, cashews, walnuts, dried cherries, 1 tablespoon of the sugar, all but 1 teaspoon of the blood orange zest, the blood orange juice, and 1 cup water in a food processor or high-speed blender and blend until a crunchy paste forms. If necessary, add up to 2 additional teaspoons of orange juice. Set aside.

3 | Combine the egg yolks and 1 tablespoon of the sugar in the bowl of a standing mixer fitted with the whisk attachment. Mix on medium-high speed until pale yellow ribbons form when you pull up the whisk, about 8 minutes.

4 | Transfer the egg yolk mixture to a large mixing bowl and set aside. Thoroughly wash and dry the whisk and bowl of the standing mixer. Place the egg whites, cream of tartar, and a pinch of the remaining sugar in the bowl and mix on medium speed until the egg whites have climbed halfway up the bowl and the whisk leaves trails in the egg whites. Add 2 tablespoons plus 1½ teaspoons of the sugar and mix for 4 to 5 minutes more, until the whites form soft but stable peaks. Raise the speed to high for the final 15 seconds of mixing. Soft peaks will flop. Stiff peaks stand up straight. You want soft.

5 | Remove the bowl from the mixer. Fold the egg yolk mixture into the egg whites, diving into the center with a rubber whisk and pulling up from the bottom, just until the yolks envelop the whites, about two folds. Place the flour in a fine-mesh sieve set over the bowl and gently tap into the egg mixture, folding it in as you go and making sure all the dry ingredients have been incorporated. Take care not to deflate the mixture.

6 | Using a large spoon, transfer the batter onto the parchment, distributing it in four equal portions. Using a large metal offset spatula and with a minimal amount of spreading, evenly distribute the batter, spreading it up to—but not touching—the edges of the pan. Immediately place in the oven and bake until a toothpick inserted at the cake's thickest point comes out clean, 10 to 12 minutes. Remove from the oven. Working quickly, use a sharp knife to separate the cake from the edges of the pan.

7 | In a small pot, cook the fresh cherries over medium-high heat until they release a little juice and are slightly softened, 5 to 8 minutes. Set aside.

8 | Place a large piece of parchment on a clean work surface with a long side facing you.

9 | Sprinkle the remaining sugar onto the parchment. Flip the cake over onto the parchment and slowly remove the top piece of parchment, using one hand to guide the paper while gently pulling it away with the other. Carefully flip the cake back over. Using a sharp knife, trim the edges to clean them up. Using a pastry brush, dab the orange juice all over the cake, all the way out to the edges.

10 | Working quickly, arrange the cherries in a 1-inch-wide strip along the edge nearest you. Spoon the fruit and nut paste in eight portions all over the cake (this prevents excessive spreading and tearing of the cake) and spread to even thickness to cover all but the long edge farthest away from you. Using your hands, roll the cake onto itself as you would a carpet, using the parchment to help you move it along and coil it as tightly as you can (it will have rolled over on itself about one and a half times). It's important to roll up quickly, while the cake—fresh from the oven—still has maximum flexibility.

11 | To serve, arrange the roulade on a platter and tap the cocoa through a fine-mesh sieve all over, then garnish with the remaining teaspoon of orange zest. The roulade will keep, covered tightly in plastic wrap, for up to 2 days at room temperature or up to 4 days in the refrigerator.

note

I like to pit the cherries and precook them before adding to the filling. To pit the cherries, just stick the outer tine of a small fork into the cherry until you feel the pit and then twist. The pit will come right out. Precooking the cherries means they take up less volume. It concentrates whole-fruit sweetness and unlocks subtle flavors.

HAPPY CAKES (LAYERED AND UNLAYERED) | *jellyless nut roll*

MATCHA GREEN TEA ROLL
with Blackberry Pastry Cream

SERVES 8 • Like everyone else who breathes on a daily basis, I am a big fan of oxygen, but when other elements in food—or your body—combine with oxygen you can often get a lot of free radicals: these are a health no-no. They can make your skin look like an old catcher's mitt. One of the best sources of antioxidants—which fight free radicals—is matcha green tea. I first encountered it while teaching about American desserts in a Tokyo *departo*—which is "Japanglish" for the food courts that you find in the basement of many large stores. Matcha cuts through a cake's richness and keeps your palate from being overwhelmed. We took sugar down by a third here and made our pastry cream with cornstarch, milk, and powdered blackberries. It binds just as well as a classic egg-based pastry cream but with far fewer calories and much less fat.

FOR THE FILLING

1¾ cups cold 2% milk

2 teaspoons blackberry powder

2 heaping tablespoons cornstarch

2 teaspoons local honey

1 teaspoon peeled, grated
  fresh ginger

½ cup heavy cream, whipped
  into soft peaks

2 cups fresh blackberries,
  plus more for serving

FOR THE SPONGE

6 large eggs

½ cup organic cane sugar

4 teaspoons matcha powder

½ cup cake flour

2 tablespoons canola oil

1 | In a small bowl, combine ¼ cup of the milk with the blackberry powder and cornstarch and whisk to make a slurry. Set aside.

2 | Fill a large bowl with water and ice. In a medium saucepan, whisk together the remaining 1½ cups milk with the honey and bring to a boil over medium heat. Add the cornstarch mixture to the center of the saucepan in a steady stream, whisking continuously. Be sure to scrape all the cornstarch from the bottom of the bowl into the saucepan. Cook until the mixture resembles thickened pan gravy, 3 minutes. Remove the pan from the heat and stir in the ginger.

3 | Transfer the mixture to a medium bowl and place the bowl in the ice water bath to speed its cooling. Place a piece of parchment or plastic wrap directly on the surface to prevent a skin from forming. Let sit until the mixture comes to room temperature and it easily pulls away from the bowl.

4 | Preheat the oven to 375°F. Coat a sheet pan with vegetable oil cooking spray. Spread a piece of parchment on top and run the edge of a rubber spatula all over it to eliminate any air pockets. Coat the parchment with vegetable oil cooking spray. Set the sheet pan on top of a second sheet pan (this prevents the sponge from drying out) and set aside.

5 | In the bowl of a standing mixer fitted with a whisk attachment, whisk together the eggs and sugar on medium-high speed until the mixture triples in size and ribbons form when you pull up the whisk, 8 to 12 minutes. Raise the speed to high for the final minute of mixing.

6 | Combine the matcha powder with the flour in a fine-mesh sieve set over parchment and tap through to sift. Remove the mixing bowl from the mixer and add the flour mixture, one third at a time, folding it in after each addition. Transfer ½ cup of the cake batter to a small bowl, add the canola oil to it, and stir until the ingredients are incorporated, about 30 seconds. Gently fold the mixture back into the cake batter.

7 | Spoon the batter onto the parchment-lined sheet pan in 4 equal portions, one in each quadrant of the pan. Using an offset spatula, spread the batter to make a level 10 × 14-inch rectangle, about ½ inch thick. Bake until the top springs back or a toothpick inserted in the center comes out clean, about 12 minutes. Let cool for just 30 seconds (it must be rolled when warm).

8 | While the sponge bakes, whip the cream on high speed in the bowl of a standing mixer fitted with the whisk attachment. Whisk one third of the whipped cream into the cooled blackberry cream until thoroughly incorporated. Add the remaining whipped cream in two more batches, whisking thoroughly after each addition.

9 | Place a large piece of parchment on a work surface with a long side facing you. Sprinkle it with the remaining 1 tablespoon sugar. Flip the sponge out onto the parchment with a long side facing you. Carefully remove the parchment from the top of the cake, guiding it with one hand while pulling it up with the other to avoid tearing the cake. Carefully flip the sponge back over. Using a sharp knife, trim the edges to make them even. Spoon the filling onto the cake in 6 equal portions. Use an offset spatula to spread it onto the cake, leaving a 1-inch rim exposed on three sides and spreading the filling to the edge of the side closest to you. Arrange the blackberries in two lines along the near edge. Roll the cake onto itself as you would a carpet, using the parchment to help you move it along and coil it as tightly as you can (it will have rolled over on itself about one and a half times).

10 | To serve, arrange the roulade on a platter and cut into 1-inch-thick slices. The roulade will keep in the refrigerator, covered tightly in plastic wrap, for up to 4 days.

 **6** | # SOFT STUFF

If crunchy crispness is the alpha of desserts, then softness is the omega. I'm not talking mushy, but luxuriously creamy and soft. Puddings, panna cottas, custards, and flans should have body but still feel airy and light. They should embrace the palate with a flood of natural flavors, and rather than being cloying, that flavor should dissipate like a puff of steam.

There is uniformity to the texture of soft desserts, so they want the accent of assertive ingredients. I nearly always add a strongly tart counterpoint, the singing high notes of spices or herbs, and a bit of crunch. Often with cool or cold soft desserts one has to oversweeten (in the same way that one over-seasons cold savory recipes) because cold dampens the palate. In this case, instead of more sweetness I've introduced ingredients that broaden the flavor spectrum and, if I'm playing my cards right, seduce the palate.

Black Sesame Parfait with Red Fruits • Dos Leches with Tropical Fruits

Strawberry Trifle with Lemon Verbena Cream • No-Bake Herbed Flan

Steamed Lemon Pudding with Wild Blueberries

Fancy Bread Pudding • Thai Tapioca Pudding • Kataifi Pudding

Fromage Blanc Cake with Elderflower Cream • Not a Cassata (with Ricotta)

Almond Milk Panna Cotta with Tamarind-Macerated Strawberries

Pickled Lychee Panna Cotta with Lemon Verbena

Spiced Mocha Semifreddo • Lemon Kaffir Semifreddo

Farmers' Cheese Dumplings with Raspberry–Black Pepper Compote • Dessert Frittata

BLACK SESAME PARFAIT
with Red Fruits

SERVES 6 • When I was the dessert meister at Citarella, a short-lived restaurant across the street from Radio City Music Hall, I created a sort of butterscotch with black sesame seeds and tahini. One enthusiastic critic was love-struck by it and wrote, "Sesame is the new vanilla!" He may have jumped the gun a bit—it's still nowhere near as ubiquitous here as it is in Japan—but it's slowly making its way from the kitchens of avant-garde restaurants into the dessert mainstream. Black sesame seed has an aromatic and tantalizing woodsy, smoky, and nutty flavor. There is an element of bitter in its taste, but that's also true of cacao. Like chocolate, black sesame pairs beautifully with red fruits. The version of the parfait in the photograph is my super-extra-deluxe interpretation. It works fine without the toppings, but if you are moved to create something special, you won't be disappointed.

3 cups almond milk, preferably homemade (see page 244)

½ cup organic cane sugar

¼ cup black sesame seed paste

5 teaspoons (2 envelopes) gelatin, bloomed in cold water

½ cup fresh black cherries, pitted (see page 141 for pitting technique)

FOR SERVING

Blackberry Chia Sauce (page 240), optional

Pavolva (page 89), optional

Black Cherry–Chocolate Pain d'Epice (page 113), cut into cubes and toasted, optional

Cherry and Flower Petal Granita (page 221), optional

1 | In a deep saucepan, combine the almond milk and sugar and bring to a boil over medium-high heat. Add the sesame paste and return to a boil, breaking up the paste as best you can with the back of a spoon; it will not dissolve easily or entirely.

2 | Remove the milk mixture from the heat and add the bloomed gelatin. Using an immersion blender, blend until the sesame paste is thoroughly incorporated. Divide the mixture among six parfait glasses and drop some cherries into each. Chill in the refrigerator until set, about 4 hours. Let sit on the counter for a few minutes before serving to take the chill off.

3 | For a more elaborate presentation, top with your choice of Blackberry Chia Sauce, Pavlova, Pain d'Epice, and Cherry and Flower Petal Granita—or all of the above!

note You will have leftover yolks. They freeze well and can be used in other recipes such as Fancy Bread Pudding (page 156), Lavender Honey Castella (page 115), or any custard or flan.

DOS LECHES
with Tropical Fruits

MAKES TWO 9 × 5-INCH LOAVES/EACH LOAF SERVES 6 • The forbearer of this cake is tres leches, beloved throughout the Hispanic world. The original relies on a yolk-heavy sponge cake plus whole, condensed, and evaporated milk. I opted instead for a fat-free angel food cake and only dos leches ("two milks"): coconut and almond. Sweet/tart passion fruit juice pumps up the flavor. Having removed 50 percent of the sugar, I needed to thicken the milk so that it wouldn't drip out of the cake cubes. Xanthan gum—a useful thickener from the Modern Cuisine pantry (available online) does the trick.

1¼ cups cake flour

1¾ cups egg whites (14 eggs), at room temperature

¼ cup local honey

1½ teaspoons cream of tartar

¼ teaspoon kosher salt

½ cup superfine sugar

3 cups almond milk (page 244)

1½ cups full-fat coconut milk

½ teaspoon vanilla paste

½ teaspoon xanthan gum

Fresh tropical fruits, such as pineapple, mango, and papaya, chopped

2 tablespoons shredded fresh mint (optional)

Whipped Coconut Cream (page 242)

1 | Preheat the oven to 330°F. Lightly coat two 9 × 5-inch loaf pans with vegetable oil cooking spray, then line the bottoms and sides with parchment paper (see page 116).

2 | Tap the flour through a fine-mesh sieve set over parchment to sift. Set aside.

3 | In the bowl of a standing mixer fitted with the whisk attachment, beat together the egg whites, honey, cream of tartar, and salt on medium-high speed until the tines of the whisk appear in the whites. Gradually add the sugar and beat until stiff peaks form. Using a rubber spatula, fold in the flour in three additions. Divide the batter between the pans and bake until the tops of the loaves are golden brown and spring back when tapped, 55 to 60 minutes. Remove from the oven and set aside on the counter, sliding a fork underneath each pan to allow airflow. Let cool until the cakes pull away from the sides of the pans, then transfer onto a serving plate and remove the parchment.

4 | In a medium-size deep bowl, whisk together the almond milk, coconut milk, and vanilla. Add the xanthan gum and mix with an immersion blender until thoroughly incorporated.

5 | Using a serrated knife, trim away the browned edges of the cakes. Slice the cakes into 2-inch cubes and arrange in a large rectangular glass or ceramic baking dish. Pour the milk mixture over the cubes and let sit for 2 to 3 hours, turning the cubes so that the liquid is fully absorbed and the cubes are soaked through. Layer the cubes with the fruits in a wide-mouth glass bowl or glasses, add the shredded mint, if desired, and serve with the Whipped Coconut Cream.

STRAWBERRY TRIFLE
with Lemon Verbena Cream

MAKES ONE 9-INCH DOUBLE-LAYER CAKE/SERVES 10 • This dessert sprung from a desire to do something with strawberries other than strawberry shortcake. And just like that summer staple, this fruity, creamy, light, and herbal dessert is just the ticket for a hot July night as a chaser to a Southern fried chicken main course. I've always seen strawberries served with mint, but I think you'll find that lemon verbena is more subtle. Freeze-dried strawberries add a tart punch of concentrated flavor to plump fresh strawberries.

FOR THE CAKE

3 duck eggs or 6 large chicken eggs
    (see Note)

½ cup organic cane sugar

½ cup plus 2 tablespoons cake flour

FOR THE FILLING

3 pints fresh strawberries, hulled

2 tablespoons local honey

10 lemon verbena leaves,
    plus more for garnish

FOR THE CREAM

1 cup plain full-fat Greek yogurt

1 cup mascarpone

1 cup heavy cream

2 tablespoons local honey

FOR GARNISH

Grated zest of 1 lemon

½ cup freeze-dried strawberries

note • If you can find duck eggs at a farmers' market, I highly recommend them because they froth faster and higher than chicken eggs, resulting in an airier texture. You may never go back to chicken eggs!

1 | Preheat the oven to 350°F. Line the bottom of two 9-inch cake pans with parchment (see page 125).

2 | **Make the cake.** In the bowl of a standing mixer fitted with the whisk attachment, whisk together the eggs and sugar on high speed for 10 minutes, or until the eggs reach at least halfway up the bowl. Remove the bowl from the mixer.

3 | Place the flour in a fine-mesh sieve and tap into the bowl to sift, folding it in with a rubber spatula. Transfer the batter to the cake pans and bake until a toothpick inserted in the center comes out clean, 20 to 30 minutes. Remove from the oven and set aside on the counter to cool, sliding a fork each pan to allow airflow.

4 | **Prepare the filling.** Sort through the strawberries and set aside 1 pint of the smallest berries for garnish. Halve the rest and place in a large heatproof bowl. In a small saucepan, combine 1 cup water with the honey and lemon verbena and bring to a boil over high heat. Strain out the lemon verbena and pour the liquid over the halved strawberries. Let sit for 10 minutes. Strain the strawberries from the juices and reserve both.

5 | **Make the cream.** In a large bowl, whisk together the yogurt and mascarpone. Place the heavy cream in the bowl of a standing mixer fitted with the whisk attachment. Add the honey and whisk until soft peaks form. Using a rubber spatula, fold the whipped cream into

(RECIPE CONTINUES)

the yogurt mixture in three additions. Cover and refrigerate until ready to use.

6 | Remove the cakes from the cake pans. Transfer one of the cakes to a 9-inch trifle bowl that is at least 6 inches deep. Brush half the reserved strawberry cooking liquid (consommé) all over the sponge. Spread a ½-inch-thick layer of the cream over the soaked sponge. Spoon all but 2 cups of the strawberries over. Set the second cake on top of the strawberries, pour the remaining consommé over, and spread with the remaining cream, smoothing it with an offset spatula.

7 | Refrigerate for 2 hours to set. Sprinkle with the lemon zest and portion onto serving plates. Scatter some of the reserved whole strawberries and freeze-dried strawberries onto each and serve.

tip

To more easily smooth creams, frostings, and batters, wet your spatula in hot water and shake off the excess.

NO-BAKE HERBED FLAN

MAKES ONE 10-INCH CHEESECAKE/SERVES 8 TO 10 • Compared to the supersize calorie bomb of many cheesecakes, this is a relatively thin wisp of a cake that packs a big flavor punch and delivers both crunchy and creamy textures. All that and no baking required! Gelatin holds it together, so once you mix the filling and pour it over the crust, the whole thing goes straight into the fridge to set. We build flavor with lemon verbena and some wonderful olive oil–based crackers for the crust.

FOR THE CRUST

3 Ines Rosales Savory Rosemary and Thyme Tortas (about 3 ounces) or any thin non-garlicky cracker, broken into pieces

6 tablespoons (¾ stick) unsalted high-fat European-style butter, melted

FOR THE FILLING

8 ounces cream cheese

½ cup organic cane sugar

2½ teaspoons (1 envelope) gelatin

3 large pasteurized egg yolks

1 large pasteurized egg

1½ cups whole milk

15 large anise hyssop or mint leaves

Raspberry–Black Pepper Compote (page 238)

note For safety, in recipes where eggs are uncooked or only partially cooked, use pasteurized eggs (the ones that have a little red stamp on them).

1 | **Make the crust.** Combine the crackers and butter in the bowl of a food processor and pulse until the crackers are finely ground and the mixture comes together. Press firmly into a 10-inch pie plate, evenly distributing the crumbs along the bottom and sides. Set aside.

2 | **Make the filling.** In the bowl of a standing mixer fitted with the paddle attachment, beat together the cream cheese and ¼ cup of the sugar on medium-high speed until the mixture is light and airy, about 10 minutes. Transfer to a large mixing bowl.

3 | In a small bowl, combine the gelatin with 3 tablespoons water. Set aside to bloom.

4 | In the bowl of a standing mixer fitted with the whisk attachment, whisk together the egg yolks and egg on medium speed for 5 minutes. Combine the milk, remaining ¼ cup of sugar, and anise hyssop in a small saucepan and bring to a boil. Remove from the heat and set aside to steep for 10 minutes. Strain.

5 | With the mixer running, pour the hot milk into the eggs in a thin stream. Add the gelatin to the bowl and mix thoroughly. Remove the bowl from the mixer and fold the cream cheese into the egg mixture. Pour into the prepared crust and refrigerate overnight or until set. Bring to room temperature and serve with the Raspberry–Black Pepper Compote.

note

A water bath is necessary to steam the egg mixture evenly to produce a smooth custard. Check periodically to make sure the water has not evaporated. Also, mind the oven temperature. If the mixture boils, it will curdle the eggs.

STEAMED LEMON PUDDING
with Wild Blueberries

SERVES 6 • I have served this dessert all through the year with whatever fresh blueberries are available, but I always go crazy with it whenever I encounter wild blueberries: one of the compensations that Mother Nature bestows on the fine citizens of Maine for enduring February. I love the look of this dessert: light custard on the bottom, an ethereal crumb on top, and blueberries nestled mid-pudding like sapphires in a tiara. It may not look so precisely layered as you fill each ramekin or cup, but then it will magically arrange itself into layers of custard, biscuit, and berries.

3 tablespoons unsalted high-fat European-style butter, melted and cooled, plus room-temperature butter for the ramekins

⅓ cup organic cane sugar

⅓ cup unbleached all-purpose flour

2 teaspoons corn flour, purchased or home-milled

3 large eggs, separated

1 cup whole milk

1 tablespoon grated lemon zest

6 tablespoons fresh lemon juice

¼ teaspoon kosher salt

1 cup fresh blueberries

1 | Generously grease six 6-ounce oven-safe custard cups or ramekins with the room-temperature butter. Set a folded kitchen towel into a baking pan large enough to hold the six ramekins. Bring a kettle of water to a boil and preheat the oven to 350°F.

2 | In a medium bowl, whisk together 3 tablespoons of the sugar and the flours. In another, large bowl, combine the remaining sugar, the egg yolks, and the melted butter and whisk until smooth. Add the milk, lemon zest and juice, and salt and whisk until incorporated. Add the flour/sugar mixture to the bowl and whisk until thoroughly blended; the batter will be very, very loose. Set aside.

3 | In the bowl of a standing mixer fitted with the whisk attachment, beat the egg whites until stiff peaks form (they should stay in place when the whisk is turned upside down).

4 | Fold the egg whites into the batter until they disappear. Working quickly, ladle the batter into the custard cups, distributing it evenly among the cups. Sprinkle the blueberries on top, dividing them evenly.

5 | Arrange the cups on the towel in the baking pan. Set the pan on the oven rack, then pour enough hot water into the pan to reach halfway up the custard cups. Bake until the puddings are golden and puffy, about 50 minutes. Remove from the water bath and serve warm.

FANCY BREAD PUDDING

SERVES 8 • Bread pudding, one of my favorites since childhood, has the virtue of being quite easy to prepare and universally appealing. It also has a tendency to be dense with eggy calories. I find that you can create a lighter, airier version by using fewer eggs and separating the yolks and the whites. The result is an aerated bread pudding—kind of a soufflé with half the sugar of Grandma's version. Though a portion may take up the same space on the plate, there are fewer calories and less fat per forkful. Poppy seeds deliver a concentrated pop of nutrition, subtle sweet/bitter nuttiness, and a bit of texture.

Butter for the casserole dish

⅔ cup whole milk

2 tablespoons poppy seeds

Grated zest and juice of 2 lemons

4 large eggs, separated

3 tablespoons organic cane sugar

2 cups cubed French bread, crust and all

Fresh red currants or raspberries, for serving

1 | Preheat the oven to 350°F. Grease a 1½-quart baking dish with butter.

2 | In a large bowl, combine the milk, poppy seeds, lemon zest and juice and stir to blend. In the bowl of a standing mixer fitted with the whisk attachment, whisk together the egg yolks and sugar on medium-high speed until the mixture is thick and lemon colored. Pour the egg yolk mixture into the bowl and mix together.

3 | Thoroughly wash and dry the whisk and bowl of the standing mixer, then whisk the egg whites on medium-high speed. When the tines begin to show in the whites, add the sugar and continue to whisk until the whites form stiff peaks. Immediately fold the whites into the egg yolk mixture, incorporating until no patches of white remain. Incorporate the bread cubes, then pour the pudding mixture into the prepared dish and bake until set, about 30 minutes. Remove from the oven and set aside on the counter to cool slightly, sliding a fork underneath the dish to allow airflow. Serve warm with the red currants.

THAI TAPIOCA PUDDING

MAKES SIX 7-OUNCE PUDDINGS • While I was pastry chef at Bouley, Queen Sirikit of Thailand came to dine. She was so delighted by her meal that afterward, she invited us to her kingdom to prepare a series of dinners. (It's great to be queen, isn't it, when you can leave an all-expenses-paid trip as a tip?) In the course of one of our food crawls in Bangkok we ate at a place where dessert was served in a bell jar: inside, a fragrant candle perfumed a pudding. I know it may seem like a stretch to hunt down a Thai dessert candle, but they are readily available online and the aroma transforms a very good dessert into a more sublime experience laced with the brightness of Kaffir lime leaves and lemongrass and the sweetness and piquancy of passion fruit.

One 13-ounce can unsweetened coconut milk

3 Kaffir lime leaves, fresh or frozen

1 lemongrass stalk, finely chopped

½ cup tiny quick-cook tapioca pearls

2 tablespoons coconut sugar or muscovado sugar

Thai scented candle (importfood.com)

¾ cup large coconut flakes, lightly toasted, for garnish

Juice and seeds of 4 passion fruits, for garnish

Whipped Coconut Cream (optional, page 242), for serving

1 | In a small saucepan, combine the coconut milk, lime leaves, and lemongrass and bring to a boil. Remove from the heat and let steep for 5 to 10 minutes. Strain and set aside.

2 | Fill a large bowl with water and ice. In a large saucepan, bring 2 cups of water to a boil over medium-high heat. Add the tapioca and cook until all the beads are translucent, 5 to 6 minutes. If some beads take longer to become translucent, add another ½ cup of water and continue cooking until they do.

3 | Set a fine-mesh strainer into the bowl of ice water and pour the cooked tapioca into the strainer to cool it quickly; this prevents the pearls from clumping together. Spoon a few of the ice cubes into the strainer and stir the pearls from the bottom. Return the tapioca (including the few ice cubes if they remain) to the saucepan and add the infused coconut milk and the sugar. Stir over medium-high heat to bring back to a boil.

4 | Divide the tapioca among six 7-ounce parfait glasses and refrigerate until set. To serve, either light the candle at the table for atmosphere or let the puddings sit with the lighted candle under a bowl for a few minutes to infuse them with an exotic aroma. Garnish with the coconut flakes and fresh passion fruit juice and seeds. If desired, serve with the Whipped Coconut Cream.

KATAIFI PUDDING

MAKES ONE 9-INCH PUDDING/SERVES 6 TO 8 • Kataifi is made from shredded baked phyllo. It looks like deconstructed Shredded Wheat. It adds an irresistible crunch that can't be imitated by any other ingredient. I first came across kataifi when I visited the late Michel Richard at Citrus in Los Angeles. Michel was a true genius, one of the giants of modern gastronomy who poured the playful spirit of a dessert chef into savory recipes. I use kataifi for added snap in my version of the classic Greek semolina and phyllo pastry known as *galataktaboureko* (a word you would only find in a crossword puzzle devised by a true sadist). I replace butter with oil, and cut the sugar and honey by nearly three quarters.

FOR THE CRUST

4 ounces kataifi

¼ cup canola oil

1 tablespoon organic cane sugar

Grated zest of 1 orange

FOR THE FILLING

1½ pounds whole-milk ricotta or quark cheese, drained overnight in the refrigerator if loose

¼ cup semolina flour

¾ cup Fat and Happy Raisins (plain or one of the variations, page 250)

¼ cup local honey

Grated zest and juice of 1 lemon (about 2 tablespoons juice)

¼ cup pistachios

1 drop food-grade bitter orange (petit grain) essential oil

1 | Preheat the oven to 350°F. Spray a 9-inch pie plate with vegetable oil cooking spray.

2 | **Make the crust.** Place the kataifi in a large bowl and loosen by pulling the strands apart with your fingers. Add the oil, sugar, and orange zest and toss until the strands are evenly coated. Arrange the kataifi evenly over the bottom of the pie plate. Bake until golden and crisp, about 20 minutes. Set aside.

3 | Reduce the oven to 300°F and prepare the filling.

4 | **Make the filling.** In a large bowl, combine the ricotta, semolina, raisins, honey and lemon zest and juice, and stir until thoroughly blended. Add the pistachios and essential oil, if using, and mix until evenly distributed. Pour over the prepared crust and set the pie plate in a roasting pan. Slide the pan into the oven, then pour enough water into the pan to reach three quarters up the side of the pie plate. Bake until the filling is golden brown, 50 to 55 minutes. Remove from the oven, then from the water bath, and slide a fork underneath the plate to allow airflow. Let cool slightly. Cut into wedges and serve warm.

FROMAGE BLANC CAKE
with Elderflower Cream

MAKES ONE 9-INCH CHEESECAKE • How, I wondered, could I reconcile my quest for healthier desserts with my love for the super-dense and justly renowned cheesecake that entices pilgrims from Manhattan across the Brooklyn Bridge to Junior's on Flatbush Avenue? The answer came in a thunderclap of inspiration—"Use *fromage blanc* (white cheese)." Fromage blanc (aka *fromage frais,* or fresh cheese) has just a fraction of the calories of cream cheese and strikes the right balance between sour and sweet. I trust this will satisfy your cheesecake cravings without making you feel you'll need to buy a new bathing suit.

Vegetable oil cooking spray, for the pan

⅔ cup confectioners' sugar

⅓ cup cornstarch

3 large eggs, separated

1 tablespoon organic cane sugar

1 tablespoon local honey

⅓ cup heavy cream

1½ cups (13.4 ounces) fromage blanc (or ricotta, which is less tart but will work)

Grated zest and juice of 1 orange

Elderflower Cream (page 243)

1 | Preheat the oven to 350°F. Spray a 9-inch springform pan with cooking spray and line with parchment (see page 125).

2 | Combine the confectioners' sugar and cornstarch in a fine-mesh sieve set over parchment and tap through to sift. Set aside.

3 | In the bowl of a standing mixer fitted with the whisk attachment, whisk together the egg yolks and sugar until fluffy and pale yellow, at least 5 minutes. Transfer to a large mixing bowl.

4 | Thoroughly wash and dry the whisk and bowl of the standing mixer and whisk the egg whites on medium-high speed until the tines of the whisk show in the whites. Add the honey and whisk until stiff peaks form, about 2 minutes more.

5 | Meanwhile, bring the cream to a boil in a large, heavy saucepan. Whisk in the confectioners' sugar mixture followed by the fromage blanc. Whisk until smooth. Pour into the egg yolk mixture and whisk to combine. Stir in the orange zest until evenly distributed. Fold in the egg whites until no white patches remain.

6 | Pour the batter into the prepared pan and bake until a toothpick inserted in the center comes out clean, about 40 minutes. Transfer to a rack to cool in the pan for about 5 minutes. Run a knife around the rim of the cake and remove the collar. Transfer the cheesecake to a serving plate. Pour the orange juice over the cake while it's still warm. Serve with the Elderflower Cream.

NOT A CASSATA (WITH RICOTTA)

MAKES ONE 6-INCH SINGLE-LAYER, VERY DEEP CAKE/SERVES 6 • As happens with many traditional desserts, this Sicilian specialty has been pummeled with added sugary touches over the generations. As best I can tell, it started out as a simple sponge cake soaked with fruit juice and layered with ricotta. Then some enterprising Palermo baker added a shell of marzipan, and someone else tossed in cannoli cream, until we arrived at today's overly sweet version. This cake is the lightest cassata I've ever tried, and truer to the original, with the added touch of dried tropical fruits for a bright finish.

4 large eggs, separated

2 tablespoons organic cane sugar

7 tablespoons cake flour

2½ tablespoons cornstarch

15 ounces whole-milk ricotta

¼ cup heavy cream

Grated zest and juice of 1 lemon

¾ cup diced dried mango, papaya, and pineapple

1 | Preheat the oven to 350°F. Coat a 6-inch cake pan or springform pan with vegetable cooking spray and line the bottom with parchment (see page 125).

2 | In the bowl of a standing mixer fitted with the whisk attachment, beat the egg yolks and 1 tablespoon sugar on medium-high speed to frothy ribbons, about 5 minutes.

3 | Combine the cake flour and cornstarch in a fine-mesh sieve set over parchment and tap through to sift. Set aside.

4 | In a large bowl, mix together the ricotta, cream, and lemon zest and juice with a spoon. Fold the egg yolk mixture into the ricotta mixture until thoroughly incorporated. Gradually add the flour mixture, stirring to incorporate.

5 | Thoroughly wash and dry the whisk and bowl of the standing mixer. Whisk the egg whites on medium-high speed until the tines of the whisk show through in the whites. Add the remaining 1 tablespoon sugar and whisk until stiff peaks form.

6 | Fold the egg whites into the ricotta mixture until there is no trace of whites. Fold in the dried fruits until they are evenly distributed. Transfer the mixture to the prepared pan and smooth the top with the back of a spoon or an offset spatula. Bake until a toothpick inserted in the center comes out clean, about 45 minutes. Remove from the oven and set aside on the counter, sliding a fork underneath the pan to allow airflow. Let the cake cool in the pan for 1 hour. Remove from the pan, cut into wedges, and serve with a cup of hot tea. After cooling to room temperature, you may refrigerate. Remove from the refrigerator 1 hour before serving.

ALMOND MILK PANNA COTTA
with Tamarind-Macerated Strawberries

MAKES SIX 6-OUNCE PANNA COTTAS • Panna cotta is beloved for its smooth, silky texture that damn near caresses your palate and sings it a love song. Like ice cream, it provides a canvas on which to paint other flavors. Fresh fruit and a flavored drinking vinegar or high-quality balsamico serve to focus and enhance flavor and texture. Unlike a classic panna cotta, this one is made with almond milk rather than cream and thickened with agar, so it's completely vegan.

1 teaspoon agar powder

2 cups almond milk, preferably homemade (page 244)

3 tablespoons organic cane sugar

3 drops almond extract, such as Nielsen-Massey

1 pint fresh strawberries, hulled and coarsely chopped

3 tablespoons tamarind vinegar, such as Pok Pok Som (or homemade, page 251), tamarind syrup, or aged balsamico

1 | Pour ½ cup water into a medium saucepan and sprinkle the agar onto the surface of the water, as if you were feeding fish. Bring to a boil over medium-high heat. Add the almond milk, sugar, and almond extract and return to a boil. Remove from the heat.

2 | Strain the mixture through a fine-mesh sieve into a large spouted vessel. Divide the mixture evenly among six 6-ounce glasses. Set the glasses on a tray, cover each with plastic wrap or a dish towel, and refrigerate until set, 1 to 2 hours.

3 | In a small bowl, toss the strawberries with the vinegar and set aside to macerate until the panna cotta is set. To serve, top each panna cotta with some of the strawberry mixture.

PICKLED LYCHEE PANNA COTTA
with Lemon Verbena

MAKES SIX 4-OUNCE SERVINGS • Lychees are one of the first exotic Asian fruits I tasted. Those first bites evoked the heady scent of tropical Asia. My coauthor Peter Kaminsky makes the same association, explaining that his lychee voyage commenced over dinner with an Indian friend, Gautum Apa, who had just returned from a summer at his grandmother's house in Mumbai. "Grandmama always had lychees with her breakfast. 'It's good for the brain,' she said, 'and with you, Gautum, it wouldn't hurt!'" I can't promise that this reduced-sugar panna cotta will enable you to speed-read Proust in forty-five minutes, but the pickled lychees are sure to get your attention! I hope it's just the beginning for adding the health benefits of fermentation to the dessert menu.

FOR THE LYCHEE CREAM

1 teaspoon gelatin

1 cup Pickled Lychees (page 253)

¼ cup heavy cream

¼ cup organic cane sugar

Grated zest of 2 oranges

1 cup plain full-fat Greek yogurt

FOR THE LEMON VERBENA CREAM

1 cup whole milk

1 cup heavy cream

12 stems fresh lemon verbena or 1 cup dried leaves

2 tablespoons organic cane sugar

1 teaspoon gelatin

1 mango, peeled, pitted, cubed, and pureed in a blender, or 1 cup mango juice, such as Odwalla

3 passion fruits, halved and flesh scraped from the skin

1 | **Make the lychee cream.** In a small bowl, combine the gelatin and 2 tablespoons water and set aside to bloom. Divide the lychees (reserving 6 for garnish) among six 6-ounce glasses and set aside.

2 | In a small saucepan, combine the cream, sugar, and zest and bring to a boil over medium heat. Remove from the heat and whisk in the gelatin until thoroughly distributed and no clumps remain. In a large bowl, place the yogurt and pour the hot mixture over. Whisk until smooth. Pour the mixture through a fine-mesh sieve into the glasses, dividing it evenly among them.

3 | **Make the lemon verbena cream.** In a large saucepan, combine the milk, cream, verbena, and sugar and bring to a boil over medium-high heat. Remove from the heat and set aside to steep for 15 minutes. Pour the mixture through a fine-mesh sieve into a large spouted vessel. Add the gelatin and whisk to thoroughly distribute. Divide the mixture among the glasses, pouring it over the back of a spoon so that it lands softly on the lychee cream. Cover with plastic wrap and refrigerate until set, at least 3 hours or overnight.

4 | Remove from the refrigerator 30 minutes before serving. Pour 2 tablespoons of the mango juice in the center of each panna cotta and, using the back of a spoon, spread it out to the edges of the glass. Top with the passion fruit and reserved Pickled Lychee and serve.

note

Many stores now offer semi-dried fruits as well as traditional dried fruits. I prefer the semi-dried here because they are more succulent. If you can't find them, regular dried fruits will work.

SPICED MOCHA SEMIFREDDO

MAKES EIGHT 3-OUNCE SERVINGS • If there is a Holy Trinity of desserts, surely it be must chocolate, coffee, and fruit, here accented with a heady mix of spices. This dessert reminds me of an exotic Fudgsicle. Quinoa plus the sugar in dark chocolate are sufficient to create structure so that there is no call for egg yolks and only a little added sugar. I often wonder how chocolate, which is a bitter bean, came to be the foundation of so many desserts. I think the answer is like the one my childhood catechism teacher, Father Brogan, had when I questioned how you could feed a multitude with a little bit of bread and a bucket of fish. Peering over his wire-rimmed spectacles he would answer, "It's a mystery, Bill." I make these in 3-ounce flexipat molds but any small vessel will do, even a teacup.

3 tablespoons good-quality coffee beans, ground to a powder in a clean coffee grinder

2 cardamom pods, ground to a powder in a clean coffee grinder

1 teaspoon fennel seeds, ground to a powder in a clean coffee grinder

1 teaspoon anise seeds, ground to a powder in a clean coffee grinder

2 cups whole milk

3 tablespoons quinoa flour, purchased or home-milled

1 tablespoon unsweetened cocoa powder

1 teaspoon kosher salt

3 ounces dark (70%) chocolate, chopped into small pieces

3 large egg whites

2 tablespoons organic cane sugar

½ cup heavy cream

Quick and Easy Shiny Chocolate Glaze (page 247), for serving

Good-quality chocolate almond bark (optional), for serving

Semi-dried fruits, such as mango, papaya, and cherries, for serving

1 | In a medium saucepan, combine the coffee beans, cardamom, fennel, and anise with the milk and bring to a boil over medium-high heat. Turn off the heat, cover, and let steep for 10 minutes. Strain and return the liquid to the saucepan.

2 | Combine the quinoa flour, cocoa, and salt in a fine-mesh sieve set over parchment and tap through to sift. Whisk the flour mixture into the milk mixture and return to medium heat. Cook, whisking constantly, until the mixture returns to a boil and thickens. Add the chopped chocolate to the saucepan and whisk until it is thoroughly melted and incorporated. Strain into a bowl and set aside to cool.

3 | In the bowl of a standing mixer fitted with the whisk attachment, whisk the egg whites on medium-high speed for 3 minutes. With the mixer running, slowly add the sugar and continue beating until stiff peaks form, about 4 minutes more. Immediately fold the egg whites into the cooled chocolate mixture in thirds, incorporating gently until no egg whites show in the chocolate mixture.

4 | Thoroughly wash and dry the whisk and bowl of the standing mixer and whip the cream to soft peaks. Fold the whipped cream into the chocolate mixture. Divide the semifreddo among eight 3-ounce Flexipat molds or freezer-safe teacups. Freeze overnight.

5 | To serve, unmold onto dessert plates if using the Flexipat molds or serve in the teacups. Spoon the Shiny Chocolate Glaze on top and serve with the chocolate almond bark and dried fruits.

LEMON KAFFIR SEMIFREDDO

MAKES TEN 2-OUNCE SERVINGS IN FLEXIPAT CUBE MOLDS OR FOUR 5-OUNCE SERVINGS IN ESPRESSO CUPS • A demitasse serving of this semifreddo to finish a meal leaves you sated but not stuffed. It's much more satisfying than a sorbet (which is typically frozen, oversweetened fruit juice). I think creaminess explains why I prefer it. Quinoa adds body and a silky texture that is enhanced by the cream. Kaffir lime leaves impart citrus notes without upping tartness, which would have required more sugar to balance. I find they also have a hint of smokiness as well as an ineffable quality I can't put my finger on. I simply call it Asian *je ne sais quoi*.

2 cups whole milk

¼ cup local honey

8 Kaffir lime leaves, fresh or frozen (importfood.com)

¼ cup quinoa flour, purchased or home-milled

Pinch of kosher salt

Zest and juice of 8 lemons (about 2 tablespoons zest and ½ cup juice)

6 large egg whites

¼ cup organic cane sugar

1 cup heavy cream

Plum Compote (page 237) or fresh berries, for serving

1 | Place a medium metal mixing bowl in the freezer to chill.

2 | In a medium saucepan, combine the milk, honey, and lime leaves and bring to a boil over medium-high heat. Turn off the heat and let steep for 5 minutes. Strain out the leaves and discard. Return the liquid to the pan. Tap in the flour through a sieve and whisk constantly over medium heat until the mixture comes to a boil. Continue whisking until the mixture reaches the consistency of Cream of Wheat. Whisk in the salt and the lemon juice and return to a boil. Turn off the heat and stir in the zest. Set aside to cool.

3 | In the bowl of a standing mixer fitted with the whisk attachment, whisk together the egg whites with 1 tablespoon of the sugar on medium-high speed until the tines of the whisk show. Add the remaining sugar and beat until stiff peaks form.

4 | Whisk the heavy cream in the chilled bowl using a hand whisk until soft peaks form. Fold the whipped cream into the quinoa cream. Fold the egg whites into the mixture in thirds, incorporating them gently until no egg whites show. Divide the mixture among ten 2-ounce Flexipat molds or 4 freezer-safe espresso cups. Freeze overnight. To serve, unmold a few onto each dessert plate or serve in the teacups along with the Plum Compote or fresh berries.

FARMERS' CHEESE DUMPLINGS
with Raspberry–Black Pepper Compote

MAKES 24 DUMPLINGS/SERVES 6 • I first made a version of these at Vienna Park, a wonderful and sorely missed restaurant in New York City. Having been trained in French pastry technique, I was pleasantly surprised to learn how light and unsugary many traditional Austrian desserts are (quite the opposite of what you'd expect from the land that brought us schnitzels, goulash, and, occasionally, a touch of heartburn). I have reduced the sugar even further than tradition dictates but find I don't miss it, no doubt in part because of the lactose (naturally occurring dairy sugar) in the light and airy farmers' cheese. The cream cheese gives body to the recipe and helps the dumplings hold their shape. The fruit and black pepper provide a scintillating wake-up call to your taste buds, a nice contrast with the smooth, mild-tasting dumplings.

15 ounces farmers' cheese

3 tablespoons cream cheese, at room temperature

5 tablespoons unsalted high-fat European-style butter, at room temperature

1 teaspoon vanilla paste

1 tablespoon organic cane sugar

½ teaspoon kosher salt

2 large eggs

¾ cup plus 1 tablespoon unbleached all-purpose flour, plus a little more for dusting

¾ cup semolina flour

3 to 4 tablespoons canola or other neutral oil

Raspberry–Black Pepper Compote (page 238)

1 | Crumble the farmers' cheese into the bowl of a standing mixer fitted with the whisk attachment. Add the cream cheese, 1 tablespoon of the butter, and the vanilla and mix at medium speed until smooth. Add the sugar and salt and mix until incorporated. With the mixer running, add the eggs, one at a time, scraping down the sides of the bowl after each addition. Beat for at least 2 minutes, until frothy.

2 | Combine the all-purpose flour and ¼ cup of the semolina flour in a fine-mesh sieve set over parchment and tap through to sift. Reduce the mixer speed to low and gradually add the flour mixture. Raise the mixer speed to medium and mix until smooth and thoroughly incorporated, about 1 minute. Cover the bowl and refrigerate for at least 2 hours or overnight so that the flour can fully absorb the moisture in the dough.

3 | When you are ready to cook the dumplings, bring a large pot of water to a nice simmer (you never want the water to go above a simmer). Place the remaining ½ cup semolina flour in a shallow bowl.

4 | Make a test dumpling to check the consistency of the dough. Dust your work surface with all-purpose flour. Scoop up a spoonful of the dough and use your index finger to scrape it onto the floured surface. Using the spoon, roll the dollop of dough around; if it picks up flour

(RECIPE CONTINUES)

and forms a ball without sticking, you're good to go. If the dough sticks, add a little more flour to the batch of dough and mix to combine.

5 | Working with a tablespoon of dough at a time, roll the dough into balls and dredge them in the semolina flour, gently tossing each one back and forth in your hands to shake off excess flour. Lower the balls into the water with a slotted spoon. Do not crowd the pot; the dumplings should move around freely. Stir carefully with the slotted spoon to prevent them from sticking together. Simmer, uncovered, until the dumplings puff up and rise to the surface, about 5 minutes.

6 | Lift the dumplings out of the water with a slotted spoon and drain on a paper towel–lined tray. Repeat with the remaining dough.

7 | In a large skillet, combine 1 tablespoon of the remaining butter with 1 tablespoon of the oil over medium-low heat. Working in batches so as not to crowd the pan, place the dumplings in the skillet and sauté until golden, turning once. Transfer to a warmed platter. Repeat with the remaining dumplings, adding butter and oil as needed. Serve warm with the Raspberry–Black Pepper Compote.

note | I have a very deliberate reason for using two kinds of flour: all-purpose makes the dumplings airier, while semolina contributes texture and a more pronounced flavor.

DESSERT FRITTATA

MAKES ONE 10-INCH CAKE • I have always had a special place in my heart for the traditional desserts of France. Everyone knows the tarte tatin, and clafoutis (cherries baked in custard) is also reasonably well known. My hope is that this updated version of an old-time fruit-filled frittata of Brittany known as Far Breton can now join them in the dessert Legion of Honor. You can make this with any nice prune, but for me the *prunes de résistance* are the wonderful Armagnac-soaked *pruneaux* of Agen in the Southwest of France. We Americans tend to regard prunes as an old person's food, but in Gascony, prunes are held in the same esteem as foie gras and truffles. There is even a shop called La Maison de la Prune in Agen. Stop in the next time you're in the neighborhood.

3 large eggs

2 cups whole milk

½ cup organic cane sugar

2 tablespoons hazelnut oil

½ teaspoon vanilla paste

¼ teaspoon kosher salt

¾ cup unbleached all-purpose flour

1 tablespoon extra-virgin olive oil

8 prunes, halved and soaked in bourbon for 1 hour

1 | Preheat the oven to 375°F.

2 | In a medium bowl, whisk together the eggs, milk, sugar, hazelnut oil, vanilla, and salt to break up the eggs and until the batter is smooth and uniform. Tap the flour through a fine-mesh sieve into the milk mixture, whisking as you go. Set aside.

3 | Slick a 10-inch cast-iron pan with the olive oil by swirling it around in the pan. Arrange the prunes in the pan and pour the batter over them. Bake until a toothpick inserted in the center comes out clean, 35 to 40 minutes. Remove from the oven and set aside on the counter to cool slightly, sliding a fork underneath the pan to allow airflow. Serve warm, straight from the pan.

 **7** | COOKIES

i come from the good-things-can-come-in-small-packages school of hand-held desserts: a little treat that satisfies you with a cup of tea, or a mid-afternoon coffee or after a big meal when you just don't have room for a slice of pie. In terms of sensual satisfaction and waist management, these do the trick in just one or two bites. Too often, cookies are the dessert equivalent of potato chips: You can't stop eating them, but eating more doesn't increase your pleasure one bit. A good cookie should have a little bit of snap to it but not leave a trail of crumbs down your shirt. You're looking for some crunch, concentrated flavor, and, like a good wine, a clean finish as you breathe out.

Here's my one attempt at sharing a White House scandal. Every afternoon, a cookie platter was sent up to the First Family's quarters. Although the family usually did not return until later, the cookie platter was often empty by 2:00 PM. This leaves the only suspects as the long-serving, loyal, discreet, cookie-loving butlers. I was fine with that; they are the unsung heroes of the Executive Branch.

Nutty Cherry Biscotti • Casbah Cookies
Fennel Snaps • High-Percentage-Chocolate Cookies
Gingered-Up Cookies • Popped Quinoa Chocolate Cookies
Coco-Choco-Aprico Cookies • Malted Oatmeal Cookies
Springerle Cookies • Bilateral Cupcakes

NUTTY CHERRY BISCOTTI

MAKES 42 BISCOTTI • Ideal biscotti strike a balance between crunch (from the baking) and chewiness (from the fruits) and, to strike that balance, biscotti need to be thin. Whole wheat flour is well suited to this recipe because the flavors and textures are so nutty. This butterless recipe features about half as much sugar as the standard formula, but when you make this recipe your own, feel free to cut down even further. It won't affect the crunchy texture of the finished cookie.

⅓ cup pistachios

⅓ cup macadamia nuts

1 cup whole wheat flour

1 cup unbleached all-purpose flour

¼ cup firmly packed dark brown sugar

1 teaspoon baking powder

3 drops wild sweet orange essential oil, or 1 tablespoon grated tangerine zest

3½ tablespoons canola oil

2 large eggs, lightly beaten

¼ cup whole milk

2 tablespoons local honey

½ teaspoon almond extract, such as Nielsen-Massey

1 cup mixed dried fruits (cherries, apricots, raisins, dates), finely chopped

1 | Preheat the oven to 350°F. Line a baking sheet with parchment paper.

2 | Combine the pistachios and macadamia nuts on a baking sheet and roast until fragrant, about 4 minutes. Set aside to cool, then coarsely chop.

3 | In the bowl of a standing mixer fitted with the paddle attachment, mix together the flours, sugar, and baking powder on low speed until combined. Combine the essential oil with the canola oil, then add to the bowl. Add the eggs, milk, honey, and almond extract, raise the speed to medium, and mix just until the dough comes together. Do not overmix. Remove the bowl from the mixer and stir in the dried fruits and nuts. Mix together with a wooden spoon until evenly distributed throughout the dough.

4 | Place the dough on a 16-inch-long sheet of plastic wrap. Bring one long side of the plastic wrap over the dough and shape into a 12-inch-long log 2 to 3 inches in diameter. Remove the plastic wrap and transfer the log to the baking sheet. Bake until browned, rotating the pan halfway through, about 30 minutes. Set aside to cool thoroughly.

5 | Using a serrated knife, slice the log on the diagonal into ¼-inch-thick slices. Arrange the slices on a baking sheet, cut side down, and bake until browned and crisp, 25 to 30 minutes. Let cool completely. The biscotti can be stored in an airtight container at room temperature for up to 1 week.

CASBAH COOKIES

MAKES ABOUT TWENTY-FOUR 3-INCH COOKIES • Here is a version of a cookie inspired by my Moroccan friend Najat Kaanache, who cooks as flamboyantly as she dresses. Mine has less butter, less sugar, and a flavor boost from bergamot essential oil (or you can "season" to taste with orange or tangerine zest). Chickpea flour, which is gluten-free, makes it properly crumbly. The cardamom and bergamot transport you straight to a Moroccan medina.

½ cup (1 stick) unsalted high-fat European-style butter

4½ cups chickpea flour, purchased or home-milled, plus more for dusting

1 tablespoon ground cardamom

¾ cup confectioners' sugar

½ cup grapeseed or other neutral oil

4 drops food-grade bergamot essential oil

2 tablespoons chopped, toasted pistachios

½ cup pomegranate seeds

1 teaspoon local honey

1 | **Clarify the butter.** Melt the butter in a small saucepan over medium heat, then pour into a heatproof measuring cup. Refrigerate until set, then scoop off the cold solidified butter and reserve. Discard the liquid.

2 | Line two cookie sheets with parchment paper.

3 | Combine the chickpea flour and cardamom in a fine-mesh sieve set over parchment and tap through to sift. Set aside.

4 | In the bowl of a standing mixer fitted with the paddle attachment, mix together the sugar, clarified butter, and grapeseed oil on medium speed until fully combined. Reduce the speed to low and gradually add half the flour mixture. Mix until incorporated. Add the remaining flour and the essential oil and mix just until incorporated. Add ⅓ cup of water and mix just until the dough comes together. Fold in the pistachios.

5 | Transfer the dough to a 16-inch-long piece of plastic wrap. Top with a second piece of plastic wrap and roll the dough out to ½-inch thickness. Wrap the dough tightly and chill in the refrigerator for 30 minutes.

6 | Preheat the oven to 350°F. Keeping the dough between the two plastic sheets, roll it out to ¼-inch thickness. Remove the plastic and dust the top of the dough with chickpea flour. Using a 3-inch cookie cutter dusted with chickpea flour, cut out the cookies. Place on the cookie sheets and bake until golden brown around the edges, about 15 minutes. Remove from the oven and set aside on the counter, sliding a fork underneath each cookie sheet to allow airflow. Let cool for 5 minutes.

7 | Stir together the pomegranate seeds and honey. Transfer the cookies to a platter and spoon some of the honey mixture onto the center of each cookie. The cookies will keep, completely cooled and tightly sealed, for up to 1 week.

Emerald Iced Tea, page 197

Popped Quinoa
Chocolate Cookies,
page 183

Gingered-Up Cookies,
page 182

High-Percentage-
Chocolate Cookies,
page 181

Fennel Snaps,
page 180

Casbah Cookies,
opposite

179

FENNEL SNAPS

MAKES THIRTY-SIX 3-INCH COOKIES • Why, you might ask, are some cookies—for example, gingersnaps—known as snaps? My theory is that, due to the molasses, these cookies will bend until they snap rather than break the second you apply any pressure. The idea behind this cookie is to use sweetness-loving licorice-flavored ingredients to cut down on the amount of sugar. If you have some Pernod that's been sitting in the back of your liquor cabinet for ten years, dig it out and add a few teaspoons to this recipe. (See photo, page 179.)

3¾ cups unbleached all-purpose flour

2½ teaspoons ground ginger

1½ teaspoons baking soda

1 teaspoon fennel seed, ground to a powder in a clean coffee grinder, plus more, finely chopped, for garnish

1 teaspoon anise seed, ground to a powder in a clean coffee grinder, plus more, finely chopped, for garnish

¾ cup (1½ sticks) unsalted high-fat European-style butter, at room temperature

½ cup organic cane sugar

2 large eggs

½ cup unsulphured molasses

2 teaspoons white distilled vinegar

1 tablespoon fennel pollen

note

If you use your coffee grinder to grind spices, you can clean out any residual spices by whirring ½ cup of raw white rice to a coarse powder before using it to grind coffee again.

1 | Preheat the oven to 325°F. Line two rimmed baking sheets with parchment or coat with vegetable oil cooking spray.

2 | Combine the flour, ginger, baking soda, and fennel and anise powders in a fine-mesh sieve set over parchment and tap through to sift.

3 | In the bowl of a standing mixer fitted with the paddle attachment, beat the butter on medium speed until smooth and creamy, about 1 minute. Gradually add the sugar and beat on medium speed until combined, about 2 minutes. Add the eggs, one at a time, beating until incorporated after each addition. Add the molasses and vinegar and beat until combined, about 1 minute. Reduce the speed to low and gradually add the flour mixture, occasionally stopping the mixer to scrape down the sides of the bowl. Beat until blended. Remove the bowl from the mixer and finish mixing with a wooden spoon to avoid overbeating.

4 | In a small bowl, combine the chopped fennel and anise and the fennel pollen. Scoop a rounded tablespoon of the dough into your palm, roll it into a ball, and place it on a cookie sheet. Repeat with the remaining dough, placing each ball 2 inches apart. Flatten with the palm of your hand. Sprinkle a pinch of the fennel seed mixture on each cookie. Bake until slightly browned around the edges, about 15 minutes. Remove from the oven and set aside on the counter, sliding a fork underneath each cookie sheet to allow airflow. Let cool for 5 minutes. Transfer the cookies to a plate to cool further. The cookies will keep, completely cooled and tightly covered, for 5 to 7 days.

HIGH-PERCENTAGE-CHOCOLATE COOKIES

MAKES 3½ DOZEN COOKIES • This is a love letter to chocolate. In much the same way that a Côtes du Rhône is called for to stand up to rich braised beef, cherries and pistachios hold their own against the high cacao content in chocolate. I wanted the chocolate flavor to be very defined, so I used half 80% chocolate and half milk chocolate instead of the 70% called for in my other chocolate recipes. (See photo, page 179.)

½ cup tart dried cherries

8 ounces dark (80%) chocolate

2 tablespoons unsalted high-fat European-style butter, at room temperature

2½ tablespoons whole wheat flour

½ teaspoon baking powder

Pinch of kosher salt

2 large eggs

⅓ cup lightly packed light brown sugar

½ teaspoon vanilla paste

½ cup pistachios, toasted and coarsely chopped

6 ounces milk chocolate cut into Toll House–size chunks

Sea salt flakes (optional)

1 | Preheat the oven to 350°F. Line two rimmed baking sheets with parchment.

2 | Bring a small saucepan of water to a boil. Add the cherries and cook for 2 to 3 minutes to plump. Drain and spread on a paper towel.

3 | Combine the dark chocolate and butter in a small microwave-safe bowl and melt in the microwave in 5-second intervals, stirring after each, until it is thoroughly melted and looks smooth and glossy. Monitor the chocolate closely, as it can easily burn. Set aside to cool for at least 10 minutes.

4 | Combine the flour, baking powder, and salt in a fine-mesh sieve set over parchment and tap through to sift. Set aside. In the bowl of a standing mixer fitted with the paddle attachment, beat together the eggs and brown sugar on medium-high speed until the mixture is frothy. Add the flour mixture, vanilla, cherries, pistachios, and milk chocolate and mix until just incorporated.

5 | With the mixer running, add the cooled melted chocolate to the bowl and mix until just incorporated. Remove the bowl from the mixer and finish mixing with a wooden spoon to avoid overbeating.

6 | Spoon walnut-size portions onto the prepared baking sheets, leaving an inch between them. Bake until the cookies form a crust with a slightly browned edge, about 8 minutes. For fudgier cookies, bake 6 to 7 minutes. Slide the parchment onto a marble or wooden countertop or onto a cold sheet pan to stop the baking. If desired, sprinkle a few flakes of sea salt onto each cookie while still soft. The cooled cookies will keep, tightly covered, for up to 4 days.

GINGERED-UP COOKIES

MAKES TWENTY-FOUR 3-INCH COOKIES • Every holiday season at the White House was a cookie fest of shock-and-awe proportions. We made a thousand cookies a day. This cookie is a less sweet version of one of our traditional gingerbread cookies, boosted with flaxseed meal—high in cholesterol-lowering omega-3's—and sharp, spicy, fragrant, fresh ginger, a folk medicine staple prescribed for all kinds of aches and pains. I upped the fresh ginger all the way past the five-alarm-spicy level, then dialed it back a tad, but this is not for timid palates! (See photo, page 179.)

2½ cups unbleached all-purpose flour

½ cup golden flaxseed flour (aka flaxseed meal), purchased or home-milled

1 teaspoon baking soda

1 teaspoon ground cinnamon

Pinch of kosher salt

1 cup (2 sticks) unsalted high-fat European-style butter, at room temperature

¼ cup firmly packed dark brown sugar

2 large eggs

⅓ cup unsulphured molasses

1 heaping tablespoon peeled, grated fresh ginger

2 teaspoons distilled white vinegar

1 | Preheat the oven to 350°F. Line two cookie sheets with parchment paper or coat with vegetable oil cooking spray.

2 | Combine the flours, baking soda, cinnamon, and salt in a fine-mesh sieve set over parchment paper. Tap through to sift. Set aside.

3 | In the bowl of a standing mixer fitted with the paddle attachment, mix together the butter and brown sugar on medium-high speed until the mixture is light and fluffy. Add the eggs, one at a time, mixing thoroughly after each addition. Add the molasses, ginger, and vinegar and mix, scraping down the sides of the bowl as needed.

4 | Reduce the mixer speed to low and gradually add the flour mixture, mixing until combined. Remove the bowl from the mixer and scrape down the sides and bottom to incorporate all the dry ingredients. Return to the mixer and mix for 30 seconds more. Remove the bowl from the mixer and finish mixing with a wooden spoon to avoid overbeating.

5 | Using a small ice-cream scoop, scoop the dough into small balls and place on one or two large plates. Refrigerate until firm enough to roll in the palms of your hands, about 20 minutes. Roll each scoopful into a ball and place 1½ inches apart on the cookie sheet. Bake, rotating the sheets, until the cookies have spread and are firm around the edges, about 12 minutes. Remove from the oven and set aside on the counter to cool, sliding a fork underneath each sheet to allow airflow. Serve slightly warm or let cool completely before storing. The cookies will keep, tightly covered, for up to 4 days.

THE SWEET SPOT | *gingered-up cookies*

POPPED QUINOA CHOCOLATE COOKIES

MAKES EIGHTEEN 3-INCH COOKIES • When I did the final test on this recipe, I thought to myself, *This cookie is going to be my retirement fund!* The happy tale started when I came across popped quinoa in a local bodega near my apartment in Spanish Harlem. Quinoa has all the essential amino acids, one of them being theonine, which some studies say is a natural "chill pill" that helps to calm anxiety. Rye flour adds a sour and nutty background flavor. But you'll forget all that with the first bite: These cookies are just so good! (See photo, page 179.)

1 cup cake flour

1 tablespoon rye flour, purchased or home-milled

1 teaspoon baking powder

1 teaspoon kosher salt

Pinch of ground black pepper

6 tablespoons (¾ stick) unsalted high-fat European-style butter, at room temperature

⅔ cup organic cane sugar

4 large eggs

½ cup pecans, lightly toasted and finely chopped

1 teaspoon instant coffee crystals

1 teaspoon vanilla paste

16 ounces dark (70%) chocolate, melted

16 ounces high-quality milk (40%) chocolate, melted

½ cup popped quinoa

1 | Preheat the oven to 350°F. Line two cookie sheets with parchment or coat with vegetable oil cooking spray.

2 | Combine the cake flour, rye flour, baking powder, salt, and pepper in a fine-mesh sieve set over parchment and tap through to sift. Set aside.

3 | In the bowl of a standing mixer fitted with the paddle attachment, beat together the butter and sugar on medium speed until the mixture is smooth and creamy. Add the eggs, one at a time, beating well after each addition. And the pecans, coffee, and vanilla and continue to beat, scraping down the sides of the bowl, until fully incorporated.

4 | Reduce the mixer speed to medium-low, add one third of the flour mixture, and beat until well incorporated. Add the remaining flour in two additions, scraping down the bowl several times. Add the melted chocolate and quinoa and let the paddle run through the dough two or three times. Remove the bowl from the mixer and finish mixing with a wooden spoon to avoid overbeating.

5 | Scoop heaping tablespoons of the dough onto the cookie sheets, leaving a 1-inch space between them. Flatten each with the palm of your hand. Bake until the tops of the cookies are crumbly and cracked, about 12 minutes, rotating the cookie sheets once. Remove from the oven and set aside on the counter, sliding a fork underneath each sheet to allow airflow. Let cool before removing from the cookie sheets. The cookies will keep, completely cooled and tightly covered, for up to 3 days.

COCO-CHOCO-APRICO COOKIES

MAKES TWENTY-FOUR 3-INCH COOKIES • My grandma Gertrude in Toledo was generally acknowledged around town as the unofficial capo of the German American Baking Mafia and was a champion all-American chocolate chip cookie baker. No county fair in northwestern Ohio was out of her jurisdiction. I developed this smaller, more powerfully flavored version of her masterpiece for receptions and small meetings at the White House. Not to drop names, but at various times over the years Brad Pitt, Angela Merkel, and the Dalai Lama all had their hands in my cookie jar.

1 cup unbleached all-purpose flour

3 tablespoons millet flour, purchased or home-milled

⅛ teaspoon baking soda

⅛ teaspoon baking powder

Pinch of kosher salt

½ cup (1 stick) unsalted high-fat European-style butter, at room temperature

⅓ cup organic cane sugar

¼ cup firmly packed dark brown sugar

2 large eggs

½ teaspoon vanilla paste

⅔ cup sweetened coconut flakes

4 ounces dark (at least 70%) chocolate, roughly chopped

1 tablespoon cacao nibs

½ cup chopped dried apricots

1 | Preheat the oven to 350°F. Line two rimmed baking sheets with parchment paper.

2 | Combine the flours, baking soda, baking powder, and salt in a fine-mesh sieve set over parchment and tap through to sift. Set aside.

3 | In the bowl of a standing mixer fitted with the paddle attachment, beat together the butter and sugars on medium-high speed until the mixture is fluffy. Add the eggs, one at a time, and beat until thoroughly incorporated. Add the vanilla and beat until incorporated. Reduce the mixer speed to low and gradually add the flour mixture, beating until thoroughly incorporated. Remove the bowl from the mixer and scrape down the sides and bottom to incorporate all the dry ingredients. Return to the mixer and mix for 30 seconds more. Remove the bowl from the mixer and finish mixing with a wooden spoon to avoid overbeating. Fold in the coconut flakes, chocolate, cacao nibs, and apricots until evenly distributed.

4 | Using a small ice-cream scoop, drop scoopfuls onto the cookie sheets, leaving a 1-inch space between them. Bake until golden, about 15 minutes. Remove from the oven and set aside on the counter, sliding a fork underneath each cookie sheet to allow airflow. Let cool for 5 minutes. Transfer the cookies to a platter to cool further. Serve slightly warm. The cookies will keep, completely cooled and tightly covered, for up to 3 days.

MALTED OATMEAL COOKIES

MAKES ABOUT THIRTY 1½-INCH COOKIES • In theory, oatmeal cookies should be non-offenders in the health and sugar departments, but way too often they are the mealy plastic-wrapped things you have to settle for at the airport newsstand: they are super-sized commercial versions with as much sweetener as a Snickers bar. My oatmeal cookies feature a medley of dried fruits, nuts, and coconut. Malt—a venerated soda fountain ingredient—adds a bit of pleasingly complex fermented grain flavor. The next time you fly, take some in your carry-on instead of the ubiquitous granola bar (a stealthy source of sugar).

1 cup unbleached all-purpose flour

½ cup whole wheat flour

1 tablespoon plus 1½ teaspoons malted milk powder

1½ teaspoons ground cinnamon

1 teaspoon baking powder

1 teaspoon baking soda

½ teaspoon kosher salt

¾ cup (1½ sticks) unsalted high-fat European-style butter, at room temperature

½ cup muscovado sugar

2 large eggs

1½ teaspoons vanilla paste

1½ cups old-fashioned rolled oats

1 cup unsweetened coconut flakes

1 cup lightly toasted pecans, coarsely chopped

½ cup mixed dried fruits (cherries, blueberries, apricots, raisins), large pieces chopped

1 | Preheat the oven to 350°F. Line two cookie sheets with parchment.

2 | Combine the flours, malted milk powder, cinnamon, baking powder, baking soda, and salt in a fine-mesh sieve set over parchment and tap through to sift. Set aside.

3 | In the bowl of a standing mixer fitted with the paddle attachment, beat together the butter and sugar on medium speed until smooth. Add the eggs, one at a time, beating well after each addition. Add the vanilla and beat until incorporated. Reduce the speed to low and gradually add the flour mixture, beating until just combined. Remove the bowl from the mixer and add the oats, coconut flakes, pecans, and dried fruit and stir in until evenly distributed.

4 | Using a small ice-cream scoop, drop scoopfuls 1 inch apart onto the cookie sheets. Bake until golden, 15 to 20 minutes. Remove from the oven and set aside on the counter, sliding a fork underneath the cookie sheets to allow airflow. Let cool for 5 minutes. Transfer the cookies to a platter to cool completely. The cookies will keep, completely cooled and tightly covered, for up to 3 days.

COOKIES *to order*

This recipe produces a big batch. I freeze a lot of the raw dough so that I can whip up a bunch with minimal fuss.

While the batter is still soft and easy to work with (it stiffens as it cools), drop walnut-size portions onto a sheet of aluminum foil. Refrigerate for 20 minutes. Remove from the refrigerator and roll into balls between your palms. Place the balls in a resealable plastic bag and freeze for up to 3 months. To bake, arrange the frozen cookies on a baking sheet and bake a minute or two longer than directed.

SPRINGERLE COOKIES

MAKES TWENTY-FOUR 4-INCH COOKIES • Is it a Christmas ornament or is it a cookie? Actually it's both. These cookies are a German tradition brought to America by Mennonite immigrants. I first made them for an all-pastry replica of the fireplace that FDR used in the White House. He commissioned tiles on the mantel to commemorate famous landmarks in our history: the Statue of Liberty, Mount Rushmore, and his summer residence at White Sulphur Springs. (The tiles now reside in the FDR museum in Hyde Park, New York.) Leaving the unbaked cookies out to dry for at least four hours or overnight before putting them in the oven helps to preserve the embossed image as they bake. These are completely edible when first made, but any you don't eat can be used as tree ornaments year after year. My suggestion is to wash down a few with eggnog or wassail and, if you can still stand upright, hang the rest on your tree.

1½ tablespoons anise seeds, ground to a fine powder in a clean coffee grinder

3½ cups unbleached all-purpose flour, plus more for dusting

1 teaspoon baking powder

2 teaspoons salt

4 large eggs

1 cup organic cane sugar

6 drops food-grade fir balsam essential oil (optional)

½ teaspoon almond extract, such as Nielsen-Massey

1 | Combine the anise powder, flour, baking powder, and salt in a fine-mesh sieve set over parchment and tap through to sift. Set aside.

2 | In the bowl of a standing mixer fitted with the whisk attachment, beat together the eggs, sugar, essential oil (if using), and almond extract on medium-high speed until the mixture is pale and frothy, 5 to 8 minutes. Replace the whisk with a paddle, reduce the speed to low, and gradually add the flour mixture to the bowl. Mix until a thick dough forms.

3 | Line a cookie sheet with parchment paper. Turn the dough out onto a clean work surface dusted with flour. Working with one third of the dough at a time, roll it out to a ⅜-inch-thick circle using a liberally dusted rolling pin. Sprinkle some flour onto the Springerle mold, then tap on the work surface to release the excess. Using a cookie cutter the size of the entire Springerle mold (not just the impression) or a sharp knife, cut out the dough. Press the cutouts into the mold. Peel the dough away and place on the cookie sheet. Air-dry for 4 hours. If you want to turn the cookies into ornaments, make a small hole in the top for threading a ribbon through before you set them out to air-dry.

4 | Preheat the oven to 250°F.

5 | Bake the cookies until they are firm and crisp, 25 to 30 minutes. Remove from the oven and set aside on the counter, sliding a fork underneath the cookie sheet to allow airflow. Let cool for 5 minutes. Transfer the cookies to a platter to cool completely. Store the cookies in an airtight container for up to 7 days or indefinitely if using for decoration (and not to be consumed).

BILATERAL CUPCAKES

MAKES THIRTY-SIX 1½-INCH CUPCAKES • At the White House I would, from time to time, find myself making cupcakes, because how are you gonna have kids over for a holiday party and not give them a cupcake? Nevertheless, the French-trained chef in me rebelled. Simply stated, the French don't do cupcakes. I know this must be true, because I have pored over the State Department treaty collection, searching in vain for a Transatlantic Cupcake Concordat.

So I took matters into my own hands for my contribution to Franco-American culinary cooperation: a cupcake/financier made with healthful almonds (whole and ground to a flour), plus cacao nibs. No frosting required . . . or desired!

4 large egg whites

⅓ cup cake flour

1¼ cups almond flour, purchased or home-milled

¼ cup roasted almonds, finely chopped

2 tablespoons organic cane sugar

1 tablespoon local honey

3 drops food-grade bergamot essential oil or zest and juice of 1 lemon

Zest and juice of 1 orange

½ cup (1 stick) unsalted high-fat European-style butter

3 tablespoons cacao nibs

1 | In the bowl of a standing mixer fitted with the whisk attachment, mix together the egg whites, cake flour, almond flour, chopped almonds, sugar, honey, essential oil, and orange zest and juice on medium speed until thoroughly incorporated.

2 | Meanwhile, brown the butter. In a small skillet (a light-colored interior is helpful), cook the butter over medium heat until the liquid turns brown on the bottom (these are the milk solids burning a little bit), stirring occasionally so that the solids don't actually carbonize. Stir the browned butter into the batter until thoroughly incorporated. Cover and let rest in the refrigerator for at least 2 hours and preferably overnight to allow the flours to fully absorb the liquid.

3 | Preheat the oven to 350°F. Prepare three mini-muffin tins with mini-cupcake liners, then spray with vegetable oil cooking spray.

4 | Divide the batter evenly among the muffin tins and sprinkle a few cacao nibs on top of each. Bake until a toothpick inserted in the center of a cupcake comes out clean, 10 to 12 minutes. Open the oven door periodically during baking to release any steam that builds up; this will ensure proper browning of the tops. Remove from the oven and set aside on the counter, sliding a fork underneath each tin to allow airflow. Let cool for 30 minutes, then gently remove the cupcakes from the tins.

variation:

For a fruity version, replace the cacao nibs with 1 cup fresh blueberries, 1 cup fresh strawberries, hulled and quartered (see photo, page 254).

 **FANCY BITES**

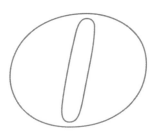

ne of the hallmarks of "fine dining" is the little sweets that arrive after more substantial desserts. For special occasions, you can offer the same at home. If French chefs hadn't already used the words *amuse bouche* to describe those little canapés that they send out before the meal, I would call these bite-sized sweets *amuses* because desserts are much more amusing than chorizo and cheese on a toothpick. Alas, I believe I am a dessert prophet crying in the savory wilderness.

The fanciful bites that follow are innovative takes on traditional *petits fours*. They are an elegant touch after dessert at a dinner party, or they can be served instead of a heftier dessert. (I'd certainly rather have one or two of these than a molten chocolate nemesis before I get up from the table.) They go well with a bit of bubbly, but then, what doesn't? Many would also make a lovely hostess gift. The satisfying part of working out these recipes, like everything else in this book, was meeting the challenge of sweet deliciousness with less sweetener and novel, healthful, ingredients.

Grapefruit Jelly Bites • Cool Orange Oreo • Jellies in a Kataifi Nest
Emerald Iced Tea • Blitz Puff Pastry Napoleon • Elegant Jell-O Shots
Olive Oil Truffles • Honey Truffles • Earl Grey Truffles
Health Bar Cohibas • Fizzicals

tea time **TRIO**

A perfect array to serve with an afternoon tea. I think of these bites as something to tide you over to the next meal if you are one of those sophisticates who don't dine until nine.

Jellies in a Kataifi Nest, page 196

Cool Orange Oreo, page 194

Grapefruit Jelly Bites, opposite

GRAPEFRUIT JELLY BITES

MAKES TWENTY-FOUR 1¼-INCH MOLDED GELÉES • A cool melt-on-your-tongue grapefruit jelly on a thin butter cookie. I make it with agar powder, which, unlike gelatin, won't melt at room temperature.

1½ teaspoons gelatin

2½ tablespoons organic cane sugar

1 teaspoon agar powder

1 cup pink grapefruit juice

½ recipe Almond Crust dough (page 68)

½ cup finely chopped candied papaya, for garnish

1 | Have ready two 12-slot Flexipat molds or two silicon ice cube trays.

2 | In a small bowl, combine the gelatin with 2 tablespoons of cold water and set aside to bloom.

3 | In a medium saucepan, bring 1½ cups of water to a boil over medium-high heat. Whisk together the sugar and agar powder and sprinkle the mixture over the boiling water as if you were feeding fish. Boil for 2 minutes. Add the grapefruit juice and return to a boil, whisking occasionally. Remove from the heat and thoroughly whisk in the bloomed gelatin. Strain the mixture through a fine-mesh sieve into a spouted vessel and pour into the molds. Refrigerate until opaque and stiff, about 1 hour.

4 | Meanwhile, preheat the oven to 350°F. Spray two rimmed baking sheets with vegetable oil cooking spray or line with parchment.

5 | On a flour-dusted work surface, roll out the tart dough to a ⅜-inch thickness. Using a 2-inch circle cookie cutter, cut out 24 circles. Transfer the circles to the baking sheets and bake until they are golden brown around the edges, about 12 minutes. Remove from the oven and set aside on the counter, sliding a fork underneath each baking sheet to allow airflow. Let cool for 5 minutes. Transfer the cookies to a platter to cool further.

6 | Use your index finger to coax the gelées away from the edges of the molds, then flip the mold over and tap onto a clean tray to release the gelées. Turn them over and place one on each cookie. Garnish with the papaya.

variations:
CHERRY JUICE, POMEGRANATE JUICE, EARL GREY TEA—just about any liquid or fruit puree substituted for the grapefruit juice will make enchanting jellies.

COOL ORANGE OREO

MAKES EIGHTEEN 2-INCH SANDWICH COOKIES • The Oreo is perhaps the most popular cookie in America. I wanted to do a reverse version (chocolate inside and white outside) using the complementary flavors of orange and chocolate, two of my favorites. The result has a sandwich cookie's dual attractions of creamy filling and crunchy exterior. (See photo, page 192.)

FOR THE COOKIES

½ cup (1 stick) unsalted high-fat European-style butter, at room temperature

½ cup organic cane sugar

2 large eggs

1 teaspoon vanilla paste

½ teaspoon kosher salt

3 cups unbleached all-purpose flour

Grated zest of 1 orange

2 tablespoons cacao nibs

FOR THE CHOCOLATE COINS

5 ounces dark (70%) chocolate, finely chopped

5 teaspoons organic cane sugar

2 large egg yolks

½ cup whole milk

½ cup heavy cream

1 | **Make the cookie dough.** In the bowl of a standing mixer fitted with the paddle attachment, mix together the butter and sugar on medium-high speed until the mixture is light and fluffy. Add the eggs, vanilla, and salt and mix until incorporated. Add the flour in thirds, mixing minimally after each addition. Turn the dough out onto a piece of plastic wrap and cover, flattening it to a ½-inch thickness. Refrigerate for at least 4 hours.

2 | **Make the chocolate coins.** Spray two mini-muffin tins with vegetable oil cooking spray or have ready two circular Flexipat molds in the same size. Place the chocolate in a large heatproof bowl and set aside.

3 | Combine the sugar and egg yolks in the bowl of a standing mixer fitted with the whisk attachment. Mix on high speed until the mixture is pale yellow and frothy, about 3 minutes.

4 | Meanwhile, combine the milk and cream in a medium saucepan and bring to a boil over medium-high heat, whisking constantly. Remove from the heat. Pour the egg yolk mixture into the cream, whisking constantly. Return the pan to medium heat and cook, whisking constantly, until the mixture thickens. DO NOT let it boil as it heats. Pour the hot liquid over the chocolate and whisk from the center outward to create an emulsion, pulling in the chocolate from the edges as you whisk. Pour the mixture through a fine-mesh sieve into a spouted vessel. Fill 18 of the mini-muffin wells ¼ inch deep. Freeze until solid, about 1 hour.

5 | Preheat the oven to 350°F. Coat two cookie sheets with vegetable oil cooking spray. Roll out the dough to ¼-inch thickness and cut out circles with a 2-inch circular cookie cutter. Transfer to the cookie sheets. Sprinkle half the cookies with the orange zest and cacao nibs.

Bake until lightly golden around the edges, about 12 minutes. Remove from the oven and set aside on the counter, sliding a fork underneath each cookie sheet to allow airflow. Let cool for 5 minutes. Transfer the cookies to a platter to cool completely.

6 | To make the cookie sandwiches, place a chocolate coin on the plain cookies and top each with an adorned cookie. Cover and refrigerate until ready to serve. The cookies will keep in the refrigerator, tightly covered in a rigid container, for up to 3 days.

I HAVE *mixed emulsions*

An emulsion is a mixture of one liquid in droplet form suspended in another with which it cannot evenly mix. We see emulsions every day: mayonnaise, milk, cream, even chocolate (yes, emulsions can be in solid form if the melting temperature of the fat is high enough). These emulsions are all based on fats dispersed in another liquid. In order to stabilize the mixture we use "emulsifiers," which may act in different ways. In the case of egg yolks, which have been used in this way since the seventeenth century, their lecithin molecules attach to both water and fat and therefore keeps both in a stable balance—voilà! Hollandaise!

JELLIES IN A KATAIFI NEST

MAKES 24 JELLIES • It looks like hard-boiled egg inside a nest of straw, but it's actually a silky concoction of agar, orange juice, and coconut milk on a bed of kataifi, Middle Eastern shredded wheat. Painters are fond of a technique called *trompe l'oeil* (fooling the eye). These jellies look enough like real eggs that I call them *trompe l'ouefs* (fooling the eggs). (See photo, page 192.)

(See photo, page 192.)

FOR THE JELLIES

1½ teaspoons gelatin

1 teaspoon agar powder

2½ tablespoons organic cane sugar

½ cup orange juice

½ cup coconut milk

FOR THE KATAIFI NEST

3 tablespoons neutral oil,
    such as grapeseed or canola

2 tablespoons local honey

One 12-ounce package kataifi

1 | Have ready two 12-slot 2-inch domed Flexipat molds.

2 | In a small bowl, combine ¾ teaspoon of the gelatin with 1 tablespoon of cold water and set aside to bloom. Whisk together half the agar powder and half the sugar and set aside.

3 | In a medium saucepan, bring ¾ cup of water to a boil over medium-high heat. Sprinkle the agar-sugar mixture over the water as if you were feeding fish. Boil for 2 minutes. Add the orange juice and return to a boil, whisking occasionally. Remove from the heat and thoroughly whisk in the bloomed gelatin. Strain the mixture through a fine-mesh sieve and into a spouted vessel.

4 | Pour the orange juice gelée halfway up a 2-inch domed mold and refrigerate until set, about 1 hour. When the "yolks" have set, prepare the coconut gelée in the same manner. Bloom the remaining ¾ teaspoon of gelatin in 1 tablespoon cold water. Whisk together the remaining sugar and agar. Bring ¾ cup of water to a boil and sprinkle the agar-sugar mixture over. Boil for 2 minutes. Add the coconut milk and return to a boil, whisking occasionally. Remove from the heat and thoroughly whisk in the gelatin. Pour through a fine-mesh sieve into a spouted vessel. Pour the "whites" over the "yolks" in the molds and refrigerate until opaque and firm, about 1 hour.

5 | Preheat the oven to 350°F. Coat a mini-muffin or cupcake tin with vegetable cooking spray. Combine the oil and honey in a small, lidded jar and shake vigorously. Pull off a chunk of kataifi the size of a Ping-Pong ball from the batch. Gently gather it into a round ball and lightly press it into the cupcake mold. Using scissors, cut away any stragglers hanging out over the edge. Pour a few drops of the honey mixture over the top of each nest. Bake until golden and crisp, 12 to 14 minutes. Cool in the pan for 5 minutes, then transfer to the rack and cool completely. Set an egg into each nest.

EMERALD ICED TEA

MAKES ABOUT 1 QUART • I am one of the few primates who never liked milk with my cookies. Actually, I'm being gentle here. I *loathed* milk and cookies. I don't know where you come down on this burning issue, but I think you will find that this herbaceous beverage is a sprightly palate cleanser between cookies. Serve ice-cold to keep the gorgeous color longer. (See photo, page 179.)

2 tablespoons local honey

1 teaspoon vitamin C powder or 1 crushed vitamin C pill (to keep the greens bright)

4 cups of your favorite soft, sweet herbs, such as mint (chocolate, cinnamon, spearmint, peppermint), lemon verbena, lemon balm, anise hyssop, or basil, leaves only

1 cup tender watercress leaves, tough stems discarded

1 | Combine the honey, vitamin C, and 1 quart water in a pitcher and stir well to combine. Set aside.

2 | Fill a large bowl with water and ice.

3 | Bring 2 quarts water to a boil. Plunge the herbs and watercress into the boiling water for 30 seconds. This is enough to break the cell walls and release the chlorophyll (aka, the green stuff). Using a large slotted spoon, scoop out the greens and immediately plunge into the ice water bath. Let cool for 10 seconds. Transfer the wet greens to a blender and pour the honey water over, scraping all the honey from the bottom of the pitcher. Blend for 30 seconds to liquefy. Strain the mixture through a fine-mesh sieve and serve cold.

BLITZ PUFF PASTRY NAPOLEON

MAKES 8 • Few home bakers have the patience to submit to the exercise in culinary masochism known as mille-feuille (aka Napoleon) with its 729 layers of flour and butter. Professional bakers often feel the same. Here's a workaround that grateful bakers affectionately characterize with the term "blitz." It incorporates all the flour, water, and butter into one glorious oversize blob and is so much easier on you and your rolling pin. You don't have to roll out layers of butter that precisely match the squared-off layers of dough like hospital bedsheet corners. Mind you, you will have to let the dough rest for the same amount of time as the classic dough, but the demands on your technique are much fewer. This labor-saving shortcut doesn't shortchange on results: The pastry comes out of the oven super airy and crisp and there's no sugar in the dough.

1½ cups unbleached all-purpose flour, plus more for dusting

1 cup (2 sticks) cold unsalted high-fat European-style butter, cut into ½-inch cubes

2 tablespoons unsweetened cocoa powder

½ teaspoon kosher salt

1 ounce dark (70%) chocolate, melted

¾ cup ice water, strained of ice

Miracle Ganache Frosting (page 245)

Quick and Easy Shiny Chocolate Glaze (page 247)

1 | Place the flour, butter, cocoa powder, and salt in the bowl of a standing mixer. Toss together with your hands until the butter is thoroughly coated. Using the standing mixer fitted with a hook attachment, mix on low speed until the butter is mashed together with the flour. With the mixer running, add the chocolate and mix until it is incorporated (it will be a patchy mix). Add the water all at once and mix until the flour has evenly absorbed the water. Scrape down the sides of the bowl, raise the speed to medium, and mix for another 10 seconds.

2 | Using a rubber spatula, scrape the dough out onto a liberally floured work surface and shape it into a ball with your hands. With well-floured hands, flatten the dough into an 8 × 12-inch rectangle. Cover with plastic wrap and refrigerate for 1 hour.

3 | Remove the dough from the refrigerator and let it rest for 3 minutes. Place the dough on a floured work surface with the short side facing you and a quarter of it hanging off the edge of the work surface (gravity helps to stretch the dough). Using a floured rolling pin, roll out the dough, pushing the dough away from you *only* (do not roll the rolling pin back toward you) to make a 16-inch-long rectangle. Brush the dough with flour if it becomes sticky. Flip the dough over frequently to prevent it from sticking to the counter.

(RECIPE CONTINUES)

4 Rotate the dough 90 degrees so that a long side faces you. Roll the dough away from you (not back and forth) to increase its width. Try to keep the edges square. Brush away any excess flour with a pastry brush. Fold the dough into thirds, from right to left, to make three layers. Roll the dough out again, rolling away from you, to make a 14-inch-long rectangle. Rotate the dough 90 degrees and roll away from you again until the rectangle is 10 × 14 inches. Fold into thirds again. Cover with plastic wrap and refrigerate for 2 to 4 hours or overnight and repeat the rolling, folding, and chilling process two more times.

5 Preheat the oven to 375°F. Line a baking sheet with parchment.

6 Roll the dough out to ⅜-inch thickness (about an 8 × 12-inch rectangle). Cut the dough into 8 equal-size pieces. Flip them over (this allows for more lift) and place on the baking sheet. Bake until fully dry on the inside, 25 to 30 minutes. Remove from the oven and set aside on the counter to cool completely, sliding a fork underneath the pan to allow airflow.

7 Using a serrated knife, slice the pieces in half horizontally. Place a spoonful of the ganache frosting on one half of the pastry and top with the other half. Drizzle with the Quick and Easy Shiny Chocolate Glaze and serve.

8 Rolled out to ½-inch thickness and triple wrapped in plastic wrap, the dough can be frozen for up to several weeks.

note

Why do we say flip the puff pastry pieces over to provide more "lift"? When you cut through the multi layers of puff pastry with a knife or cookie cutter, you are crushing the layers together where the cutting edge goes through the dough. Those layers crushed downward will stick to one another and hold the baking dough down. If you flip the piece of puff pastry over, the layers will open in the heat of the oven and lift the pastry upward.

ELEGANT JELL-O SHOTS

MAKES SIX 1¼-INCH CUBES/SERVES 6 • Those of you who regularly tailgate at NFL games will no doubt be familiar with Jell-O shots—usually gin, vodka, or tequila mixed with Jell-O that is chilled and molded in small paper cups. My tribute to this fine tradition is a beautiful combination of cocoa powder, Thai chili, Banyuls sweet wine, and good-quality high-percentage chocolate that preserves the wiggly texture but without such a boozy bang. On a recent visit to Mexico, I was really taken with the way the Zapotec people of Oaxaca use the combination of sugar and many chilies to great effect in their supernal *mole negro*. Serve with High-Percentage-Chocolate Cookies (page 181).

½ teaspoon gelatin

5 teaspoons organic cane sugar

1 teaspoon agar powder

1 tablespoon cocoa powder

1 fresh or dried Thai chili pepper, seeded and chopped

1 tablespoon fortified dessert wine, such as Banyuls

1 ounce dark (70%) chocolate, chopped

Cacao nibs, for garnish

1 | Have ready a 2½-ounce Flexipat cube mold or a silicone ice cube tray or six parfait glasses.

2 | In a small bowl, combine the gelatin with 1 tablespoon cold water and set aside to bloom.

3 | Place 2 cups of water in a medium saucepan. Whisk together the sugar and agar powder, then tap the mixture into the water as you would fish food. Bring to a boil over medium-high heat. Continue to boil for 2 minutes. Add the cocoa powder, chili, and wine and return to a boil, whisking occasionally. Continue to boil for 3 minutes—do not walk away; the mixture boils over readily. Whisk in the bloomed gelatin and chocolate. Immediately remove from the heat and stir until the gelatin is fully melted into the liquid. Pour the mixture through a fine-mesh sieve into a spouted cup or pitcher, which makes it easier to pour into the Flexipat mold. Refrigerate until set, 1 to 3 hours. Gently unmold onto dessert plates and garnish with the cacao nibs.

note

All Banyuls are fortified sweet red wines that go very well with chocolate. Mas Amiel is the current fave among sommeliers, but any Banyuls will work. Port will also serve nicely.

truffles, TRIED AND TRUE

My intention with these truffles is to deliver such powerful flavors and pleasing textures that one or two are a dessert in themselves—at the same time that I reduce the amount of sugar and butter, in some cases even eliminating them entirely. I have calibrated the ratio of sweetener to oil (or butter) so it melts slowly on the palate, which allows the interesting aromas, tastes, and textures in the coatings to come forward. Here are three great truffles and some suggestions for coatings. Use your imagination, because the coating possibilities are limitless.

OLIVE OIL TRUFFLES

MAKES 24 TRUFFLES • The combination of chocolate and olive oil has passed the test of centuries of pairing in Catalonia. I never thought of it until I went to Barcelona, where I became a devotee.

½ cup heavy cream

1 tablespoon plus 1 teaspoon local honey

7 ounces dark (70%) chocolate, finely chopped

1 tablespoon extra-virgin olive oil

1 In a medium saucepan, combine the cream and honey and bring to a boil over medium-high heat. Place the chocolate in a medium mixing bowl. Pour the hot cream over the chocolate and let sit for 20 seconds. Whisk the chocolate from the center, pulling the liquid in from the edges until all the cream is incorporated into the chocolate. Whisk until smooth and well incorporated.

2 Line a baking sheet with parchment. Whisk the oil into the chocolate mixture, pouring it in a thin stream, and whisk until smooth and well incorporated. Using a teaspoon, scoop small mounds of the chocolate onto the baking sheet. Refrigerate for 30 minutes. Roll the mounds of chocolate between the palms of your hands to form smooth balls. Return to the baking sheet and refrigerate for 30 minutes more. Roll the truffles in your coatings of choice. Refrigerate until ready to serve. These truffles can be stored in a rigid, tightly covered container in the refrigerator for up to 5 days.

truffle DUSTERS

Truffles want a coating. Coatings start off the truffle experience with a bit of flavor and texture that contrasts with the smoothness of the interior and keep your fingers from getting covered with melted chocolate. Over the course of my career, I have tried literally hundreds of coatings, from simple cocoa powder to the gamut of nuts, flours, and other powders. Here are some of my favorites.

- Organic dried rose petals
- Cacao nibs
- Cornflowers
- Bee pollen
- Raspberry fruit powder

- Blackberry fruit powder
- Chopped pumpkin seeds
- Popped quinoa
- Dried coconut flakes

HONEY TRUFFLES

MAKES 24 TRUFFLES • I find that honey—for reasons known only to Mother Nature—broadens the flavor of chocolate more harmoniously than simple cane sugar, which is sweet and little else.

½ cup heavy cream

3 tablespoons local honey

7 ounces dark (70%) chocolate, finely chopped

Coating or coatings of your choice (see Truffle Dusters, page 205)

1 | In a medium saucepan, combine the cream and honey and bring to a boil over medium-high heat. Place the chocolate in a medium mixing bowl. Pour the hot cream over the chocolate and let sit for 20 seconds. Whisk the chocolate from the center, pulling the liquid in from the edges until all the cream is incorporated into the chocolate. Whisk until smooth and well combined.

2 | Line a baking sheet with parchment. Using a teaspoon, scoop small mounds of the chocolate onto the baking sheet. Refrigerate for 30 minutes. Roll the mounds of chocolate between the palms of your hands to form smooth balls. Return to the baking sheet and refrigerate for 30 minutes more.

3 | Roll the truffles in your coatings of choice. Refrigerate until ready to serve. The finished truffles can be stored in a rigid, tightly covered container for up to 5 days.

EARL GREY TRUFFLES

MAKES 24 TRUFFLES • Infusing chocolate with Earl Grey tea imparts a delicate smokiness that pairs well with the roasted flavor of cacao nibs.

¾ cup heavy cream

1 Earl Grey tea bag

¼ cup agave syrup

13 ounces dark (70%) chocolate, finely chopped

3 tablespoons unsalted high-fat European-style butter, at room temperature

Coating or coatings of your choice (see Truffle Dusters, page 205)

1 | In a small saucepan, bring the cream to a boil over medium-high heat. Add the tea bag. Turn off the heat, cover, and let steep for 5 minutes. Strain the cream and discard the tea bag. Return the cream to the saucepan, add the agave, and return to a boil over medium-high heat. Place the chocolate in a medium mixing bowl. Pour the hot cream over the chocolate and whisk from the center outward, forming an emulsion. Continue pulling the cream from the edges of the bowl with the whisk, bringing it toward the center until thoroughly incorporated. Set aside and cool to room temperature.

2 | Line a baking sheet with parchment. Add the butter to the chocolate mixture and whisk it until smooth and well incorporated. Using a teaspoon, scoop small mounds of the chocolate onto the baking sheet. Refrigerate for 30 minutes. Roll the mounds of chocolate between the palms of your hands to form smooth balls. Return to the baking sheet and refrigerate for 30 minutes more.

3 | Roll the truffles in your desired coating. Refrigerate until ready to serve. These truffles can be stored in the refrigerator, in a rigid, tightly covered container, for up to 5 days.

HEALTH BAR COHIBAS

MAKES 4 TO 6 BARS, DEPENDING ON THICKNESS • With apologies to Sigmund Freud, sometimes a cigar is not just a cigar. Case in point: these bad boys. They are my version of those health bars that cost ten times more than a Milky Way but which push the same flavor buttons. I think you will find these far more sophisticated but no less healthful. One day, I noticed some rice paper lying around my kitchen in Queens and I decided to wrap the bars in the rice paper—a natural product, just like the supple tobacco leaf that wraps Cuban cigars, which were originally reserved for Fidel's private stash. Added benefit: After eating one of my cohibas your significant other won't shy away from a kiss because you have serious cigar breath!

¼ cup whole roasted almonds

¼ cup dried cherries

¼ cup pistachios, lightly toasted

Grated zest and juice of 1 orange

1 tablespoon chia seeds

2 tablespoons walnut oil

1 tablespoon unbleached all-purpose flour

1 tablespoon local honey

Two 8½ × 11-inch rice paper sheets

4 ounces dark (70%) chocolate, melted

1 tablespoon unsweetened cocoa powder

2 tablespoons buckwheat flour, purchased or home-milled

1 | Place the almonds, cherries, pistachios, orange zest and juice, chia seeds, and oil in the bowl of a food processor and pulse to create a chunky paste. Scrape down the sides and pulse again until the texture is uniform.

2 | Dust a clean work surface with the all-purpose flour and turn the mixture out onto it. Shape the dough into a cylinder with a 2-inch diameter.

3 | Place the fruit paste cylinder on the work surface and, using your palm with fingers extended and applying gentle pressure, roll it into an even slimmer cylinder. Tear off a 12-inch piece of plastic wrap and place it on the work surface. Set the cylinder on the plastic wrap and roll it in the plastic wrap, using the wrap to keep the cigar rounded as you roll it to about a ¼-inch diameter. Using scissors, cut the fruit paste into 4 pieces, each about 4 inches long. Remove the plastic wrap.

4 | Cut each piece of rice paper into a 3 × 5-inch rectangle. With a long side facing you, place a fruit paste cylinder on a piece of rice paper, about ½ inch from the long side facing you. Use a pastry brush to moisten the opposite long side with water. Bring the paper up over the fruit paste to cover it entirely, rolling it as tightly as possible, then continue to roll and press along the moistened edge of the paper to seal. If necessary, brush again with a little water. Repeat with the remaining rice paper and fruit paste cylinders.

(RECIPE CONTINUES)

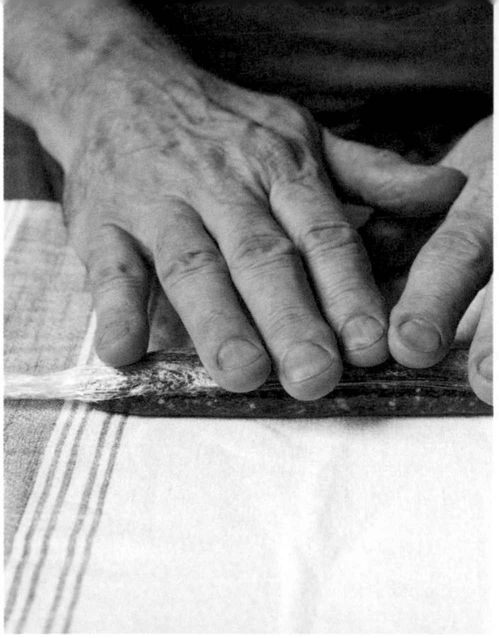
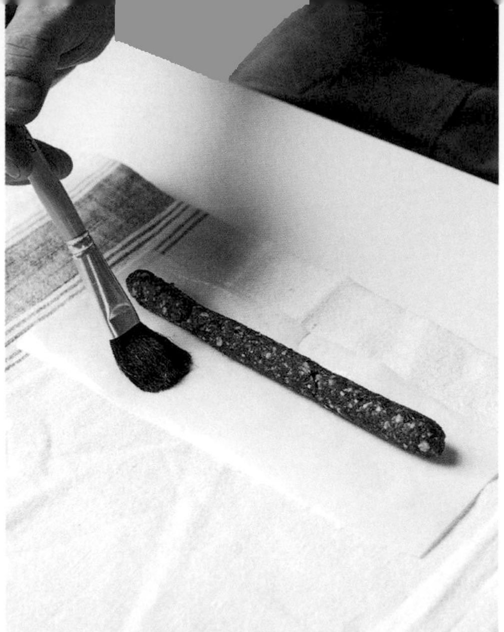
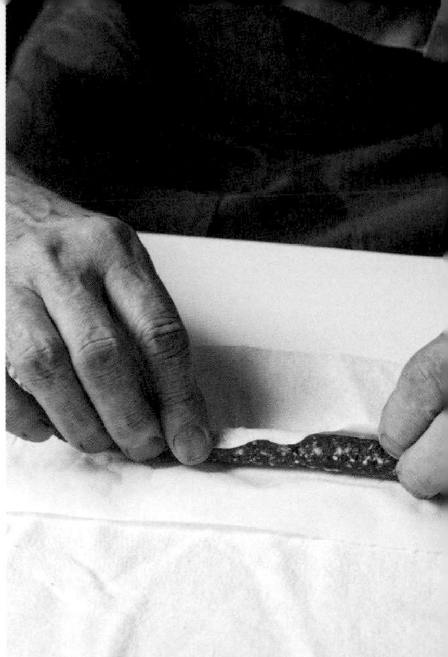
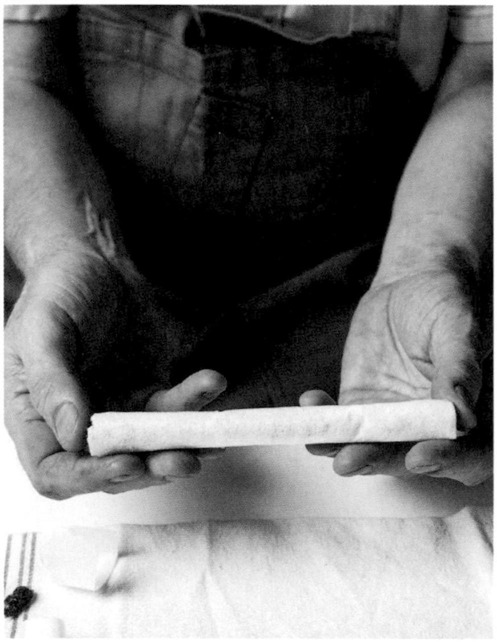
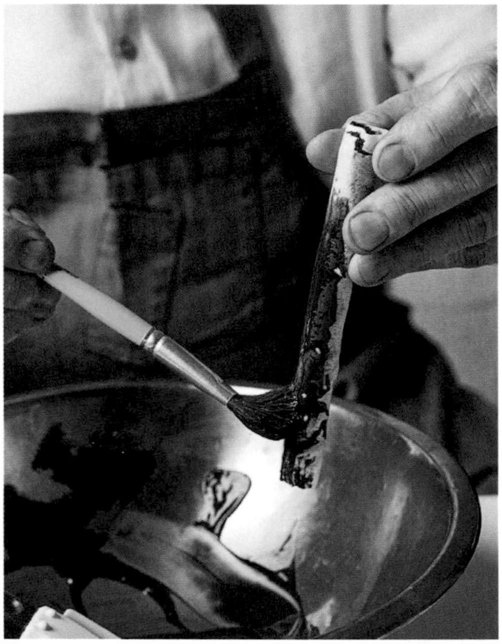
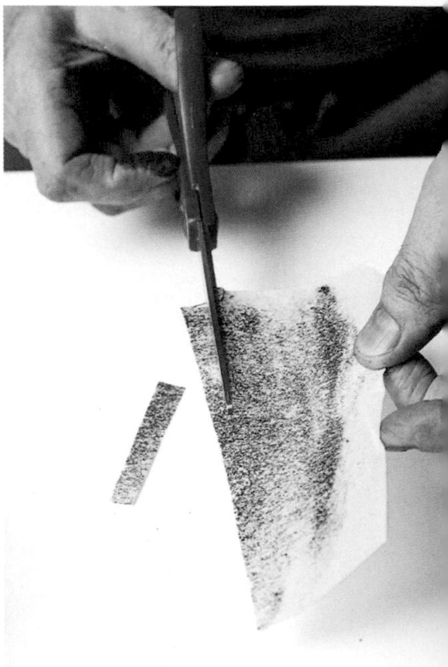
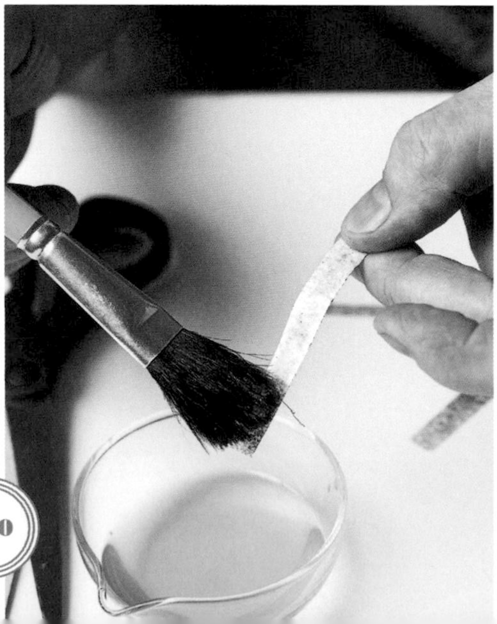
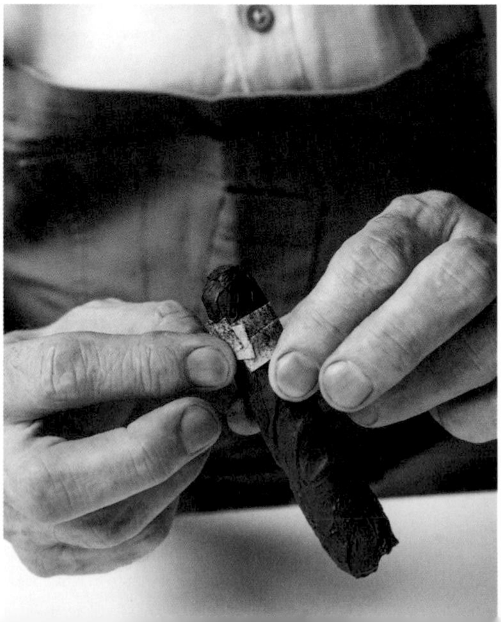
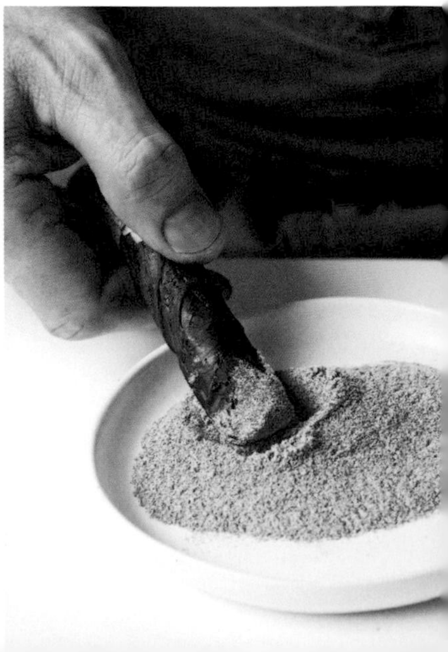

5 | Working with one cigar at a time, hold the cigar vertically over the bowl of melted chocolate and use a clean pastry brush to "paint" the chocolate onto it, working in vertical strokes and allowing the excess chocolate to drip back into the bowl. Set the cigar on the parchment-lined tray. Let dry for about 30 minutes.

6 | **Make the cigar band.** Cut thin strips of the rice paper into 3 × ½-inch rectangles. Using your thumb, rub some cocoa powder into the strip, pressing firmly so that it sticks. Place the band cocoa side down and set the cigar on top, about 1 inch from one end of the cigar. Carefully brush the band with water and roll it around the cigar. Roll the opposite end of the cigar in the buckwheat flour (to simulate ashes) and shake off the excess. Serve in a shallow soup bowl or other ashtray-like dish with a glass of good port. The cigars will keep in the refrigerator, tightly covered in a rigid container, for up to 10 days.

note

There are vast discrepancies between chocolates, even between different chocolates at different times of year. If your melted chocolate is too thick to use as a paint, add a tiny amount of neutral oil; it will be more fluid yet still shiny. Grapeseed or canola oil will not detract from the flavor of the chocolate. Two teaspoons of oil is enough for 8 ounces of melted chocolate, and will not prevent the chocolate from setting.

note Agar does not
absorb water easily in
acidic liquids, so the first
bit of water in the recipe is
what you use to boil the agar.
Once it is activated in that
water, almost any fruit or fruit
juice or puree can be added and
cooked to blend thoroughly.
Pick your favorite. Don't use
olive oil, which will solidify.
Peanut, canola, grapeseed,
and safflower all remain
liquid when cold and
you want cold.

FIZZICALS:
Concord Grape Pearls for Champagne

MAKES ABOUT ½ CUP OF PEARLS • This is straight out of the molecular cuisine playbook. Fruit juice, agar, and locust bean gum become perfectly shaped spheres the size of pearls, each packed with an explosion of fruit flavor. Use them as decoration, in place of a sauce or alongside a slice of cake. Like the olive in a martini, these pearls in a glass of champagne are a delicious extra in the form of a tangy kick at the end. This recipe is good for both sweet and savory pearls. You can replace the grape juice with the juices of raspberry, blackberry, mango, or orange. It can be used with alcohol, for example, gin pearls for a gin and tonic. As Borat, everyone's favorite fake Kazakh, might have said when tasting our pearls, "SEXY TIME!"

¾ teaspoon agar powder

¾ cup concentrated Concord grape juice or other fruit juice concentrate

¼ teaspoon locust bean gum (available at Whole Foods or online)

2 cups canola oil, chilled

1 | In a medium saucepan, bring ½ cup water to a boil over medium-high heat. Meanwhile, place the agar in a paper cup. Once the water is boiling, gently tap the cup to sprinkle the agar onto the surface of the water, as if you were feeding fish. Return to a boil and whisk in the grape juice.

2 | Whisk in the locust bean gum, whisking continuously. Boil for 2 minutes to allow the agar to slowly dissolve. Remove from the heat and pour the liquid into a spouted vessel. Do not let the mixture cool too much; it will set at room temperature. Do not agitate or stir or it will weaken the gel.

3 | Pour the cold oil into a transparent plastic container; the gel will stick to metal or glass. Pour half the mixture into a paper cup and pinch the rim of the cup to form a sharp spout (this is essential for controlling the size of the droplets).

4 | Carefully hold the cup over the cold oil and tilt it so that droplets fall into the oil. Uniformly sized droplets give a better result. Allow the droplets to gel for 3 minutes.

5 | Remove the pearls from the oil to a paper towel–lined plate. I use a spherification spoon (see page 24), but if you are very dexterous and patient, you can use a soup spoon. Transfer the pearls to a rigid container and refrigerate until ready to use. The pearls will keep in the refrigerator for 3 to 5 days.

FRUITY FINISHES

Applepalooza and Beyond

*i*f you asked me what my favorite ingredient is, I'd say chocolate without a second thought. But when I reflect a little more, fruit beats chocolate by a country mile. It would take a lifetime to master the possibilities of the hundreds of fruits that humans consume. I have always used fruits extensively, Nature's true gift to sweetness.

Fruits were the original dessert—no cooking necessary. The truly astonishing thing about fruit is how many varieties there are of our favorites, each with their own flavor, texture, and cookability. Eve gave Adam an apple, but sadly, the book of Genesis neglects to tell us what variety. Was it a Mac? A Granny Smith? There are many kinds of apples. Ditto oranges, grapes, strawberries, and pears, and every one of them can work beautifully in a well-crafted recipe.

Cornmeal-Crusted Fried Apples • Cranberry-Orange Sautéed Apples

Pan-Roasted Apples and Figs with Balsamic Vinegar and Rosemary

Baked Apples with Blue Cheese and Hazelnuts • Lemon-Poppy Apple Hash

Spiced Roasted Apples • Cherry and Flower Petal Granita

Floating Islands in Watermelon Coulis • Greenita • Poached Whole Pineapple

PB's and J (Poached Bartletts, Blue Cheese & Jasmine Tea) • Autumn Fruit Packet

Cranberry-Orange
Sautéed Apples,
page 218

Cornmeal-
Crusted
Fried Apples,
opposite

Lemon-Poppy
Apple Hash,
page 219

Pan-Roasted
Apples and Figs,
page 218

Baked Apples
with Blue Cheese
and Hazelnuts,
page 219

Spiced
Roasted
Apples,
page 220

APPLES, EVERY WHICH WAY

As First Lady, one of Mrs. Obama's signature efforts was a mentorship program that she started quite early in the administration. As the mother of young children, no one had to sell her on the importance of exposing kids to interesting experiences and believing that something would light a spark in them. Two or three times a year a group of students, mostly tweens and young teens from the area, would come to the White House, where they would meet with artists, scientists, entertainers, and so on. One of those sessions was devoted to healthy eating and exercising. With *healthy* as the key word there, she wasn't about to have me serve gooey cupcakes and roasted marshmallows. I chose to show-case apples. Pretty soon variations on the apple theme worked their way into the dessert rotation for receptions and special events.

For most baking applications I recommend Fuji, Golden Delicious, and Granny Smith apples. They hold their shape when cooked, while a Mac or a Macoun will fall apart.

Cornmeal-Crusted Fried Apples

SERVES 8 • The late, great Edna Lewis used to make an old-time apple fritter at the venerable Gage and Tollner, now sadly gone from Brooklyn. This is my modernized take. Cayenne gives it a slight kick, and with the optional jicama, this will boldly go where no apple fritter has gone before.

2 cups canola or other neutral oil

2 cups buttermilk

1 cup unbleached all-purpose flour

1 cup cornmeal

¼ teaspoon cayenne

4 Honeycrisp apples, peeled, cored, and cut into ½-inch-thick rings

¾ cup walnut halves, toasted

Jicama Pickles (page 252)

1 | Pour 2 inches of oil into a straight-sided skillet and heat until it reads 350°F on a deep-fry thermometer.

2 | Pour the buttermilk into a medium bowl. In a separate, shallow bowl, whisk together the flour, cornmeal, and cayenne. Dip the apple rings in the buttermilk, then dredge in the cornmeal mixture. Gently slip the apples into the hot oil a few at a time, taking care not to overcrowd the pan, and fry until deep golden, about 5 minutes, turning once. Using a slotted spoon, transfer the apple rings to a paper towel–lined plate. Repeat with the remaining apple rings. Arrange on a dessert plate, sprinkle with the walnuts, and serve warm with a few pickles.

Cranberry-Orange Sautéed Apples

SERVES 8 • Mediterranean-style (olive oil and honey) takes a spin through Cape Cod (cranberries) and upstate New York (apples) for this easy dessert. Bitter sweetness from the cranberries, citrusy aroma from the orange zest, and texture and sweetness from the apples are pushed forward by semi-burnt honey. The olive oil ties it all together. (See photo, page 216.)

¼ cup extra-virgin olive oil

4 to 6 Golden Delicious apples, peeled, halved, and cored

1 cup fresh cranberries

⅓ cup local honey

1 tablespoon grated orange zest

In a large skillet, heat the oil over medium heat until hot. Add the apples and cranberries and reduce the heat to low. Cook, covered, for 10 minutes. Remove the cover, raise the heat to medium-high, and add the honey and orange zest. Bring to a boil. Arrange the apples cut side up on a dessert plate and spoon the honeyed cranberries over them.

Pan-Roasted Apples and Figs with Balsamic Vinegar and Rosemary

SERVES 8 • Pan roasting the apples pulls out their juices and heightens the custard-like texture of fresh figs. The sweet-and-sour vinegar brings out the flavor of peak ripeness in almost any fruit. I love the way that rosemary—normally reserved for savory dishes—adds an evergreen flourish. (See photo, page 216.)

1 tablespoon extra-virgin olive oil, plus more for the pan

4 Granny Smith apples, halved and cored

10 fresh figs, halved

¼ cup aged balsamic vinegar or tamarind drinking vinegar (see page 251)

1 tablespoon finely chopped fresh rosemary

½ cup plain full-fat Greek yogurt, for serving

1 | Slick a 9 × 13-inch skillet with olive oil.

2 | Place the apples and figs cut side down in the skillet over low heat. Drizzle with the olive oil and balsamic vinegar. Sauté until the apples resist slightly when a skewer is inserted into them, about 12 minutes. Turn the apples over, sprinkle with the rosemary, and cook until soft, 5 minutes more. Transfer to dessert plates, pour the pan juices over, and serve warm with a dollop of Greek yogurt.

Baked Apples with Blue Cheese and Hazelnuts

SERVES 8 • This makes the apple, which is normally a footnote to a cheese plate, the centerpiece. Baking the apples concentrates their natural sweetness, so there is no need to add sugar. The meltiness of the cheese is very seductive, and the nuts deliver a pleasant punctuating crunch. (See photo, page 216.)

1 tablespoon hazelnut or grapeseed oil

4 Fuji apples, peeled, halved, and cored

3 ounces crumbled blue cheese

1 cup hazelnuts, lightly toasted and coarsely chopped

1 | In a large skillet, heat the oil over medium heat until hot. Arrange the apples cut side down in the skillet, reduce the heat to low, and cook until lightly browned, about 12 minutes.

2 | Preheat the oven to 350°F. In a small bowl, combine the blue cheese and ½ cup of the hazelnuts. Using a slotted spoon, transfer the apples from the skillet to a baking dish, arranging them cut side up. Spoon the cheese mixture onto the apples and bake until the cheese melts, about 12 minutes. Garnish with the remaining ½ cup of hazelnuts. Serve warm or at room temperature.

Lemon-Poppy Apple Hash

SERVES 6 • When apples are cut into small dice, the little cubes absorb flavor more readily in the same way that home-fried potatoes provide more surface area for crisping. Poppy seeds are normally used for pastry filling or a crunchy topping, but here they are more than just an "also." They have crunchy texture, slight bitterness, and flavor-boosting umami. Granny Smiths and Galas will hold their shape and soften but not melt. (See photo, page 216.)

6 Granny Smith or Gala apples, peeled, cored, and cut into ½-inch dice

2 tablespoons canola or grapeseed oil

1 tablespoon organic cane sugar

1 tablespoon poppy seeds

Grated zest of 1 lemon

2 tablespoons apple cider vinegar

1 | Preheat the oven to 375°F.

2 | In a large bowl, combine the apples and the oil and toss to coat. Spread the apples on a rimmed baking sheet and roast for 10 minutes. Meanwhile, mix together the sugar, poppy seeds, and lemon zest in a small bowl. Add the mixture to the pan and toss well with the apples to coat. Divide the mixture evenly among 6 ramekins, drizzle the vinegar over each, and return to the oven to bake until the apples are tender, 5 minutes more. Serve warm or at room temperature.

Spiced Roasted Apples

SERVES 4 • Firm-fleshed Mutsu apples soften enough during baking to be easily scoopable. Their spongy texture is perfect for absorbing other flavors—in this case, North African spices. The fruits, nuts, and optional flower petals would not be out of place in a Bedouin tent. (See photo, page 216.)

FOR THE APPLES

4 Mutsu apples, peeled and stemmed

2 tablespoons extra-virgin olive oil

1 tablespoon peeled, minced fresh ginger

1 teaspoon ground cumin

½ teaspoon ground coriander

½ teaspoon ground cinnamon

FOR THE FILLING

½ cup fromage blanc

½ cup chopped dried dates

1 tablespoon lightly toasted, chopped pistachios

1 tablespoon pomegranate molasses

2 tablespoons fresh pomegranate seeds, for garnish

2 tablespoons organic dried rose petals, for garnish (optional)

1 | Preheat the oven to 350°F.

2 | **Prepare the apples.** Use a melon baller to scoop the seeds from the apples, working from the stem end. Slightly trim the bottom of each apple so that it stands upright.

3 | Combine the apples and the olive oil in a large bowl and toss to coat. Arrange the apples on a rimmed baking sheet and roast until softened, about 10 minutes.

4 | Whisk together the ginger, cumin, coriander, and cinnamon. Remove the apples from the oven, sprinkle with the spice mixture, and toss to coat evenly. Return the apples to the oven and roast for 10 minutes more, or until the apples are tender.

5 | **Make the filling.** In a mixing bowl, combine the fromage blanc, dates, pistachios, and pomegranate molasses and stir with a wooden spoon to make a thick paste. Divide the paste evenly among the apples, placing a spoonful in the center of each. Garnish with the pomegranate seeds and rose petals, if using, and serve warm.

CHERRY AND FLOWER PETAL GRANITA

MAKES 2½ CUPS • A most elegant fruit and flower extravaganza. Marrying them in this recipe makes for a divine palate freshener. Serve along with Black Sesame Parfait with Red Fruits (page 146).

2 cups distilled or mineral water

2 cups fresh Bing cherries, pitted (see page 141 for pitting technique)

1 cup fresh blackberries

¼ cup organic cane sugar

3 tablespoons organic dried rose petals

1 | In a medium saucepan, bring the water to a boil over high heat. Add the cherries, blackberries, and sugar, then reduce the heat to medium and bring to a simmer. Continue to simmer for 5 minutes more. Remove from the heat and set aside to steep for 10 minutes.

2 | Transfer the fruit to a blender and blend until liquefied (be careful—the liquid is still hot). Strain the mixture through a fine-mesh sieve, pressing lightly with a spoon to extract as much flavor from the solids as possible. Discard the solids. Pour the mixture into a rigid, freezer-safe container and scatter the rose petals over it. Cover and freeze until partially frozen, about 1 hour, then scrape the mixture with a fork to create flaked ice. Use the fork to crush any lumps. Freeze for 1 hour more, scraping periodically with a fork after 30 minutes and 1 hour. The granita will keep in the freezer for up to 3 weeks.

FLOATING ISLANDS in Watermelon Coulis

SERVES 6 • Classical floating islands is one of the most visually enticing desserts: a dollop of sugary meringue set adrift in a Great Lake of cholesterol. My reimagined version is a low-sugar, yogurt-enriched meringue bobbing in a velvety watermelon coulis. I've graced it with every summer fruit that was in my fridge, and any that you have on hand will do nicely.

When you are dialing back sugar in a meringue recipe you need to replace it with something that the egg whites can cling to. In this case I've used yogurt powder.

FOR THE MERINGUE

2 tablespoons yogurt powder
  (or nonfat dried milk powder)

½ cup organic cane sugar

6 large egg whites

Pinch of kosher salt

½ cup almonds, roasted and
  chopped

½ cup dried tart cherries

FOR THE WATERMELON COULIS

2 cups pureed watermelon

1 teaspoon xanthan gum

2½-inch-thick slices golden
  watermelon, rind removed and
  cut into chunks

1 cup fresh strawberries, hulled
  and halved

½ cup fresh blackberries, halved

Grated zest of 1 lime, for garnish

6 lemon verbena leaves, for garnish

1 | Preheat the oven to 300°F.

2 | Coat six 4½-ounce ramekins with vegetable oil cooking spray.

3 | **Make the meringue.** In a small bowl, whisk together the yogurt powder and 1 teaspoon of the sugar and set aside. In the bowl of a standing mixer fitted with the whisk attachment, whisk the egg whites and salt on medium-high speed for 3 minutes. Add the remaining sugar and continue to whisk until stiff peaks form, about 5 minutes more. Add the yogurt powder mixture, raise the speed to high, and whisk for 2 minutes.

4 | Transfer the whites to a pastry bag fitted with a large star tip and pipe the meringue into the individual ramekins in a tight spiral, like soft-serve ice cream. Sprinkle the meringues with the nuts and cherries.

5 | Set the ramekins in a baking dish and slide into the oven. Pour enough water into the dish to reach halfway up the sides of the ramekins. Bake until the meringues are golden on top, 25 to 30 minutes. Remove the dish from the oven and remove the ramekins from the water bath. Let cool for 10 minutes.

6 | **Make the watermelon coulis.** Place the watermelon in a deep medium bowl. Sprinkle the xanthan gum over the watermelon, as if you were feeding fish. Using an immersion blender, blend for 2 to 3 minutes to ensure the xanthan gum is hydrated. Divide the coulis among six rimmed dessert plates.

7 | Using a wet paring knife, separate the meringues from the ramekins, then use a fork to coax them onto the dessert plates. Divide among the plates and sprinkle with the lime zest. Use scissors to snip a bit of lemon verbena onto each.

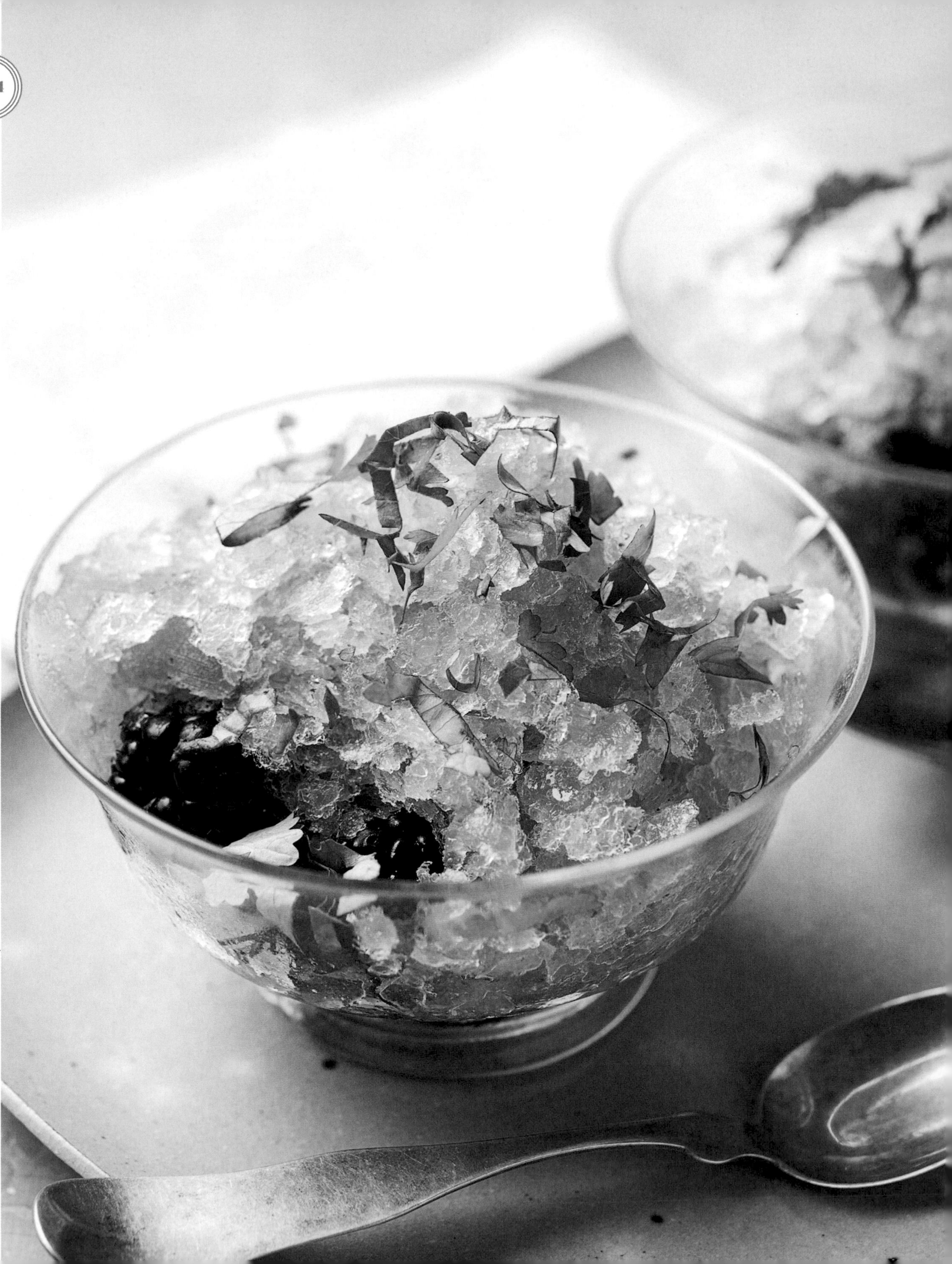

GREENITA

MAKES 1 QUART • We need more green in our lives. When you consider the cucumber and fresh cilantro called for in this recipe, you would be forgiven if you thought a salad had found its way into a dessert book. In fact, this green granita is wonderful as a palate-cleansing intermezzo or as a topping on our Very Fresh Green Cake (page 130). It is brimming with antioxidants and is bracingly green, always a cheering color.

2 teaspoons kosher salt

1 handful tightly packed cilantro leaves and stems

1 handful tightly packed watercress leaves and soft stems (tough stems discarded)

1 mixed cup lemon verbena, sage, and tarragon (optional)

1 green apple, peeled, cored, and diced

1 large cucumber, peeled, seeded, and coarsely chopped

1 tablespoon local honey

1 | Fill a large bowl with ice and water. Place a shallow 2-quart container in the freezer. In a large saucepan, combine 1½ quarts of water with the salt and bring to a boil. Plunge the herbs in the boiling water for 20 seconds. Use tongs to transfer to the ice water to stop the cooking.

2 | Combine 1 cup of water with the apple, cucumber, the blanched herbs, and the honey in a high-powered blender and puree. Let the blender run for 30 seconds. Pour the mixture through a fine-mesh sieve, using a wooden spoon to push the liquid through. Discard the solids.

3 | Pour the liquid into the chilled container and freeze for 1 hour or until it is slightly hardened. Vigorously drag a fork across the frozen liquid to create shavings. Return to the freezer. Just before serving, scrape down again. To serve, scoop into chilled dessert bowls. The greenita will keep in the freezer, tightly covered, for up to 10 days.

POACHED WHOLE PINEAPPLE

SERVES 6 TO 8 • I was trying to think of the dessert equivalent of a Thanksgiving turkey or a standing rib roast, something that makes for an unusual and dramatic presentation at the table, where it gets carved and served. A pineapple has the size and appearance to make such a bold statement. I've poached it in liquid that is boldly spiced and the resulting broth is a riot of aroma. It infuses the pineapple and turns it a color that I call Lamborghini Yellow in honor of the world's sexiest car. To serve, I place it on equally bright mango slices and flaming-red goji berries.

½ cup local honey

1 cup dried jasmine flowers

1 star anise

1 stalk lemongrass, finely chopped

2 tablespoons Szechuan
  peppercorns, crushed

1 tablespoon ground turmeric

1 tablespoon ground ginger

Pinch of saffron

1 pineapple

1 mango, peeled, pitted, and cut into
  eighths, for garnish

½ cup dried goji berries, for garnish

Zest of 1 lime, for garnish

1 | Preheat the oven to 350°F. Adjust the racks in your oven to accommodate a stockpot.

2 | Prepare the poaching liquid. Combine 4 quarts water with the honey, dried jasmine, star anise, lemongrass, peppercorns, turmeric, ginger, and saffron in an oven-safe stockpot and bring to a boil over medium-high heat.

3 | Meanwhile, on a clean work surface, trim the top and bottom away from the pineapple. Set it upright on the work surface and trim away the skin and eyes. Set the pineapple in the poaching liquid vertically so that it is completely covered by the poaching liquid. To keep the pineapple submerged, place a circle of parchment directly on the surface of the liquid (see page 125). Place the pot in the oven and bake for 1 hour, adding more water periodically if necessary to keep the pineapple covered. Remove the pot from the oven and set aside to cool in the liquid for 2 hours.

4 | Remove the pineapple from the liquid by plunging a meat fork into the core, then transfer it to a rimmed serving platter. Bring the pot of liquid to a gentle simmer and continue to cook until it is reduced by half. Drizzle the poaching liquid onto the pineapple until it fills the platter. Garnish with the mango slices, goji berries, and lime zest. Slice vertically into wedges and serve with some of the sauce.

PICK YOUR PEARS
purposefully

My favorite pear for poaching is the full-flavored Bartlett, though Comice and Bosc work as well. Always choose pears that are a little hard so that they don't turn mushy. And please note, poaching means a gentle simmer. Don't walk away from the pot with your pears boiling away.

PB'S AND J (Poached Bartletts, Blue Cheese & Jasmine Tea)

MAKES 6 • Pears get a colorful flavor boost from a filling of chopped hazelnuts and blue cheese and the combination of blackberries plus jasmine and hibiscus teas in the poaching liquid. The broad flavors of the pear and cheese are counterbalanced by the tannins in the teas. This is a complete and pretty dessert. If you are going all-out to impress your guests, pair it with our Hazelnut Mocha Loaf (page 117).

FOR THE PEARS

6 Bartlett, Comice, or Bosc pears, not too ripe

1 pint fresh blackberries

3 hibiscus tea bags

1 jasmine tea bag

2 tablespoons local honey

1 cardamom pod, crushed

FOR THE FILLING

2 ounces blue cheese, crumbled, plus a 4-ounce wedge for serving

3 tablespoons quinoa flour, purchased or home-milled

½ cup plain full-fat Greek yogurt

¼ cup hazelnuts, lightly toasted and chopped

1 | **Prepare the pears.** Using a paring knife or vegetable peeler, peel the pears, leaving the stems intact. Slice away the bottom so that the pears stand upright. Using a melon baller, remove the base stem, then hollow out the pear from the bottom to create a cavity for the cheese.

2 | In a 4 quart-saucepan, combine 3 quarts water with the blackberries, hibiscus and jasmine tea bags, honey, and cardamom. Bring to a boil over medium-high heat. Reduce the heat to a simmer and set the pears in the liquid. Cut out a circle of parchment to fit the pan and place it directly on the liquid. Reduce the heat to low and simmer until the pears are soft but not mushy, about 30 minutes.

3 | Using a slotted spoon, transfer the pears to a plate. Strain the cooking liquid through a fine-mesh sieve and reserve for another use (it makes an excellent sangria—just add red wine and chopped oranges, limes, and strawberries).

4 | Preheat the oven to 350°F. Line a baking sheet with parchment paper.

5 | **Make the filling.** In a small bowl, combine the crumbled blue cheese, quinoa flour, yogurt, and hazelnuts and mix with a sturdy wooden spoon until thoroughly combined. Transfer the mixture to a pastry bag or a resealable plastic bag snipped in one corner.

6 | Pipe the cheese mixture into the cavity of each pear and set upright on the baking sheet. Bake for 20 minutes. The skin will start to blister and dry.

7 | To serve, place the pears on plates and accompany with the wedge of blue cheese.

AUTUMN FRUIT PACKET

SERVE 4 • Fall, when the first chill of autumn has me breaking out the hats and sweaters, is so well suited to this presentation. When you open this packet of fruits baked in Armagnac (or booze of your choice), an inebriating cloud of sweet, tantalizing perfume wafts over you. I've really cut back on the sugar we used when we made this at Bouley. As long as you have Concord grapes—with their beautifully colored juices—you don't absolutely need to include all these fruits, but take it from me, using them all is quite special. I like to serve this over a slice of tea cake.

1 quince, peeled, cored, and cut into sixths

1 persimmon, peeled, pit removed, and cut into sixths

Handful of Concord grapes

1 Pink Lady or Honeycrisp apple, peeled, cored, and halved, or 3 lady apples, peeled, cored, and halved

1 pear, peeled, cored, and halved or 3 Seckel pears, stems on, peeled, cored, and halved

2 plums, halved, pitted, and cut into eighths

3 tablespoons pomegranate seeds

1 fresh vanilla bean, split lengthwise and seeds scraped out

2 teaspoons organic cane sugar

2 tablespoons Armagnac, rum, or bourbon

1 thumb-size piece fresh ginger, peeled and very thinly sliced

1 | In a small saucepan, bring 2 cups of water to a boil over medium-high heat. Add the quince and simmer until soft, about 15 minutes. It will turn pinkish yellow. Remove with a slotted spoon.

2 | Preheat the oven to 400°F. Line a pie plate with two 14-inch-long pieces of Carta Fata cooking paper (see below) or foil and turn up the edges to form a cradle. Arrange the quince, persimmon, grapes, apple, pear, plums, and pomegranate seeds on top. Spread the vanilla seeds on the fruit, then sprinkle them with the sugar and Armagnac. Scatter the ginger slices all over.

3 | Gather the paper together in your fist and tie with butcher's twine to make a tight packet. If using foil, bring the edges together and fold. Bake until the fruits are just softened, about 15 minutes. To serve, bring the dish to the table and open in front of guests. Spoon onto dessert plates, making sure to drizzle each serving with some of the juices.

note | Carta Fata cooking paper is a transparent "parchment." It's especially useful for this recipe as it allows you to visually monitor the fruits as they cook.

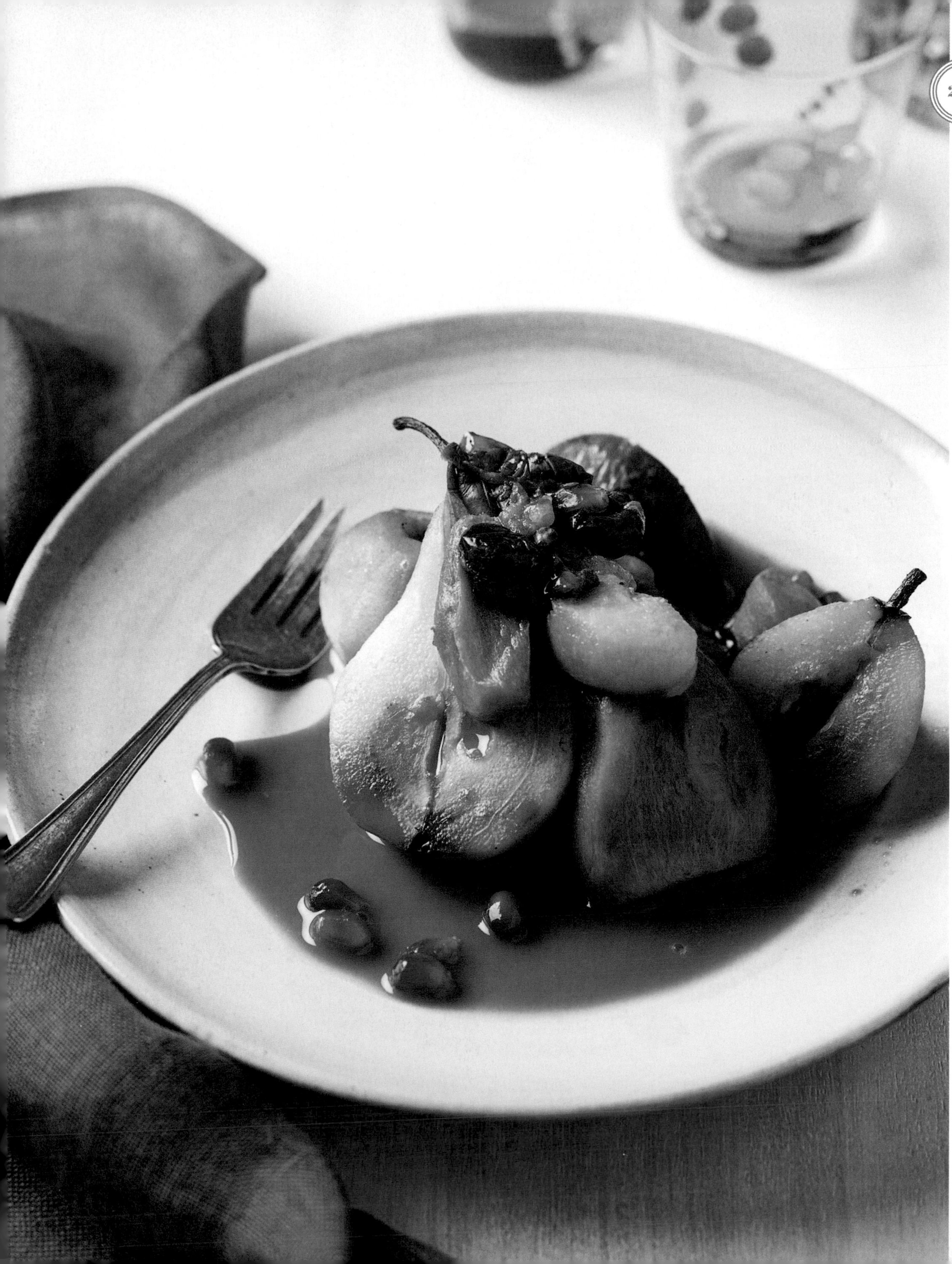

TOPPINGS, FROSTINGS, FILLINGS & GARNISHES

ith their quirky diversity, these often simple recipes lend desserts additional flair and personality. Think of a tuxedo without a smart bow tie, or Janis Joplin without a feather boa. Something would be missing . . . right? These recipes give the desserts in this book much of their attitude and swagger. Their flavors are so focused, clean, and concentrated that you don't miss a surfeit of sugar or fat generally present in sweet embellishments and toppings. And that's a cherry on the sundae you can really love.

Clementine Coconut Mango Compote • Plum Compote • Kumquat Compote

Cherry Compote • Raspberry–Black Pepper Compote

Mango Lime Chutney with Goji Berries • Blackberry Chia Sauce • Cherry Licorice Sauce

Blackberry Whipped Cream • Maple Whipped Cream • Whipped Coconut Cream

Hazelnut, Maple & Coffee Whipped Cream • Elderflower Cream

Cashew Cream • Maiz Morado Cream • Almond Milk • Miracle Ganache Frosting

Like Mineral Water for Chocolate Ganache • Quick and Easy Shiny Chocolate Glaze

Airy Chocolate Foam • Yuzu Curd • Fat and Happy Raisins

Tamarind Vinegar • Jicama Pickles • Pickled Lychees

Clementine Coconut Mango Compote

MAKES ABOUT 3 CUPS • When there's snow on the ground and not a leaf on the trees, what's a fruit fancier to do? All the fruits in this recipe are available even when bone-rattling cold air blows off the East River and straight down my street. Yeah, I know, they're not local, but they are in season somewhere and we do live in an age when transportation and refrigeration can bring great fruits to the market. So rather than be a doctrinaire locavore, I cut myself a little slack. Also, looks count here—the colors go so well together.

4 clementines

1 heaping tablespoon local honey

3 ripe mangoes, peeled, pitted, and cut into confetti-size pieces

6 ounces (1 can) unsweetened coconut cream or coconut milk

1 | Trim the top and bottom of the clementines and stand upright on a work surface. Using a sharp knife, trim away the skin and all the pith, working vertically around the fruit. Slice the clementines crosswise into ¼-inch-thick disks, then cut those into half-moons. Cut the skins into ⅛-inch-wide pieces about 1 inch in length.

2 | Bring a medium pot of water to a simmer. Add the strips of clementine peel to the pot and bring the water to a rolling boil. Drain and repeat the process two more times, refilling the pot with fresh water each time. Drain the pot one last time and refill it with 4 cups of water. Place the peels back in the pot and add the honey. Bring to a boil. Reduce the heat and cook until the liquid has reduced by two thirds. Using a slotted spoon, transfer the peels to a plate and continue to reduce the liquid to about ¼ cup syrup.

3 | Add the clementines and mangoes to the syrup and bring to a boil over medium heat. Add the coconut cream and return to a boil, then reduce the heat to medium, and simmer for 10 minutes. Let cool before serving. The compote will keep in the refrigerator, tightly covered, for up to 7 days.

Plum Compote

MAKES 2 CUPS • When you cook plums you coax out color, flavor, and texture as they melt in the pan. This is true even when it's not that one week each summer when they are at their best. I use star anise to accentuate sweetness and sage to impart a fresh top note. If you can find the herb known as pineapple sage, it is really the way to go, but common sage will do.

2 tablespoons local honey

1 whole star anise

6 fresh plums (whatever type is in season), halved, pitted, and each half quartered

4 large fresh sage leaves, preferably pineapple sage, coarsely chopped

In a large saucepan, bring 1 cup water, the honey, and star anise to a boil. Reduce the heat to low, add the plums to the boiling syrup, and cook until soft, about 3 minutes. Remove from the heat and cool to room temperature, then cover and chill in the refrigerator. Serve garnished with the sage. The compote will keep in the refrigerator, covered, for up to 5 days.

Kumquat Compote

MAKES ABOUT 3 CUPS • Bitter kumquats cut through sweetness, with their essential oils providing a citrusy lift. No need to remove the ginger after cooking; it will soften and become sweet in this very concentrated flavor mash-up.

24 kumquats, washed, stems removed, and halved

3 penny-size slices peeled fresh ginger

Zest and juice of 2 oranges

2 tablespoons local honey

In a medium saucepan, combine the kumquats, ginger, orange zest and juice, and honey with 3 cups water and bring to a boil over medium-high heat, stirring occasionally. Reduce the heat to medium-low and simmer until the fruit is softened, about 30 minutes. Serve warm. The compote will keep in the refrigerator, tightly covered, for up to 5 days.

Cherry Compote

MAKES 3 CUPS • Cherries have a long season. This recipe is a way to take advantage of their bounty and store them for winter. Almonds and cherries are part of the same genus—botanical kissin' cousins, in a manner of speaking—and a relationship I encourage here. If you are ever stumped on what to serve with a dessert, cherries and almonds are an infallible combo.

2 tablespoons local honey

1 pound mixed fresh or frozen Bing and sour cherries, pitted (see page 141 for pitting technique)

½ teaspoon almond extract, such as Nielsen-Massey

In a medium saucepan, bring 1 cup water and the honey to a boil over medium-high heat. Reduce the heat to medium-low, add the cherries to the boiling syrup, and cook until the cherries burst, about 10 minutes. Remove from the heat, cool to room temperature, then cover and chill in the refrigerator. The compote will keep in the refrigerator, covered, for up to 5 days.

Raspberry–Black Pepper Compote

MAKES ABOUT 1¼ CUPS • Instead of serving Farmers' Cheese Dumplings (page 169) with thick jam, as the Austrians do, I use fresh raspberries soaked in tamarind syrup.

2 cups fresh raspberries, halved

2 tablespoons tamarind syrup or well-aged balsamic vinegar

Fresh ground black pepper (about 4 twists of the pepper mill)

In a small saucepan, combine the raspberries with ½ cup of water over medium heat and cook until the berries just begin to release their juices. Remove from the heat. Drizzle in the tamarind syrup and season with the pepper. Serve warm. The compote will keep in the refrigerator, tightly covered, for 5 to 7 days.

Mango Lime Chutney with Goji Berries

MAKES ABOUT 4 CUPS • Chutneys, by definition, are spicy and kind of sour—a perfect complement to a lamb shank or short rib. Sometimes, desserts want a similar wake-up call by way of a strong counterpoint. I am a big believer in limes for that purpose, and they pair well with all tropical fruit. Gojis, often touted as a superfood, are high in vitamins, protein, and antioxidants. Because of their concentrated sweet-and-sour taste, gojis lend this chutney complexity and a pleasing texture.

Serve with any panna cotta or pudding. Nut cakes, with their subtle flavors, come alive with a bright chutney, too.

1 cup mirin or rice wine vinegar

5 whole cardamom pods

1 Kaffir lime leaf

2 tablespoons organic cane sugar

2 teaspoons kosher salt

1 jasmine tea bag

Grated zest and juice of 1 lime

1 mango, peeled and cut into dime-size cubes

¼ cup goji berries

In a medium saucepan, combine the mirin, 1 cup water, the cardamom, lime leaf, sugar, salt, tea bag, lime zest and juice and bring to a boil over medium-high heat. Continue to boil until the liquid has reduced by half. Using a slotted spoon, remove the cardamom and the tea bag. Add the mango and goji berries and continue to simmer for 10 minutes on low heat, until the chutney has thickened.

sterilizing

There are several ways to preserve food, the most common being salting, fermenting, drying, smoking, and canning (my preferred method). These methods are used to retard the growth of bacteria.

To can the chutney, bring a pot filled with water and large enough to clear the height of a 16-ounce jar to a boil. Use tongs to submerge two 16-ounce mason jars, filling them with hot water, 15 minutes. Turn off the heat and let the jars stand in the water until you are ready to fill them. Remove the jars with the tongs, pour out the water, and let the jars air-dry completely. Meanwhile, wash the lids and rubber rings in hot, soapy water and rinse thoroughly. Set aside to air-dry.

Divide the chutney between the jars and seal tightly with the lids. Wrap each securely on the bottom and sides with a kitchen towel. Place them in the pot and fill the pot with enough water to cover the jars by 1 inch. Bring the water to a boil over high heat, then reduce the heat to medium-high and boil for 45 minutes. Using the tongs, remove the jars from the water. The chutney will keep for up to 3 months. Once opened, store in the refrigerator for up to 2 weeks.

Blackberry Chia Sauce

MAKES 1 GENEROUS CUP • Blackberries often play second fiddle to raspberries but not in my orchestra. In season they have a natural balance between sweet and sour that lends dynamism to whatever you pair them with, and their strong character stands up to big flavors. Smushing the cooked blackberries through a sieve gets rid of the floss-defying seeds.

2 cups fresh blackberries, plus more for garnish

1 tablespoon organic cane sugar

2 tablespoons chia seeds

1 | In a medium saucepan, combine the blackberries and sugar with 1 cup of water and bring to a boil over medium-high heat. Transfer the blackberries to a fine-mesh sieve set over a bowl and strain, pressing the liquid from the mixture through the sieve with a spoon.

2 | Return the liquid to the saucepan and stir in the chia seeds. Bring to a boil over high heat and continue to boil for 1 minute. Remove from the heat and bring to room temperature. Transfer to a bowl and chill in the refrigerator for 4 hours or until the liquid thickens. The sauce will keep in the refrigerator, tightly covered, for up to 1 week.

Cherry Licorice Sauce

MAKES ABOUT 2 CUPS • In my childhood, I thought licorice was just those black jellies you found at the candy counter. It never crossed my mind that there was an actual botanical specimen known as licorice root. Then, while shopping in one of the Middle Eastern markets on Atlantic Avenue in Brooklyn, I discovered licorice root. As you will see here, it was born to mate with cherries.

Four 8-inch sticks licorice root, smashed decisively with a hammer or the bottom of a heavy pot, or 2 star anise

1 tablespoon local honey

2 cups fresh cherries, pitted (see page 141 for pitting technique)

1 | In a medium saucepan, combine the licorice and 1 cup of water and bring to a boil over medium-high heat. Continue to boil until the liquid reduces by half.

2 | Strain the liquid and return it to the pot. Add the honey and cherries and return to a boil. Continue to cook until the cherries soften and collapse but do not fall apart, about 5 minutes. Set aside to cool. Serve warm. The sauce will keep in the refrigerator, tightly covered, for 5 to 7 days.

Blackberry Whipped Cream

MAKES ABOUT 1¼ CUPS • In the search for less fatty fillings and frostings I discovered that dried fruit powder in whipped cream absorbs excess water and produces a stable result. It tastes like a lighter, more delicate "real frosting," with less fat per mouthful and less refined sugar. It's best when applied just before serving, though you can make it in advance; just give it a quick pass with a whisk to aerate it.

1 cup heavy cream

2 teaspoons confectioners' sugar

2 teaspoons blackberry powder

1 │ Place the bowl and whisk attachment of a standing mixer in the refrigerator for 10 minutes.

2 │ Combine the cream, sugar, and blackberry powder in the chilled bowl and mix on medium-high speed until soft peaks form. The cream will keep in the refrigerator, covered, for up to 2 days. It will separate; simply whisk before serving.

Maple Whipped Cream

MAKES 1 CUP • When Pierre Hermé, the pastry god of France, came to work with us at Bouley, his Gallic *sangfroid* evaporated when confronted with the quintessentially American taste of maple sugar. In this recipe, I use granulated maple sugar rather than syrup because the water in maple syrup will collapse the whipped cream. You can use this to top just about any pie or cake in this book.

½ cup heavy cream

2 teaspoons granulated maple sugar

1 │ Place the bowl and whisk attachment of a standing mixer in the refrigerator for 10 minutes.

2 │ Return the bowl and whisk to the mixer and pour the cream into the bowl. Whisk on medium-high speed until soft peaks form and the tines of the whisk begin to show in the cream. Add the sugar and whisk for 30 seconds more. Remove the bowl from the mixer, and using a hand whisk, finish whisking to stiff peaks. The whipped cream will keep in the refrigerator, tightly covered, overnight. Whisk before serving.

Whipped Coconut Cream

MAKES 1½ CUPS • A welcome substitute for dairy-based whipped cream that stays whipped and frothy for days. While coconut cream is high in saturated fat, studies have shown that the particular type of fat is more likely to be converted to energy rather than stored as a fatty deposit. If your coconut cream is rock hard, run it through a blender to break it up before whisking in a standing mixer.

8 ounces coconut cream,
   chilled but not solid

1 tablespoon confectioners' sugar

Place the bowl and whisk attachment of a standing mixer in the freezer for 15 minutes. Return the bowl and whisk to the mixer and combine the coconut cream and confectioners' sugar in the bowl. Mix on medium-high speed until the mixture is smooth and creamy and resembles whipped cream. Serve immediately. The cream will keep in the refrigerator, tightly covered, for up to 5 days.

Hazelnut, Maple & Coffee Whipped Cream

MAKES 1½ CUPS • The recent mania for flavored coffees served with a pile of whipped cream and syrup on top has passed me by. I think the idea of loading up on cream and sweetness is way more suited to a dollop on a dessert than my morning joe. This topping has the same pleasing flavor and texture of your favorite coffee splurge.

1 cup heavy cream

¼ cup hazelnuts, skins on, lightly
   toasted and finely chopped

1 teaspoon instant coffee crystals

1 tablespoon grade B maple syrup

1 | In a medium saucepan, combine the cream, hazelnuts, coffee, and syrup and bring to a boil over medium-high heat. Remove from the heat, cover, and let steep for 5 minutes.

2 | Pour the mixture through a strainer and refrigerate for 2 hours. Pour the chilled cream into the bowl of a standing mixer fitted with a whisk attachment and whisk until soft peaks form. Remove from the mixer and finish whisking to stiff peaks using a hand whisk. The cream can be made 2 hours in advance, covered tightly, and refrigerated until ready to use.

Elderflower Cream

MAKES 1¼ CUPS • The taste and aroma of elderflower is an intoxicating combination of honey, apricots, and jasmine. The Swiss are very fond of their elderflowers, and after a helping of this, you'll be yodeling like Heidi.

1 cup heavy cream

1 tablespoon confectioners' sugar

3 tablespoons elderflower syrup, such as Darbo (available in gourmet stores or online)

1 | Place the bowl and whisk attachment of a standing mixer in the refrigerator until thoroughly chilled, about 30 minutes.

2 | Return the bowl and whisk to the mixer, combine the cream and sugar in the bowl, and whisk on medium-high speed until soft peaks form. Remove the bowl from the mixer, and using a hand whisk, spoon ¼ cup of the whipped cream into a small bowl. Add the elderflower syrup and mix to incorporate. Pour the mixture back into the mixer bowl with the whipped cream and mix on medium-high speed to incorporate. The cream can be made 1 day in advance and kept tightly covered and refrigerated.

Cashew Cream

MAKES ABOUT 2 CUPS • This is a very full-flavored frosting and filling that calls for very little sugar. It owes its richness to the high percentage of healthy fat in cashews. We rely on aeration to pump up the volume and decrease the density of calories.

3 tablespoons cashew butter

2 cups heavy cream

1 tablespoon confectioners' sugar

1 | Place the mixing bowl and whisk attachment of a standing mixer in the refrigerator until thoroughly chilled, about 30 minutes.

2 | Return the bowl and whisk to the mixer, place the cashew butter and 3 tablespoons of the heavy cream in the bowl, whisk on medium speed until the mixture is loosened and smooth. Add the remaining cream and sugar and whisk until soft peaks form. The cream will keep in the refrigerator, covered, overnight. Whisk again before serving.

Maiz Morado Cream

MAKES 1¼ CUPS • Maiz morado lends a beautiful hue to this rich and complexly flavored cream. It's quite special for its deep flavor and bold fuchsia color, and worth seeking out. Use this cream with any nut or sesame cake.

2 cups heavy cream

1 tablespoon local honey

½ cup maiz morado kernels

2 drops food-grade bitter wild orange essential oil or grated zest of 1 clementine or tangerine

1 | Place the bowl and whisk attachment of a standing mixer in the refrigerator to chill.

2 | In a medium saucepan, combine the heavy cream, honey, and the corn kernels and bring to a boil over medium heat. Remove the saucepan from the heat, cover, and set aside to steep for 20 minutes. Strain the liquid through a fine-mesh sieve and allow to chill in the refrigerator for 2 hours.

3 | Return the bowl and whisk to the mixer, pour the liquid into the chilled bowl, and add the essential oil, if using. Beat the mixture on medium speed until soft peaks form. The cream will keep in the refrigerator, tightly covered, overnight. Re-whip if the liquid separates from the cream.

Almond Milk

MAKES ABOUT 3 CUPS • Commercial almond milk often has additives, and homemade tastes infinitely better. The pulverized nuts can be dried in the oven and added to oatmeal, smoothies, or cookie doughs.

1 cup raw almonds, skins on

4 cups filtered or mineral water

Pinch of sea salt

1 teaspoon apple cider vinegar

1 tablespoon grade B maple syrup (optional)

1 | In a small bowl, combine the almonds with 1 cup of the water and cover with plastic wrap, punching a little hole in the top. Refrigerate the nuts at least overnight or until plump, up to 24 hours. Drain the nuts and rinse well.

2 | Combine the nuts with the remaining 3 cups of water in a high-powered blender and pulverize for 3 minutes on high speed. Strain through a double layer of cheesecloth or a nut milk bag, twisting it to extract all the liquid. Stir in the salt, vinegar, and maple syrup, if using. The almond milk will keep in a covered container in the refrigerator for up to 3 days.

Miracle Ganache Frosting

MAKES 4 CUPS • In creating this frosting, my aim was to offer something as smooth and spreadable as the processed frostings you get out of a jar and come loaded with enough chemicals to start your own pharmacy. Admittedly there is a large proportion of cream and chocolate here, but by aeration you double the volume, decreasing the sweetener per bite. You'll love the way your spatula glides along as you spread it and how the frosting stays in place with each swirl.

2¾ cups heavy cream

5 ounces dark (70%) chocolate, chopped

1 | Place 1¾ cups of the cream in a container, cover, and chill in the refrigerator. Place the chocolate in a medium heatproof bowl. Bring the remaining 1 cup heavy cream to a boil in a small saucepan over medium-high heat. Pour the boiling cream over the chocolate and, using a whisk, stir from the center outward until the chocolate is thoroughly melted. Using an immersion blender, blend for 2 minutes more on high speed. Whisk the chilled heavy cream into the chocolate mixture until thoroughly incorporated, then cover and refrigerate overnight.

2 | Transfer the chilled chocolate mixture to the bowl of a standing mixer fitted with the whisk attachment and whip just until soft peaks form. Do not overmix. Remove the bowl from the mixer and give the ganache a few good stirs with a rubber spatula or whisk. Stir just until it is spreadable. Cover and refrigerate for 3 to 4 hours or ideally overnight.

3 | To spread, spoon large dollops onto the surface of the cake and use an offset spatula to spread the ganache all over with as few movements as possible. The ganache will keep in the refrigerator, tightly covered, for 5 to 7 days.

note | The cream is added in two parts because you want to make sure the emulsion takes place and that there is a smooth distribution of chocolate and cream. Only then do we add the rest of the cream. If you added all the cream at once, you could stir forever and it would never completely emulsify.

Like Mineral Water for Chocolate Ganache

MAKES 3 CUPS • Every pastry apprentice is told the day they first work with chocolate, "Don't let any water get in the chocolate. Never, ever!" And then in 1982 I met the great Michel Richard, who began his career as a pastry chef. "Pastry chefs are stupid," said Michel with characteristic frankness. "What matters is *how* you add water." And throwing my training to the winds, I did just that. Like a mechanic who takes a '57 Chevy apart in order to figure out how to rebuild it, I deconstructed a regular ganache to produce this version that contains no eggs, no butter, and no added sugar. Think of using it as you would whipped cream but with a chocolate kick.

10 ounces dark (60%–80%)
   chocolate, chopped

1 teaspoon gelatin

1¾ cups mineral water

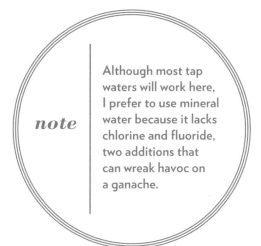

note

Although most tap waters will work here, I prefer to use mineral water because it lacks chlorine and fluoride, two additions that can wreak havoc on a ganache.

1 | Place the chocolate in a 1-quart bowl. Sprinkle the gelatin over it. Sprinkle 1 tablespoon of the mineral water over the gelatin.

2 | Fill a second bowl of similar size with hot tap water. Set the bowl of chocolate in the second bowl and walk away.

3 | While the chocolate melts, bring the remaining mineral water to a boil over high heat in a small saucepan. Immediately remove from the heat (to avoid too much of the water evaporating).

4 | Remove the bowl of chocolate from the hot water bath. Replace the hot water bath with a cold water bath by filling the bowl with ice cubes and a little water. Set aside.

5 | Pour half the hot mineral water into the bowl of chocolate and whisk to loosen the chocolate stuck to the bottom of the bowl. Whisk until it is fully incorporated. Add the remaining mineral water and stir, scraping the bottom as you go.

6 | Once the mixture is thoroughly blended, place it in the ice bath and immediately begin to blend with an immersion blender, submerging the blade into the chocolate to avoid spattering. Move the blender around the chocolate without lifting the blender. Blend until it thickens; after 4 or 5 minutes, it will resemble chocolate milk. Continue to blend and it will soon become the consistency of thick ganache. At this point, move the immersion blender quickly throughout the mass of chocolate to combine well, scraping down the sides with a rubber spatula every so often. Blend until thick and smooth. Pay attention to the consistency of the ganache; if you overblend, the mixture will break.

7 | Use immediately (if you let it sit, the gelatin will set and it will be too stiff to spread) to frost any of the nut flour cakes or alongside the Elegant Jell-O Shots (page 202). To use the ganache as a garnish, cover with plastic wrap and refrigerate for 2 hours. Using a metal teaspoon dipped in very hot water to create a sheen on the surface of the chocolate, scoop a little to serve with any dessert you desire.

Quick and Easy Shiny Chocolate Glaze

MAKES 2½ CUPS • A glaze gives your desserts a lustrous professional finish with cake-shop shine. Water and gelatin have been substituted for some of the heavy cream you would normally find in a chocolate glaze recipe. It's easy to work with because it grips the surface of the cake. Spread it in a very thin layer (or two to ensure an even, glassy glaze).

You will have leftovers. Freeze them to use later; frost cookies or dip fresh fruit in it.

2 teaspoons gelatin

1½ cups organic cane sugar

1 cup heavy cream

¾ cup unsweetened cocoa powder

1 | In a small bowl, combine the gelatin with 2 tablespoons cold water and set aside to bloom, 3 to 5 minutes.

2 | In a medium saucepan, combine the sugar, ⅔ cup water, and the heavy cream and bring to a boil over medium-high heat. Briskly whisk in the cocoa powder, keeping a close eye on the pot to prevent it from boiling over. Cook, whisking constantly, for about 2 minutes to completely cook the starches in the cocoa powder.

3 | Remove the chocolate mixture from the heat and whisk in the bloomed gelatin until thoroughly incorporated. Pour the mixture through a fine-mesh sieve. Spoon over dessert, as desired.

4 | The glaze will keep in the refrigerator, tightly covered, for up to 1 week. It will firm up when chilled. To liquefy, microwave for 5 seconds or place in a saucepan over low heat until fluid.

Airy Chocolate Foam

SERVES 6 TO 8 • If you captured the flavor of the air floating over a chocolate milkshake, this is what I imagine it would taste like. A drop of grapefruit essential oil, while optional, gives it an ephemeral floral tone.

10 ounces firm tofu

¾ teaspoon gelatin

1 cup whole, soy, or almond milk

4 ounces dark (70%) chocolate, melted

2 drops food-grade grapefruit essential oil (optional)

1 | In a medium saucepan, bring 4 cups water to a boil. Remove from the heat and submerge the tofu in the hot water. Let soak for 3 minutes, then drain through a fine-mesh sieve.

2 | In a small bowl, combine the gelatin with 2 tablespoons cold water and set aside to bloom.

3 | In a deep medium saucepan, bring the milk to a boil over medium-high heat. Whisk in the bloomed gelatin and remove from the heat. Add the chocolate, tofu, and grapefruit oil, if using, and, with an immersion blender, blend until smooth and thoroughly combined.

4 | Pour the mixture into a whipping siphon with two charges or into a whipped cream dispenser. Shake the canister and refrigerate until 1 hour before serving. Shake the canister until you hear the mixture moving around inside. Put two cartridges into the canister. Hold the canister at an angle to the plate and depress to dispense the chocolate foam.

note | This dessert can only be made with a whipping siphon, which adventuresome home chefs are starting to use everywhere. If you are not gadget inclined, my apologies.

Yuzu Curd

MAKES 1 CUP • The tangy punch of yuzu cuts through whatever you serve it with. This versatile sauce recalls the flavors of Ye Olde English lemon sauce traditionally served with figgy pudding but it has far fewer calories.

½ cup yuzu juice

¼ cup fresh-squeezed lemon juice

1 teaspoon agar powder

2 large pasteurized eggs

⅓ cup organic cane sugar

4 tablespoons (½ stick) unsalted high-fat European-style butter

1 | In a deep medium bowl, combine the yuzu juice and lemon juice. Sprinkle the agar to cover the surface of the liquid, as if you were feeding fish. Using an immersion blender, blend the mixture (it is difficult to hydrate agar—shearing it helps to encourage hydrating it). Transfer the mixture to a medium saucepan and bring to a simmer over medium heat.

2 | In a medium bowl, place the eggs and sugar and whisk to combine. Slowly pour the hot liquid into the egg mixture, whisking briskly. Return the mixture to the saucepan and bring to a boil over medium-high heat, stirring constantly. Pour into a blender and let sit for 5 minutes to cool slightly. Blend on low speed, adding the butter 1 tablespoon at a time, until it is thoroughly incorporated.

3 | Pour into a shallow container, cover, and chill in the refrigerator until the mixture is set. Transfer to the blender and mix on medium speed until smooth and creamy. The curd will keep in the refrigerator, tightly covered, for 5 to 7 days.

Fat and Happy Raisins

MAKES ABOUT ¼ CUP • When raisins are used straight from the box they never get time to soften, which, in my opinion, is the only way they can become their full selves. Plumping makes them more grapey in texture and taste. Below, you'll find five variations of raisins that amp up the taste even further. And because they start with such concentrated flavor, these soaked beauties create powerful and defined accents. Although I call for them in specific recipes, when you have some on hand, they make a great garnish for all and any nut cake, pudding, or panna cotta.

2 tablespoons local honey

4½ teaspoons dark rum

2 cups golden or dark raisins

In a medium saucepan, combine 4 cups water with the honey and rum and bring to a boil over medium heat. Pour the hot liquid into a heatproof pitcher. Working with 1 cup of liquid at a time, return it to the saucepan and add ½ cup of raisins and flavorings of your choice (see below). Continue to boil for 10 minutes more, stirring frequently. Remove from the heat and let the raisins soak for 30 minutes. Drain them from the liquid, let cool, and store them covered and refrigerated for up to 3 weeks. Repeat with the remaining liquid, raisins, and variations.

variations:

ZIPPY RAISINS: Add 5 teaspoons instant coffee crystals to the saucepan with the other ingredients.

TROPICAL RAISINS: Add ½ cup pineapple juice to the liquid before boiling, then add 2 tablespoons grated fresh ginger for the second boiling.

SPANISH RAISINS: Replace the rum with an equal amount of Madeira and add 2 tablespoons cocoa powder.

SMOKY TEA RAISINS: Add 1 lapsang souchong tea bag to the mixture as it cools and before storing in the refrigerator.

Tamarind Vinegar

MAKES 4 CUPS • One of my biggest discoveries in developing the recipes for this book was the way tart drinking vinegars, intended to be mixed with seltzer for a tangy, refreshing beverage, bring balance and fruit flavor to reduced-sugar recipes. I am especially enamored of the Som vinegars made by the Pok Pok team in Portland, Oregon, which can be purchased online or in some retail outlets. If you don't want to buy ready-made, here is my do-it-yourself workaround. Real vinegars are made by allowing fruits steeping in wine to ferment and turn sour. This process takes about eight weeks and can turn bad or not turn at all, depending on the ambient temperature. If you don't want your kitchen to look and smell like a biology lab, use a good-quality white or red wine vinegar to start and then add your flavoring: tamarind paste or pods, pineapple, peaches, berries, or whatever favorite fruit you have. These vinegars really add pizzazz to a dessert.

6 tamarind pods, washed, peeled, and cut into 1-inch pieces with scissors, or 6 ounces tamarind paste

1 quart good-quality white or red wine vinegar

3 tablespoons organic cane sugar

1 | Sterilize two 16-ounce mason jars (see page 239).

2 | In a large saucepan, combine the tamarind pod pieces and the vinegar and bring to a simmer over medium heat. Continue to simmer for 1 minute (to allow the tamarind flavor to infuse the vinegar). Turn off the heat and pour the mixture—vinegar and fruit—into the sterilized jars. Let cool with the lids off. Once cool, cover tightly and store in a cool, dark place for 3 days.

3 | Strain the mixture through a fine-mesh sieve lined with a coffee filter into a spouted container. Stir in the sugar until dissolved. Pour the liquid back into the jars, cover tightly, and refrigerate. The vinegar will keep for 1 month.

Jicama Pickles

MAKES 2 QUARTS • Pickles have always been consigned to the savory side of the menu, but I count them as one of the revelations in my pursuit of a wider range of flavors in my desserts. These are sweeter than the pickle you have with your corned beef sandwich. Jicama has the texture and snap of an apple but is happy to play a supporting part to other flavors. I can't guarantee that every picky-eating child will love this novel idea, but we're all grown-ups here. Variety is the spice of life and vice versa.

½ cup apple cider vinegar

¼ cup verjus or white wine

2 tablespoons local honey

1 tablespoon pink or white
 peppercorns

1 tablespoon cardamom pods

1 star anise

2 teaspoons kosher salt

1 jicama, peeled and cut into
 3 × ¼-inch planks

1 | Cut a circle of parchment paper to fit the inside of a large saucepan (see page 125).

2 | In a large saucepan, combine the vinegar, verjus, honey, peppercorns, cardamom, star anise, and salt with 3 cups of water and bring to a boil over medium-high heat. Reduce the heat to low and add the jicama. Place the circle of parchment over the liquid and simmer for 45 minutes. Add more water, ½ cup at a time, if the liquid no longer covers the jicama. Turn off the heat, cover, and let steep overnight.

3 | Sterilize four 16-ounce mason jars (see page 239).

4 | Using a slotted spoon, divide the jicama between the jars. Pour the liquid and aromatics over to fill. Seal tightly and complete the sterilizing process. The pickles will keep in the refrigerator for up to 2 months.

variations:
Replace the jicama with 2 pints of fresh whole figs (snip off the stem of the fig to provide an entry point for the pickling liquid); 4 or 5 unripe peaches or nectarines, depending on their size; or a dozen plums, pitted and quartered.

Pickled Lychees

MAKES 3 CUPS • Herewith, a liquid bonanza of fermented fruit flavors as we combine two different vinegars. The tamarind vinegar contributes bold flavor evocative of burnt orange and the white vinegar brings it all together. I turn to aromatic spices to wake up subtle flavors in whatever you pair them with.

1 cup white wine vinegar

½ cup tamarind drinking vinegar, such as Pok Pok Som (or homemade, page 251)

6 cardamom pods, crushed

3 star anise

2 tablespoons kosher salt

24 fresh lychees or two 14-ounce cans lychees, drained and rinsed

1 | In a medium saucepan, combine the vinegars, cardamom, star anise, salt, and 2 cups water and bring to a boil over medium-high heat. Add the lychees, reduce the heat to low, and simmer for 20 minutes. Turn off the heat, cover, and let steep for 30 minutes.

2 | Sterilize three 8-ounce canning jars (see page 239).

3 | Using a slotted spoon, divide the lychees between the jars. Pour the liquid and aromatics over to fill the jars. Seal tightly and complete the sterilizing process. The pickles will keep in the refrigerator for up to 3 months.

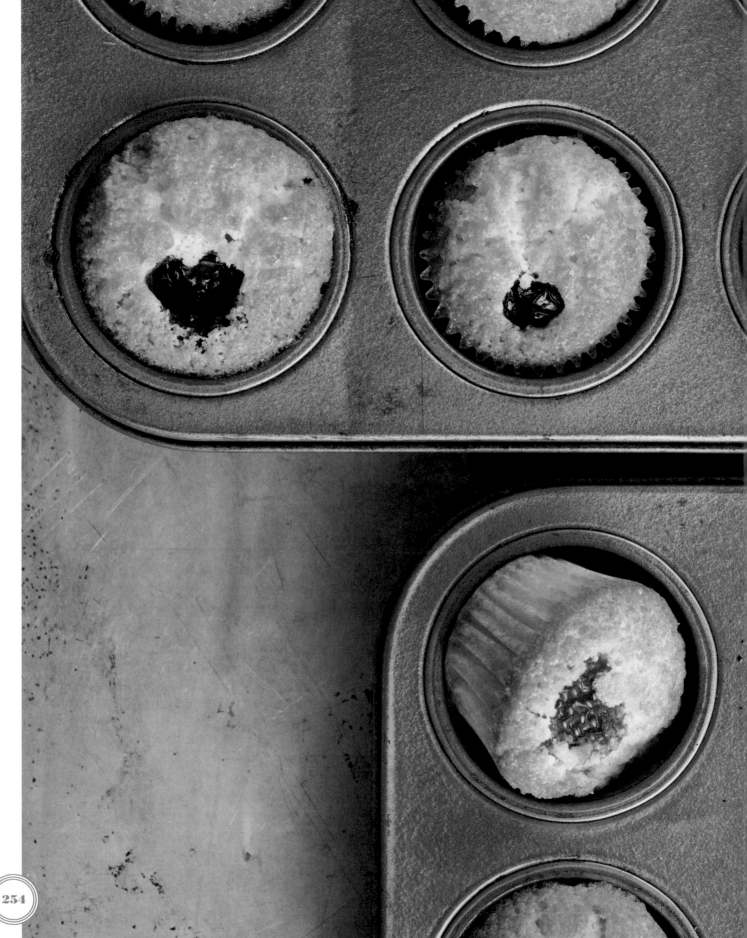

ACKNOWLEDGMENTS

Charlie Fabella

Melinda Kaminsky

James, Finn, and
Stephen Antonson

Roberto Welch

Barbara and Dick Moore

Patsy Taylor

Susie Morrison

Stephen Howell

Nuhma Tuazon

Pedro Rossel

Maya Rossi

JT Norton

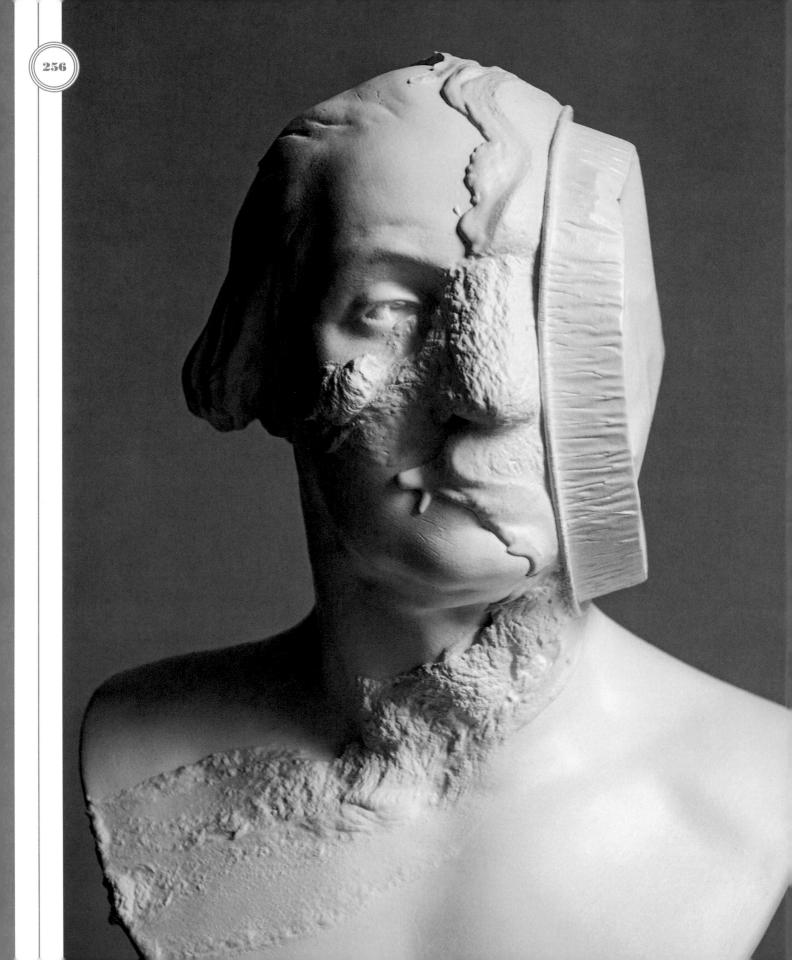

INDEX